Clothing and Fashion in Southern History

Clothing and Fashion in Southern History

Edited by
TED OWNBY and BECCA WALTON

University Press of Mississippi • Jackson

The University Press of Mississippi is the scholarly publishing agency of the Mississippi Institutions of Higher Learning: Alcorn State University, Delta State University, Jackson State University, Mississippi State University, Mississippi University for Women, Mississippi Valley State University, University of Mississippi, and University of Southern Mississippi.

www.upress.state.ms.us

The University Press of Mississippi is a member of the Association of University Presses.

Copyright © 2020 by University Press of Mississippi
All rights reserved

First printing 2020

∞

Library of Congress Cataloging-in-Publication Data

Names: Ownby, Ted, editor. | Walton, Becca, editor.
Title: Clothing and fashion in southern history / edited by Ted Ownby and Becca Walton.
Description: Jackson: University Press of Mississippi, 2020. | Includes bibliographical references and index.
Identifiers: LCCN 2020004453 (print) | LCCN 2020004454 (ebook) | ISBN 9781496829504 (hardback) | ISBN 9781496829511 (trade paperback) | ISBN 9781496829528 (epub) | ISBN 9781496829535 (epub) | ISBN 9781496829542 (pdf) | ISBN 9781496829559 (pdf)
Subjects: LCSH: Clothing and dress—Southern States—History. | Clothing and dress—Social aspects—Southern States. | BISAC: HISTORY / United States / State & Local / South (AL, AR, FL, GA, KY, LA, MS, NC, SC, TN, VA, WV)
Classification: LCC TT496.U6 C56 2020 (print) | LCC TT496.U6 (ebook) | DDC 646/.30973—dc23
LC record available at https://lccn.loc.gov/2020004453
LC ebook record available at https://lccn.loc.gov/2020004454

British Library Cataloging-in-Publication Data available

CONTENTS

Introduction
Where Should We Begin?
TED OWNBY and BECCA WALTON
vii

Patches of Resistance on the Badges of Enslavement:
Enslaved Southerners, Negro Cloth, and Fashionability in the Cotton South
KATIE KNOWLES
3

Confederate Cultures of Military Clothing Production
SARAH JONES WEICKSEL
32

WPA Sewing Projects
A Case Study in Southern Encounters with the New Deal Welfare State
SUSANNAH WALKER
54

"Thinking of you every minute (and every stitch)"
Sewing, Clothing, and Identity at the Mississippi State Penitentiary at Parchman, 1950–1969
BECCA WALTON
84

The Mississippi Poor People's Corporation
Clothing Manufacture and Consumer Capitalism in Defense of Black Voting Rights, 1965–1974
WILLIAM STURKEY
109

The Dress Makes the Band
Used Clothes, Drag Acts, and Bohemians in the Athens, Georgia Music Scene
GRACE ELIZABETH HALE
124

Afterword
JONATHAN PRUDE
142

Contributors
151

Index
153

INTRODUCTION

Where Should We Begin?

TED OWNBY and BECCA WALTON

Where should we begin, if we want to use clothing to study southern history? There is no survey text or big dominant book on the history of clothing and fashion in the South. For many topics, adding the word "southern" as an adjective leads quickly to a set of questions that those of us who study the South find predictable, whether because we ask, teach, and try to answer them or because we work hard to redefine or get beyond them. Adding the word "southern" before words like literature, politics, religion, architecture, music, history, or foodways means starting with a background of past questions we want to answer or overturn and assumptions we might want to challenge. We may be tired of the assumptions that southern religion probably means studying evangelical Protestants or that southern music probably means studying a few genres that started in the region, or that southern foodways might seem to mean studying barbecue and the products of grandparents' gardens, or that studying southern literature means comparing recent writers to a few influential writers from the past. Whether we want new approaches to those topics or completely new questions, we probably know where past conversations have begun.

If one adds the word "southern" to the word clothing, it's not clear where to begin. That fact means today's scholars have a great deal of freedom to figure out where they want to begin their work without the frustrations of scholarship they may have rejected. Of course there are terrific scholars of clothing and fashion working in academic programs in the South, and there are extraordinary creators of fashion and lots of people making clothing in the South. There is good and important scholarship on individual subjects about clothing, its production, its display, and its meanings. The point is not that such scholarship doesn't exist—the point is that the topic has not received much study as a regional question.

We might start with a curious example from popular culture. In 2013, the competitive design television program *Project Runway* had a challenge in which contestants were supposed to design a look for the "modern southern woman." Hosting (and helping evaluate) the challenge was Belk, the Charlotte-based department store chain that was sponsoring the program. The intriguing thing was the responses of the contestants, most of whom said they had never given much thought to the "modern southern woman," how to conceptualize who that would be, or certainly what she might wear. Cohost Tim Gunn suggested they should design for a woman who "dresses vibrantly and impressively. She is always fashionably put together. She knows how to use accessories, and she loves color and anything with feminine detail."[1] The contestants on the show tossed around a few bland regional stereotypes, mentioned *Designing Women* and *Steel Magnolias*, and then they all made dresses, most of which were colorful and none of which seemed outlandish, daring, interesting, or by most definitions "modern." At least to this group of designers, the fascination with the changing contemporary South, which has energized powerful and innovative scholarship on many topics, did not seem meaningful.

So, where could we begin? Maybe we begin with shoes. Numerous students in Southern Studies classes say that they first thought about regional differences when they attended events for teenagers and people from outside the region asked them if they wore shoes. They hadn't really thought about shoes and southern identity, but other people had, and many of the southern students seem offended by the accusation. The image of barefoot southerners is one of the recurring images especially of people in the Appalachian South, African Americans in the Deep South, and subjects of Works Progress Administration (WPA) photographs. New Deal Labor Secretary Frances Perkins made lifelong enemies among some southern politicians when she suggested that government policies could help put shoes on the South.[2] Shoes offer a common theme in southern music and literature, with Pauli Murray entitling her memoir *Proud Shoes*, Unita Blackwell calling her civil rights memoir *Barefootin'*, Loretta Lynn in "Coal Miner's Daughter" singing "In the Summertime we didn't have shoes to wear," and Carl Perkins and then Elvis Presley telling people to stay off their shoes. Some people might want to begin with hoop skirts, as some of the garments most likely to turn up in some museums and many pilgrimage tours. But that would be ridiculous. It would return scholars of the South to a time when they had to overturn assumptions that they should begin their work by studying rich people on antebellum plantations. Even if one starts with images from plantation life, the most famous item of clothing in the most famous film about the South, Scarlett O'Hara's post-Civil War green velvet dress made from pre-Civil War curtains, was not a hoop skirt. Instead, that dress was about creative reuse, trying to pay taxes and save the family land, and pretending that in a time of crisis, everything was going to be okay. In its celebration of reuse, Scarlett's curtain dress is probably an upper-class version of Dolly Parton's "Coat of Many Colors," a song about a poor mother patching together a coat made of rags for her daughter, who proudly wears it as both beautiful and biblical.

The challenge—and also part of the excitement—of studying clothing lies in the scholar's obligation to study the intersections of production, choice, use, and image. Every garment has a designer, maker, wearer, and viewer, and scholars can study all of them. Essays in this book, using clothing as a point of departure, show ways to approach written and object archives that are limited in what they can reveal about marginalized groups. Fashion studies long centered on the art and preservation of finely rendered garments of the upper-class, and written archival resources used in the study of southern history have gaps and silences. In this volume, scholars approach clothing as something made, worn, and intimately experienced by enslaved people, incarcerated people, the poor and working class, and by subcultures perceived as transgressive. Power structures, economics, technology, materiality, gender, class, race, desire, projection, choice, and force, all are reasonable and often essential parts of studying history by studying clothing.

One could start with global networks. Taking seriously the history of clothing means studying a complex global system; one can see the South's centuries-long engagement with a global economy through a single garment, with cotton harvested by enslaved laborers in the South, milled in Massachusetts or Manchester, designed with influence from Parisian tastemakers, and sold in the South by Jewish immigrant peddlers or merchants.

One could certainly begin at the level of production—in Native American trade with Europeans, then in cotton fields during and long after slavery, in cotton-mill work in the piedmont South, and then in garment manufacturing in larger parts of the South. One should start with women, sewing. Scholars of textile mills have shown how building mills seemed to represent an industrial "crusade" to save southern workers, specifically southern white workers, from dependence and poverty.[3] A 2015 work by Michelle Haberland shows that by the 1970s and 1980s, more southerners made their livings making garments than making cloth.[4] Mississippi led the country in the production of pajamas and Alabama led in making t-shirts. One could start with factories that moved south for inexpensive labor and later moved to Latin America or southeast Asia for the same reason.

One could begin with issues of home production and its ideals and worries. When women in the 1800s wrote in their diaries and letters that they "did my work today," they meant that they had sewed or repaired clothing.[5] Many southerners, especially on farms, worried that buying too many goods made them "indulgences" that endangered both household independence and religious understandings of personal modesty. For decades after emancipation, rural southerners tried to avoid store-bought clothing to get out (or stay out) of debts they associated with multiple forms of dependence to employers and creditors. We might start with the pride people showed in homespun clothing, whether at certain moments or in memory, as ideas of heroic thrift and making clothing from feed sacks and cotton sacks were important both to the wearers themselves and to people documenting and analyzing the South.

Or, one could start with sales, analyzing the experiences of owning, running, shopping in, or avoiding haberdasheries, millinery shops, general stores and plantation stores, department stores and fabric stores, peddlers, informal economies, shopping trips to cities by wealthy people or their representatives, mail-order catalogues, modern shopping centers and malls, and even more recent remade and multiethnic shopping centers and malls.

Many people would begin with clothing as part of the art of personal representation, the choices people make about how to look and what to project when they choose their clothing and the ways viewers attach meanings, positive or negative, to other people's clothing. The significance clothing plays in southern definitions of African American life range from enslaved people having to wear negro cloth to African American reformers who insisted on dressing for respectability with neat suits and dresses and no overalls and head rags, to the caricatures of Jim Crow and Aunt Jemima, to the drama of Mardi Gras Indians, to the importance of uniforms, whether military, prison, or related to specific jobs, displaying the importance of appearance in thinking about issues of race. Studying both the South and distant cultural centers, Tanisha C. Ford's *Liberated Threads* analyzes clothing and hairstyles as signs of liberation from multiple predictable and forced identities for African American women.[6] Clothing is almost always crucial to southern musicians, whether they are fitting into images of what blues or country or jazz performers are supposed to represent or they are choosing to overturn predictable images.

We could start with clothing and gender, whether that means rumors about what Jefferson Davis was wearing when he was arrested, or religious notions of proper clothing (and, for some, hats), or the lessons taught in school home economics and then consumer-science classes and in home extension work, to the multiple cross-dressings Grace Hale analyzes in her paper in this volume. In *Sexual Reckonings: Southern Girls in a Troubling Age*, Susan Cahn insists on the centrality of clothing as "along with shelter, a literal boundary between a person and a cold world."[7] We could study how clothing fits into ritual moments about family life, marriage, religious transitions, aging, dying, and mourning, most of which have special garments that either confirm gender differences or, occasionally, blur them.

And when do we talk about clothing as art? We would need to study, but not necessarily start with, fashion designers; the sense that for generations, the South seemed distant from fashion centers like New York, Paris, Milan; the rise of fashion districts and fashion weeks in southern cities; and designers who leave the South and those who design with an eye toward local communities and sustainability. And as scholars, do we think of the countless ways people who were not professional designers made and remade clothing to make it special, artistic, outlandish, respectable, or not at all respectable in the same terms we use to study professional designers?

So, where should we begin? We hope we begin with essays like those in this volume. Like so much scholarship in Southern Studies for the past generation or so, these essays are not looking for an essential definition, some central theme that makes clothing or fashion or style southern. Clothing itself resists such easy definition. Elizabeth Wilson notes in *Adorned in Dreams* that "fashion is ambivalent—for when we dress we wear inscribed upon our bodies the often obscure relationship of art, personal psychology, and the social order."[8] The question of what is southern clothing is probably better left unasked because it suggests there will be a short answer. Instead, these essays ask how we should study southern history by studying clothing. They take different approaches, but all use clothing to study crucial issues about power and conflict, identities and images, and the meanings of ownership, creativity, and freedom. Far from seeing sewing, clothing, and adornment as nonpolitical, they study politics, sometimes by studying law and government, sometimes by studying other ways people used clothing as part of keeping or gaining power, sometimes by showing people challenging norms about respectability and good taste. Most of the essays study clothing as an important part of understanding the intersection of necessity and creativity.

This book's first essay takes seriously the intersections of necessity and creativity as well as the necessity of studying production, remaking, and image-making. Katie Knowles details the history of so-called negro cloth, a crucial element of antebellum clothing. Knowles analyzes who produced the inexpensive cloth, who chose and distributed it, how it reflected ideas about race, power, usefulness, and fashion, and how enslaved people used, dyed, reshaped, and often reused it. Knowles argues that "contributions of African Americans to early American fashion remain undervalued: a relic of racist attempts in early nation-forming to exclude black people as creators and participants in American culture." Knowles takes a traditional archival resource like a plantation ledger and interprets it in fresh ways to see an article of clothing as a garment shaped by its maker and wearer, not just an item of property of a slave owner.

Sarah Jones Weicksel analyzes issues that arise from studying women's roles in producing clothing for Confederate soldiers. The Civil War brought many women in contact with demands from the Confederate government, and the war raised questions of which women really knew how to sew well, and many upper-class women found themselves relying on and learning from poor and enslaved women. Thus, a story emerges not just of white women sewing to support male relatives on the warfront, but of those women's efforts at mastery. "When Georgia's governor offered women the possibility of having their names recorded in the official state records," Weicksel writes, "they were to be rewarded not only for their sewing skills, but also their ability to command the work of enslaved women."

Susannah Walker's paper analyzes New Deal projects designed both for the employment of southern women and for the production of clothing for the poorest people in the South. Considerable scholarship has addressed New Deal food projects; Walker's paper is one of few to take a parallel approach to clothing. Analyzing both the multiple goals of the government—worker training, relief, providing respectable clothing to impoverished people themselves—and the segregated experiences of the white and African American women working in the projects, the paper raises questions about the challenges of developing welfare programs in the South. The essay also highlights the importance of aesthetics in New Deal programs, describing the making of attractive garments for relief recipients.

Becca Walton's essay on Mississippi's Parchman Prison uses material from the prison publication *Inside World* to analyze clothing both as a form of production for women prisoners and as a system of meaning and communication for women and men who envisioned clothing as part of various definitions of freedom. "Camp reporters," she writes, "almost never mentioned the crimes for which they were imprisoned, choosing to focus on other defining characteristics and life experiences. Both men and women wrote continually of sewing and clothing, discussing their work in camp reports, sending messages related to clothing across the penitentiary, and drawing cartoons that featured fashion as a defining element. By discussing sewing machine mishaps and ill-fitting pants, the men and women of Parchman formed relationships and maintained identities beyond and apart from their status as criminals."

William Sturkey tells the story of the Una Sewing Cooperative, a women's group that formed in Mississippi in 1965 as one way "to complicate the historiographical understanding of the connection between civil rights and economic equality." Sewing cooperatives built on the sewing knowledge of many African American women elicited extraordinary public sympathy as part of efforts by a new group called the Poor People's Corporation, and offered potential for economic empowerment as part of the late-1960s phase of the civil rights movement.

Studying Athens scene-makers including Jerry Ayers, Vanessa Briscoe Hay of Pylon, Michael Stipe of R.E.M., Mark Cline of Love Tractor, Lynda Stipe and Lynda Hopper of Oh OK, and all of the members of B-52's, Grace Hale's paper discusses the importance of clothing in the rise of a college subculture in the late 1970s and 1980s. With connections to New York art scenes and their own choices, the musicians used clothing, especially second-hand store items they reused and reconceived, to express multiple definitions of gender and sexuality in settings full of transgression, idiosyncrasy, and creativity.

Jonathan Prude ends the book by asking how one might conclude a discussion of clothing and fashion in southern history. He offers a critique of the essays and the issues they raise, highlighting interconnections among them.

The editors thank the contributors for their work on this project. The volume began with a conference called "Clothing and Fashion in Southern History," held at the University of Mississippi. Funding came from the Future of the South Endowment at the Center for the Study of Southern Culture. The conference took the form of a workshop where conference participants listened and made suggestions for the essays that made their way into this volume. Other participants included Thuy Linh Tu and Jessamyn Hatcher of New York University, Laura Edwards of Duke University, Lawrence T. McDonnell of Iowa State University, Blain Roberts of Fresno State University, New Orleans friend and documentarian Pableaux Johnson, Nancy Dunlap

Bercaw of the Smithsonian, and Coulter Fussell of Yalorun Textiles in Holly Springs. Natalie Chanin of Alabama Chanin could not attend the event, but the editors relied on her kind advice early in the project. Thanks also to our friends and colleagues at the Southern Foodways Alliance for their advice and example and to the numerous Southern Studies faculty and students who participated in the event.

For the volume itself, we thank our colleagues at the University Press of Mississippi and the Center for the Study of Southern Culture: M. Mairéad Gaffney, who helped with proofreading and editing; James G. Thomas, who helped with final preparations for the book; and Rebecca Lauck Cleary, who helped with both the conference and the manuscript.

Notes

1. https://vintageinspiredpassionista.com/2013/09/18/project-runway-belk-challenge-season-12-episode-9/.

2. Kirstin Downey, *The Woman behind the New Deal: The Life of Frances Perkins, FDR's Secretary of Labor and his Moral Conscience* (NY: Doubleday, 2009), 146.

3. Jacquelyn Dowd Hall, James Leloudis, Robert Korstad, Mary Murphy, Lu Ann Jones, Christopher B. Daly, *Like a Family: The Making of a Southern Cotton Mill World* (Chapel Hill: University of North Carolina Press, 1987); Shelley Sallee, *The Whiteness of Child Labor Reform in the South* (Athens: University of Georgia Press, 2004).

4. Michelle Haberland, *Striking Beauties: Women Apparel Workers in the U.S. South, 1930–2000* (Athens: University of Georgia Press, 2015).

5. Ted Ownby, *American Dreams in Mississippi: Consumers, Poverty, and Culture, 1830–1998* (Chapel Hill: University of North Carolina Press, 1999).

6. Tanisha C. Ford, *Liberated Threads: Black Women, Style, and the Global Politics of Soul* (Chapel Hill: University of North Carolina Press, 2015).

7. Susan K. Cahn, *Sexual Reckonings: Southern Girls in a Troubling Age* (Cambridge: Harvard University Press, 2007), 135.

8. Elizabeth Wilson, *Adorned in Dreams: Fashion and Modernity*. (New Brunswick: Rutgers University Press, 2003), 247.

Clothing and Fashion in Southern History

PATCHES OF RESISTANCE ON THE BADGES OF ENSLAVEMENT

Enslaved Southerners, Negro Cloth, and Fashionability in the Cotton South

KATIE KNOWLES

In an often-quoted line from Harriet Jacobs's autobiography *Incidents in the Life of a Slave Girl*, she states, "I have a vivid recollection of the linsey-woolsey dress given me every winter by Mrs. Flint. How I hated it! It was one of the badges of slavery."[1] Enslaved people in the antebellum South must be recognized as creators of culture and consumers of goods; they wanted "to participate more fully in a common North Atlantic world of cloth and clothing" that had developed during the colonial period into a unique fashion system.[2] They lived in a country that was increasingly reliant on a global system of industrialized manufacturing, of which the South was a crucial supplier of raw goods. When thinking about the clothing worn by enslaved people, it must be remembered that they were indirectly participating in a capitalist market when they received fabric or ready-made clothing from enslavers. Most enslaved people were also direct participants, bartering or purchasing consumer goods from local merchants, including clothing.

Enslaved people and their clothing played a fundamental role in changing the textile industry, in particular through their use of a product called negro cloth.[3] Negro cloth was cheap and rough. Unlike other fabrics of the period that were designed to last sometimes for several years with proper care, negro cloth was made to be used up, worn through, and thrown out. Both textile factory owners and enslavers embarked on a project to create fabrics that would last exactly to the next period when enslaved people were to receive new clothing, but would cost the factory owner minimal money to make and the enslaver minimal money to purchase. This is a very basic reduction of a complicated global supply system built on a capitalist economy.[4] At the heart of it were enslaved people in the American South, who provided the labor to supply factories with cheap raw cotton and were the ultimate end users of the finished cheap goods.

As end-users, enslaved people manipulated a new approach to clothing supplies, to throwaway fast fashion textiles, in order to serve their needs and desires. Enslaved people found ways to extend the usefulness of their limited, poor-quality apparel through reuse and adaptation, often using limited sewing and mending skills. In the early nineteenth century, patches and other visible mending indicated that the wearer could not afford to pay for proper clothing maintenance more than it indicated they could not afford to buy new clothes. Even quite wealthy people wore clothing refashioned to conform to style changes, and well into the antebellum period, proper education for young women included a variety of mending stitches. But these reused and mended fabrics were built to last for a few years and were not clothes worn all day, every day while doing intense physical labor.

Contributions of African Americans to early American fashion remain undervalued, an effect of racist attempts in early nation-forming to exclude black people as creators and participants in American culture. Previous scholarship on African influences within American culture have used the phrase "Africanisms in American culture." This conception moves the influences of African cultures to the margins in the process of early American cultural formation and implies that African and American (or African and European) are inherently opposite. It pushes aside the commonalities between European and African cultures that coalesced naturally in the process of creating American cultures. In addition, diverse European and African cultures are lumped together under continental nomenclature, which hides the ways in which cultural influences moved across the Atlantic from Africa, to the Americas, to Europe, and sometimes back again.[5]

What ultimately mattered most in the fashion system of the young United States was the color of one's skin. Blackness indicated an outsider status, an un-Americanness that prevented African Americans from expressing themselves as part of the nation through their clothing and style. Exclusion from fashionability also allowed white people to appropriate ways of dressing without sacrificing their cultural capital. Meanwhile, African Americans used the rules of the established fashion system to resist racism by creating alternate dress codes that had a lasting impact on the larger history of American fashion. As users of a new kind of throwaway textile, enslaved people, dressed in the what Harriet Jacobs called the "badge" of their status, forged new ways of dressing and caring for textiles and clothing.

Understanding clothing requires studying a combination of sources. Evidence of the appearance of and fabrics for slave clothing is abundant in written sources, including enslavers' account books and personal papers, narratives written by formerly enslaved people, and newspaper advertisements. Enslavers, particularly those who enslaved large numbers of people, kept careful records of food, clothing, punishment, and daily work performed on their land. Their account books, plantation record books, and personal correspondence are rich with evidence of how they approached the clothing of enslaved bodies. Advertisements for runaways are also an excellent source as many give detailed descriptions of the colors, fabrics, and styles of clothing worn by fugitives.[6] Equally rich are the narratives written by those who escaped slavery and recorded their lived experiences. The other main sources, coming from the voices of those who experienced enslavement, are the Works Progress Administration narratives.[7] These sources are particularly important in determining the attitudes of enslaved people toward their clothing.

Written sources alone are inadequate when the objects themselves survive. A surprising number of apparel items with a provenance of use by enslaved wearers remain to help reveal this history.[8] They skew toward nicer, more distinctive items, but they exist and are read using methods of material-culture studies and fashion theory. The dualities of enslaved people's lives as products and as people speak well to theories of fashion studies. Fashion is inherently contradictory as a method of expressing one's self as belonging to a group or society while also maintaining a sense of individualism.[9] In his study *Fashion as Communication*, Malcolm Barnard states, "By means of fashion and clothing, positions of dominance and subservience are made to appear and are experienced as natural, not the result of human action."[10] Barnard often draws on how fashion is used by those in power to solidify and naturalize their domination of other groups; in the case of the antebellum South, enslavers defined black bodies as unfashionable by supplying enslaved people with only rough, cheap, and ill-fitting garments.[11]

In addition to material-culture methods and fashion theory, recent scholarship on understanding the experiences of enslaved people helps push forward this knowledge and explain the contradictory ways in which clothing was used as a method of control and a method of resistance in the antebellum South. The reading of surviving clothing in particular is approached through the method of what Marisa J. Fuentes calls "reading along the bias grain," a concept particularly apt when reading textiles and clothing.[12] As Fuentes explains, "Like cutting fabric on the bias to create more elasticity, reading along the bias grain expands the legibility" of the sources, allowing the historian to interpret surviving fragments in ways that stretch beyond those small pieces to create a fuller, deeper understanding of people not always centered in the source.[13] This method is also used when approaching written sources, such as lists of cloth distributed to enslaved people, which are traditionally read in ways that present the receivers of the cloth as disembodied, inanimate, or abstract rather than as actors who will wear, manipulate, and discard the fabric.

Fully understanding negro cloth requires a worldwide lens to explore the history of this product, an economic development rooted in cultural assumptions of race and class that formed the beginnings of our modern-day consumption patterns of textiles and clothing. There has been a recent resurgence of studies on the connections between chattel slavery, capitalism, and the cotton industry.[14] These works primarily use methods of economic history and economic theories. While they analyze laborers, both free and enslaved, involved in the cotton and textile industries, they do so through a capitalist lens. They continue to devalue or ignore what capitalism considers nonproductive labor, such as women's textile work on large-scale plantations in finishing, mending, and laundering textiles, and the continuation of home textile production on many southern plantations up to the Civil War.

It is challenging to tell a history of enslaved people using methods of economic history without losing them in prolonged discussions of those who made the money and held the power that resulted from the development of negro cloth. By using material-culture methods and focusing on this product created and perfected specifically for a capitalist slavery system, we can more fully understand the experience of enslaved people who lived in this fabric each day while recognizing their importance in a global trade system. While enslaved people are not always at the center of that larger story, they are always central to it. Without enslaved southerners, there would be no way to produce and no ultimate need for negro cloth.

What exactly was this new fabric called negro cloth? The *Oxford English Dictionary* gives a definition under the heading for the word "Negro": "Designating hard-wearing, durable clothes and fabrics, originally intended or designed to be worn or used by slaves, as Negro cloth, Negro cotton, Negro shirting."[15] In her seminal work *Textiles in America, 1650–1870*, Florence Montgomery defined negro cloth as "a coarse homespun fabric used for clothing slaves in the West Indies and the southern colonies. Inexpensive grades of cloth were also imported for the same purpose."[16] *Fairchild's Dictionary of Textiles* gives a more detailed, but still ambiguous, definition for negro cloth: "A coarse hemp cloth, often containing cotton, which was imported from England by the American colonies during the seventeenth and eighteenth centuries. Used to make clothes for African slaves. American mills began to make this fabric in the beginning of the nineteenth century, and coarse wool imported from Smyrna (Izmir), Turkey, sometimes was used for filling."[17] One common difficulty with all of these definitions is their lack of sources. Aside from the examples of use given by the *Oxford English Dictionary*, it is unclear where the authors found their information and where and when the term originated.[18] Particularly intriguing is the very specific reference to Turkish wool imported to American mills in the third definition. These existing definitions of negro cloth treat the bodies of enslaved people as objects rather than actors, erasing the complex relationship between race-based slavery and the Industrial Revolution. The antebellum economy was strongly associated with slavery through the creation of products that were raced.

In the antebellum period, the term negro cloth was applied to a variety of fabrics that could be mixtures of cotton with wool, cotton with bast fibers, or all cotton. Weave structure is not often specified, though likely the cloth was a plain or twill as these were durable weave structures common in other types of work clothing, including other textile terms used to describe slave clothing. What is clear from all of these definitions is that negro cloth was an extremely low grade of fabric, and it was meant to be used as clothing for enslaved bodies only. Negro cloth was a consumer good, created specifically for the race-based slave system that developed in the Americas. The term itself helped contribute to efforts by the ruling powers to define enslaved people as raced and to define all people of African descent as slaves. To fully understand the product negro cloth, we must understand it as a raced product—one that could only exist in a racist capitalist economy.[19] As the term indicates, it was fabric that was produced specifically to clothe people with dark skin. But other people were wearing the fabrics that were sold as negro cloth; these were not textiles worn solely by enslaved people or purchased solely by enslavers. Poor and lower-class white people in the North and South purchased and wore linseys, kerseys, and plains, as did sailors from both Europe and the Americas.[20]

Westward expansion and the need for utilitarian fabrics on the frontier opened yet another market for these textiles. A book of fabric samples in the collection of the Smithsonian National Museum of American History illustrates this market in the antebellum period. The book was compiled in 1834 as a sample of fabrics sold in the Indian trade at Fort Gibson in

Indian Territory (now eastern Oklahoma). By this time there was a mixture of people living in the region, from white people in East Texas, Missouri, and Arkansas to several Native American tribes including the Cherokee, Creek, and Seminole, who were being forced off lands further east. Both white people and Native Americans in the area enslaved people of African or mixed descent. Among the checks, shirtings, and other samples in this book is one labeled "heavy negro cotton." Fabrics sold in the South as negro cloth were also sold to the Indian trade under different names; that this fabric was marketed with a racial connotation suggests it was still intended to be sold to enslavers to clothe enslaved black bodies.[21]

The important distinction between different wearers across this wide market for low end fabrics is that the textiles were only marketed as negro cloth when being sold for use by enslaved people. This specific use of a product demonstrates the close connection between the economy and culture. Enslavers and others who supported the slave labor system in the antebellum South attempted to visually differentiate enslaved people from free people through the purchase and distribution of negro cloth. Harriet Jacobs's recognition of her clothing as a "badge" demonstrates enslaved people were well aware of efforts to define and restrict their bodies through visual displays. Their attempts to individualize their clothing or to obtain higher quality goods were more than vanity; these were people resisting a product that marked them as enslaved. The word negro in the name of the fabric further solidifies its position as a product designed to reinforce race-based slavery by equating the textile with black skin.

Negro cloth appears most often in the written record in advertisements of textile manufacturers or dry-goods merchants, indicating the term was used as a sort of marketing strategy to attract buyers to the company's products. Benjamin Whitney advertised his Whitney's Cotton Factory in the *New Orleans Times-Picayune*, noting, "He is producing a fabric under the style and denomination of WHITNEY'S NEGRO COTTONS."[22] In the *Macon Weekly Telegraph* an advertisement alerted buyers to the "manufacturing near Augusta" of "first rate Negro Cloths, styled GEORGIA PLAINS, made of strong well twisted cotton warp and pure Wool filling."[23] The term appears less frequently in the business and personal writings of antebellum slaveholders, runaway advertisements, and the records of the formerly enslaved. All of these sources are more likely to describe clothing according to the fibers used to make the cloth, or use other textile terminology such as osnaburg, kersey, plains, or Jacobs's term linsey-woolsey.

The general absence of the term "negro cloth" as colloquial, but its prevalence in the capitalist textile economy, suggests that it was a term used to both attract consumers who needed a very low-quality, cheap product for their enslaved property, and to mark that same product as undesirable for use in clothing free, white bodies. The process of racing a product such as negro cloth was slowly solidified over time. In the early years of colonial settlement, enslavers did use it frequently themselves when describing the clothing of runaways in newspaper advertisements.[24] By the antebellum period, it was likely that readers of runaway advertisements assumed that fugitives were wearing negro cloth because it had been so long associated with enslaved bodies. Negro cloth is one example of how the capitalist world economy assisted in solidifying and encouraging racism and race-based slavery by creating and marketing products meant to be used exclusively by enslaved black people.

Of course, the cheap price of negro cloth was also an attractive incentive for economizing slaveholders, particularly those who needed to clothe dozens or even hundreds of enslaved laborers. What remains unclear is how this fabric differed from other kinds of low-end textiles meant for use as work clothing. If anything distinguished negro cloth from other types of apparel fabrics of the time, it was its extremely low grade. The many references formerly enslaved people made to the quality of their clothing being similar to bagging or sacking indicates that their clothing was no better than or even the very same as these utilitarian fabrics.

Enslavers conceptualized enslaved people as merely property, often treating them with the same bodily and emotional care as any other good that could be bought and sold. By housing the bodies of the enslaved in cloth with the same characteristics as sacks or bags used to contain inanimate products, enslavers attempted to reinforce their definitions of enslaved people as less than human.[25] Taking this association more literally, Sarah Laws Hill testified that the people on the plantation where she lived "were given discarded gunny sacks" as their only clothing.[26] This connection to sacking also suggested that white people of any class were above wearing negro cloth as it was a type of fabric meant to be used as clothing only if that clothed body was legal property.

Negro cloth was closely connected to the textile trade between the South and manufacturers in England and the United States.[27] The mechanization of spinning and weaving marked a profound and important shift in the American North, which became increasingly urbanized and market-oriented in part because of the solidification and expansion of the textile industry in the mid-nineteenth century. Most of these factories made cheap household and apparel fabrics, including those used by southern enslavers to clothe enslaved people. Some manufacturers began expanding into the ready-made apparel industry, paying mostly female workers by the piece to sew garments made from the fabrics manufactured in their mills, which were then sold as finished products.[28]

The burgeoning ready-made industry in New England and the Mid-Atlantic found one of its best markets in southern enslavers. In an 1848 account with a Philadelphia merchant, planter John Devereux purchased "66 large size negro Blankets" for one dollar apiece.[29] Another planter from South Carolina listed coats ordered by size, including two frock coats, in his plantation journal.[30] These enslavers reasoned that the higher cost of finished goods was worth spending because it saved them the extra labor of enslaved people, who would have otherwise made these items.

Two Brooks Brothers coats purchased by Dr. William Mercer of Louisiana for men he enslaved survive as examples of ready-made apparel. The dark tan fulled wool coats, one a frock coat and the other a livery coat, were likely purchased by Mercer during one of his many trips to New York City, where he bought plantation tools and bulk purchases of cloth and "negro shoes" each year in addition to expensive wines and fancy items from Tiffany & Co.[31] Only the frock coat has a Brooks Brothers brand label in it, but both coats were made with the same lining material and similar construction methods, though the frock coat is of a slightly higher quality wool than the livery coat. The label for Brooks Brothers of New York in the interior collar of the frock coat, a firm that was known for its men's tailored clothing, is an early example of branded labeling of ready-made clothing. The firm began selling ready-made suits in 1849 and changed the name to Brooks Brothers in 1850.[32] The buttons on the coats are decorated with a raised design of a bird, said to be the Mercer family crest. While the enslaved men who wore these coats clearly did important work for Mercer, their bodies were marked as belonging to the Mercer family through the wearing of similar looking apparel embellished with the same buttons.[33]

These coats represent a newer way of purchasing clothing that was used by lower and working-class people in addition to enslavers. In buying them, Mercer was exercising his ability to consume goods from a far-off metropolitan city in the North. He also used the coats to identify the bodies of the enslaved men who wore them as belonging to him—a uniform that signified to others that he had the monetary capital to own people and to clothe them well—thus increasing his cultural capital as a man of wealth and prestige.

Some enslavers kept their textile purchases more local. While most cotton manufacturing took place outside the South, there were a significant number of textile mills in the southern states before the Civil War. By 1850 the state of Georgia alone had over two dozen cotton mills.[34] These mills marketed to the needs of the immediate surrounding area, producing primarily rough cloth for other kinds of household use as well as negro cloth for clothing enslaved people.[35] They were relatively small mills that sometimes only operated seasonally, shutting down or reducing output during the summer months.

Mahala Jewel remembered her enslaver taking a train to Augusta, Georgia, to purchase cloth instead of from the nearer town stores: "Dere was new dresses for de gals and clothes for de boys too, and us felt mighty proud when us dressed up in dem store bought clothes f'um 'Gusty."[36] Jewel also noted that most clothing was woven on the plantation, so there was something special about the quality of the Augusta cloth that made it more valuable to her. Ellen Claibourn, who worked in the house, said, "Marster uster buy us cloth from the 'Gusta Fact'ry in checks and plaids for our dresses, but all the fiel'-hands clothes was made out of cloth what was wove on mistis' own loom."[37] The descriptions from Jewel and Claibourn suggest that while store-bought cloth was not of excellent quality, it was still better than anything manufactured by hand.[38]

Enslaved people understood that plantation managers and owners defined and divided labor according to work done that directly affected the success of a cash crop versus work done for the upkeep and maintenance of the plantation. George Womble described these divisions of labor along gendered lines. "The men worked every day in the week while the women were given Saturday afternoon off so that they might do their personal work such as the washing and the repairing of their clothing etc. The women were required to do the washing and the repairing of the single men's clothing in addition to their own. No night work was required of any of them except during the winter when they were given three cuts of thread to card, reel, and spin each night."[39] Womble described the women's Saturday's as "off" and having "no" labor in the evening because they were not doing work related to the cash crop.

This type of necessary maintenance work was often dismissed by plantation managers as inconsequential or not considered to be labor. An overseer employed on a plantation owned by Rice Ballard took notes of the work enslaved people performed each day. Several entries include information about cloth production. On November 23, 1848, the overseer wrote, "Wet day, nothing at all done of any importance the women engaged at the House Spinning, Sewing Thread, Karding Bats, & making Comforts."[40] That the overseer considered all of this labor of no importance to the overall productivity of the plantation was a common perception of women's work.[41]

Enslaved women in particular were closely involved with the production of their apparel. On some plantations, this meant growing cotton and linen and raising sheep for wool and cows for leather. John Wells recalled working as "a shepherd boy" during slavery, and Lottie Jones said that the plantation she worked on "raised sheep of different colors, dere wuz white, black and yellow, and so we didn' dye de wool."[42] Livestock such as sheep and cattle required care year-round just like the crops. Patsy Jane Bland noted that she did work related to the processing of both linen and wool textiles, stating that she "spun flax, cut wool off sheep, washed it, carded and spun it for stockings and underwear."[43]

John Boyd recalled "the winter woolens were made from the wool sheared from the sheep every May. Wool was taken to the factory at Bivensville and there made into yarn."[44] Sina Banks noted that before the wool was taken to a factory to be processed, it had to be "washed, picked apart and combed."[45] As a child, Nicey Kinney helped with the shearing of the sheep. After the animal was tied to a scaffold, Kinney was instructed to "set on de sheep's head whilst he cut off de wool."[46] Kinney noted that their wool was sent off the plantation to be cleaned and prepared for spinning.

Some planters also raised flax on a portion of their land, which was processed into linen for home use. In addition to sheep, Sina Banks lived on a plantation where flax was raised:

> Flax grew about two feet high and hemp about three high. The hands would go through and cut it down and let it lay there till it rotted. It was then gathered up and placed in the brakes. A brake was a frame on a stand with a slatted floor about three feet long and three or four feet high. The flax was laid across these slats and a lever pressed down to break the chaff from the coarse thread like skin. The chaff fell to the ground and the skins were placed in piles to be run through the heckles. Heckles were comb-like things made of wood with teeth like a comb or brush. The flax was combed through three or four heckles each one a little finer than the other. This product was called tow. This made coarse linen.[47]

Her detailed description of the plant and how it was prepared for spinning indicates she was likely involved in this labor herself.

On some cotton plantations, a portion of the cash crop was set aside for home use rather than shipped to market. Rose Williams gave an abbreviated summary of the months of work that went into transforming cotton from boll to fabric.[48] Her recollections demonstrate the close relationship enslaved people had to their clothing through this process. Williams stated, "Clothes dat we wore was made right dar what we lives, first we picks de cotton in baskets, den feeds it ter a little ole gin. . . . Den it was carded, spinned, and den weaved and made into our clothes."[49] Breaking down the many steps listed by Williams shows that nearly every day of enslaved people's lives was involved in textile production of some kind, whether it was plowing land that would eventually grow cotton to be manufactured in Manchester, or hand sewing the sleeves of a jacket.

Enslaved people often took great time and energy to color the thread, yarn, and cloth that they produced to set it apart. Dyeing was done either before the thread or yarn was woven in order to create colored designs such as stripes and checks, or it was done after weaving to achieve a solid colored fabric. Women were usually the ones to do the dyeing, sometimes with the assistance of children in gathering natural dyestuffs or tending fires.

Dyestuffs could be procured from locally available natural items, or they could be purchased. Enslavers and enslaved people procured a variety of coloring agents. Marie Askin Simpson remembered, "Yarn was dyed all sorts of pretty colors, red, black, yellow, blue, brown, and purple."[50] Indigo was a popular crop grown across the South in the antebellum period and used locally to dye textiles. A wide array of other dyestuffs was available either cultivated or wild, including sumac, walnut hulls, red clay, and poke berries.[51] Copperas was a common dyestuff in the South that could be used as a colorant or a binding agent. If properly processed, enslaved people could create a rainbow of colors, the most common being shades of yellow and brown. For brighter colors, red was the easiest to obtain in a colorfast dye from natural dyestuff. All of these dyes, particularly those available in the wild, provided opportunities for enslaved people to personalize their clothing without incurring expenses.

Knowledge about dyeing and dyestuffs came from many sources. Some of it was passed down through generations from African ancestors. In the Benin in West Africa women were the dyers, weavers, and spinners before and during the Atlantic slave trade era.[52] Dyeing, weaving, and spinning also all had a long history in Europe, where many English women knew how to spin, and increasingly also how to weave and dye as the network of the guild system was broken down over the eighteenth century.[53] Weaving and spinning were likely skills women of both races taught each other, though by the antebellum period these tasks were seen as below the station of elite white women.[54] In the North American colonies, both Europeans and Africans encountered new plants that contained multiple possibilities as dyestuffs. The natural dyes of the antebellum South were likely a combination of several world cultures adapting previous knowledge to a new environment; this was a shared knowledge of skills that created a uniquely American dye culture.

Once dyed, thread could be woven into stripes, checks, and—if someone skilled enough in weaving was available—multicolored plaids. Cloth dyed in the piece or finished garments that were dyed could set a person apart from the crowd. In places where dozens of people were given the same textile supplies or clothing allotments, such differences in appearance could have a big impact. A great amount of labor went into the dyeing of thread, fabric, and garments that were often not going to last more than a year. These efforts to create individualized fabrics and garments despite the limited time they would exist and the heavy use they would see as work clothing demonstrates the value enslaved people placed on looking unique.

The intimate knowledge enslaved people had about the production of textiles from raw materials to finished garments affected how they understood the clothing they wore. Even those who did not participate regularly in making fabric or clothing were aware of the labor done by others to provide garments for all. This was especially true on cotton plantations of the antebellum period, where enslaved people were integral in every single step of the creation of clothing, from its beginnings as a seed. Most enslaved people lived in isolated rural locations, yet they were undoubtedly aware of their importance within a global market as both producers and consumers. Knowing how to spin, weave, and dye cloth aided enslaved people in customizing their everyday work clothing, while sewing, laundering, and mending helped them in their endeavors to resist conditions of servitude.

Many factors contributed to an enslaved person's access to clothing, including whether they were enslaved in an urban or rural environment, whether they had special skills, their ability to supplement their wardrobe with cast-offs, and the basic supply levels that differed between enslavers. This varied so much across the South that it is impossible to make a general statement regarding the quality and quantity of enslaved southerners' wardrobes. What is abundantly clear is that enslaved people created their own fashions through manipulating the clothing allowance given them through altering the appearance of the cloth itself in dyeing it, repurposing worn clothing as underwear or patching material, and adding additional apparel through purchases or gifts.

The plantation books of James Heyward of South Carolina provide a good example of how slave clothing appears in the written historical record. His surviving plantation books cover the years 1852 to 1858 and contain cloth and blanket distribution lists for three different plantations he owned. Enslaved people received clothing once a year in late November or early December.[55] Many enslavers gave clothing in the late spring as well as in winter, while others distributed clothing throughout the year as it was needed. Others such as Heyward only handed out clothing in the winter, reasoning that by summer the cloth would be worn enough to be thinner, but substantial enough to last until the next winter. Although the rhythm of plantation life differed slightly by the crops grown, most of the heavy work would be done in the late spring during planting and by the midwinter after harvesting. Clothing goods would be given out at these times for a variety of reasons, such as a reward for the work done during the year or as a Christmas or New Year present.

Often, as is the case with Heyward's plantations, enslaved people received yardage and supplies for finishing it into garments. For the one hundred enslaved people on the Comingtee Plantation of the Ball family in South Carolina, an account entry titled "Cloth for 1856" lists the following items as purchased and distributed: "120 yds. Blue [fabric]; 630 yd white [fabric]; 40 Doz metal [buttons]; 40 Doz Horn [buttons]; 200 needles; 120 skeins Blue [yarn or thread]; 630 ditto White, Brown [yarn or thread]; 102 caps; 44 1st Blankets; 26 2nd [blankets]; 8 ditto [blankets] Infants; 2 Great coats."[56] On this plantation, enslaved people received clothing in December and again in May or June, indicating that this list is probably only for winter clothing given in December of 1855 for use in 1856.

The large quantities of textiles and supplies purchased were balanced out by the incredibly cheap prices of these fabrics. For an example of cost comparison of two kinds of fabrics, in 1833 a customer purchased 294 yards of osnaburg (a usually cotton or linen fabric used as summer clothing) at a total of $32.34, or roughly $0.11 cents per yard. In the same transaction he also bought six and a half yards of Paris muslin for a total of $6.50, or $1.00 per yard. A typical woman's dress of relatively simple style at this time would require between five and seven yards of fabric. Assuming a dress took six and a half yards of fabric, it cost him roughly seventy-two cents to clothe one enslaved woman in an osnaburg dress, or less than one tenth the cost of a relatively fine dress.[57]

Having time to sew the yards of cloth that were doled out presented another reason for giving it at a relatively idle time in the crop cycle since enslaved people would not be needed in the fields. On many cotton plantations the winter work of ginning and baling was done by men, while women worked indoors spinning, weaving, or sewing. Heyward's lists are organized with the first column listing male and female people by name followed by several columns with different types of apparel. These columns are labeled "white cloth," "blue cloth," "shoes," "blankets," "caps," "handkerchiefs," "great coats," and "homespun." Different yardage amounts of cloth are given under the appropriate columns, with the majority of people listed receiving five and a half yards of white cloth and six yards of homespun. Only the first four people listed received blue cloth, each receiving six yards. The first person listed has the word "driver" after his name, indicating that this man had a certain amount of authority over the others.[58] By giving enslaved people with higher authority or special skills different clothing goods, which were often of better quality than what the majority received, enslavers established a visual hierarchy among the enslaved population. Access by some to better goods could create tension within enslaved communities, which enslavers knew and worked to their advantage as a method of controlling such large numbers of people. These different fabrics were also an opportunity for enslaved people to barter and trade with each other, creating further access to a variety of textiles.[59]

People who were enslaved in towns rather than rural settings tended to have access to a higher quality and wider array of clothing. George Eason, who worked in the city and on a plantation during enslavement, told an interviewer that in the city house, "They all had good clothing," but "clothing on the Ormand plantation was usually insufficient to satisfy the needs of the slave."[60] Eason also recalled that women in the city wore calico dresses and the men had suits "of good grade cloth," while men and women on the plantation wore clothing made from homespun.[61] The terminology Eason used to describe the textiles of urban versus rural enslaved people indicates that cloth used to clothe people whose bodies were more readily on display to other whites in cities and towns was of a different quality from the cloth on the bodies of rural field hands.

A woman's sleeveless white cotton apron in the Charleston Museum's collection provides a rare surviving example of everyday work clothing typically worn by enslaved people in the antebellum South. The apron is open at the back but closes at the neck with a drawstring, and the hem is trimmed with five tucks ending with a picot edge. An old card that likely came with the apron when it found its home in the Charleston Museum says, "Slave apron, worn when serving."[62] This brief card provides a hint as to why this apron has a fancy edging. The person who wore it likely did so while serving her enslavers and their guests either in a city house or in the plantation's Big House.

A second surviving apron, made of a rougher, cheaper-quality cotton than the first apron, has sleeves, which probably served the important purpose of protecting the wearer's arms. Like the first apron, it came with a small card when it entered the collection of the Charleston Museum. The cotton fabric is referred to as "osnaberg," and the note says this apron was "worn when working."[63] The placement of the sleeves in relation to the neckline and the lack of any shaping at the shoulders are intriguing, as are the reddish stains that appear all over the garment. The stains, which might be anything from remnants of foodstuffs to some sort of cleaning agent, may provide a clue about how this apron was used. Chemical analysis could perhaps provide more conclusive answers, but like so many details of history, the specific work the apron's wearer performed will likely remain a mystery.

These two plain white aprons look similar in appearance at first glance, but they served two very different purposes. The first, higher-quality apron was worn by a woman who worked around her enslavers and their guests. Enslaved people who labored in the homes of enslavers often had better-quality clothing than their field-working counterparts. In part, this was due to the use of enslaved bodies to display wealth. A healthy, clean, and well-dressed enslaved person was a sign to white visitors that the enslaver had the income not only to own people but also to provide amply for their care. The second apron was probably used by an enslaved woman who worked out in the fields or in the kitchen of the house, away from the prying eyes of white guests. This woman's physical appearance was not as valuable to the enslaver as her physical labor.

The valuation of an enslaved person's clothed body by the enslaver of that person and the enslavers' peers speaks to Daina Ramey Berry's conception of the multiple values of enslaved bodies. Berry's framework of external values used by enslavers and internal values used by enslaved people can be applied to the used of enslaved bodies as valuable sites of display. The external values Berry discusses are based upon monetary values, but there was also a value of cultural capital that enslavers practiced upon enslaved bodies.[64] The coats purchased by William Newton Mercer from Brooks Brothers and the two aprons discussed above served to identify enslaved bodies not as their own, but as the property of an enslaver, who gained social standing and displayed his or her wealth. Frank Bell, who worked in a brothel, said of his apparel,

"The clothes I wore was some of the masters. They have holes in them and he give them to me cause I'se have to work where everybody that comes to masters could see me."[65] The value of well-clothed enslaved bodies served to indicate to other enslavers that certain enslaved bodies belonged to particular persons of importance within the social world of the ruling class.

In the antebellum South, notions of paternalism from the enslaver toward enslaved people could also be used through clothing, specifically in expectations of cleanliness. On many plantations, enslaved people were expected to spend all or part of their evenings and Saturdays cleaning their living quarters, their belongings, and themselves.[66] Tom Douglas recalled, "We had to go nice and clean. If old missus caught us dirty our hide was busted."[67] Callie Williams noted that she "must appear in clean clothes Monday morning to go to work, or else get punished for being dirty."[68] Williams also "said the slaves did not work on Saturday afternoons; that was their time to clean up their quarters and wash their clothes."[69] Here again is an example of work being done, but not considered labor. Saturday afternoons and Sundays on many plantations were times for enslaved people to care for their bodies, their homes, and their social lives. Mose Davis remarked that enslaved people did "personal work such as the washing and the repairing of clothing" after spending the day laboring, "since no work was required at night."[70] By requiring enslaved people to be clean at the risk of punishment, enslavers extended their realm of control into time that was not really available for enslaved people to spend unreservedly. This extra work served the cultural-capital value of enslaved bodies for enslavers, who could present to society material evidence of what they saw as a civilizing influence over black people and the success of the paternalistic project.

Enslaved people did not wash themselves and their clothing only because they were required to. The pride in appearance and the care taken of clothing was an important part of life during enslavement. Hattie Sugg recalled that her mother used her task of soap-making to obtain what she needed to wash her own items. Sugg said her mother would "steal a gourd full of it an' bury it some place to wash our Sunday clothes with." Sugg also remarked that it must all be washed on Sunday, the only time Sugg's mother had to do this kind of work for herself and her family.[71] The time and care Sugg's mother spent washing their clothing in good quality soap draws on the internal value Berry discusses in her work, what she terms a "soul value." Attention to appearance was a method of displaying this "intangible marker that often defied monetization yet spoke to the spirit and soul of who they were as human beings."[72] Enslavers cared about levels of cleanliness in terms of retaining their control and their investment, either through practical concerns of disease or the display of black bodies as cultural capital. By investing her limited free time in performing labor for her family, Sugg's mother was asserting her soul value for herself and reaffirming that of her family. Her labor furthered this investment by allowing them to present themselves in well-laundered clothing.

Stephanie M. H. Camp's concept that enslaved people lived within three bodies—the body of domination, the body of suffering, and the body of pleasure—is another method of thinking about the valuation of enslaved bodies.[73] All three of the bodies Camp identifies existed within the one physical body of every enslaved individual at the same time. One did not exist without the others, and the conditions of enslavement caused the existence of all three. Camp's framework allows a better understanding of how the values placed on enslaved people's bodies by enslavers are ever-present even when seeing how enslaved people valued themselves. The dominated, suffering, and pleasurable bodies Camp defines represent the experience of a single person who lived in all of those bodies. When a woman appeared neatly attired in a clean apron, she met the expectations of enslavers and how they valued her clothed body as a place to gain cultural capital while also materially expressing her soul value.

Camp uses her theories of the enslaved body to explore moments when enslaved people escaped temporarily to dress up in fine clothing and hold parties.[74] There is a difference between dressing for work and dressing for pleasure. This distinction is possibly the most misunderstood aspect of enslaved people and their clothing. Much more attention has been paid to the fashionable or fancy clothing enslaved people obtained through various means. Dressing up is often interpreted rightly as an opportunity for enslaved people to have greater individual and community expression through more colorful, higher-quality garments and accessories than their everyday work clothing.[75] The examination of fine clothing as a site for resistance against oppression has resulted in the ignoring of the importance of everyday clothing to the material life of slavery. Enslaved people spent the majority of their time laboring, thus they spent most of their lives wearing work clothing. The social and cultural habits enslaved people practiced outside of work, such as dressing in individualized clothing, certainly carried over into their social habits when working.[76]

Individualization of clothing often resulted from necessity. As clothing wore out, it would sometimes be turned into underclothes or used to patch other apparel. As noted earlier, the quality of the cloth used for enslaved people's work clothing was very poor and not meant to last. Better textile goods used for work clothing of the same period could still last years with proper maintenance, while most enslaved people had thoroughly worn out their apparel in a year. This was cloth meant to be discarded and replaced, unlike other textiles of the time that were meant to be maintained and used for longer periods. Also contributing to the throwaway nature of negro cloth was the very little time or skill available to enslaved people to maintain their clothing. Most could sew a patch, but a proper (ideally unnoticeable) mending job was beyond the sewing skills or time commitment available to the average enslaved person. In the dominant American fashion system, patches indicated that the person could not afford to pay for proper clothing maintenance more than indicating they could not afford to buy new. Even the wealthiest plantation owners paid or enslaved professional seamstresses and tailors to mend, turn, and alter clothing so that it would last a few years.[77]

An advertisement for Virgil noted that he was wearing "Virginia cloth trowsers, much patched" when he ran away.[78] Sylvia Cannon remembered that she made a "petticoat out of old dress an patch en patch till couldn' tell which place weave."[79] Cannon was not given an undergarment by her owner, so she created one for herself by repurposing an old piece of clothing and smaller rags to patch it and make it last longer. The excessively patched garment Cannon made is an example of creative consumerism indicative of the improvisation enslaved people practiced in manipulating their limited access to clothing into an opportunity for self-expression and individualization. It is likely that enslaved people turned the stigma toward patching in American fashion into a useful method of expressing individuality in their clothing. Rather than shunning obvious patches, they interpreted them as aesthetically pleasing. This creative expression through reuse and adaptation is another example of enslaved people displaying their soul value through clothing and appearance. In seeking to make space for themselves and others, they fashioned alternate dress codes that allowed them to extend their self-evaluation and that of their communities into subcultures that sometimes reached into dominant ways of dressing and styles in mainstream American fashion.

Though Callie Bracey was not born until after the end of slavery, she did know many stories of life during enslavement from her mother, Louise Terrell. Similar to Cannon, Terrell repurposed old clothing. Bracey said that her mother "was given two dresses a year," and that "her old dress from last year, she wore as an underskirt."[80] In some cases, enslaved people were provided underclothes. A few recalled a very specific undergarment known as a balmoral petticoat; Lina Hunter recalled them as being "some sight, but dey was show warm as hell."⁸¹ What Hunter means in describing these petticoats as "some sight" is partially explained in the meaning of the term. Balmoral petticoats were of a heavy woolen and usually dyed red, sometimes striped with black.⁸² They were a splash of color underneath a woman's dress and helped to keep her legs warm in the winter months.

Nothing about the clothing enslaved people wore explains the ways they could be distinguished from other poor or laboring people. Mollie Dawson recalled, "Marser [N]ewman and his folks wore a little bettah clothes den de slaves did, but de clothes dat dey wore fer evey day on de farm was jest like ours."⁸³ Newman and his family probably replaced their work clothing more often, but the only other main identifier of who was owner and who was owned had nothing to do with an item of clothing. If enslavers and other white laborers sometimes wore the same work clothing as enslaved people, then skin color was the main visual identifier of who was enslaved and who was free.⁸⁴

Runaway advertisements provide insight into how everyday clothing of the working classes served to exclude free black people as Americans. Many notices of African Americans jailed as runaways in Easton, Maryland, include the statement "says he is free" or "says she is free." Their clothing is not markedly different than that of advertisements describing people without a claim to free status noted. While this source does not necessarily reveal how all free black people dressed on a daily basis, it does demonstrate the way in which race operated as a part of the fashion system in America. An unfamiliar black person dressed in common work clothing or in ragged clothing was assumed by the white community to be a fugitive because of his or her skin color. For example, Jacob Blunt was taken up in Richmond, Virginia, as a runaway wearing "common negro clothing, and very ragged and dirty," despite his claim to be free and his even having free papers with him.⁸⁵ Thus in antebellum American culture, skin color was a part of the fashion system and the black body an unfashionable article of clothing.⁸⁶ This irremovable apparel became a more important marker of identity than clothing itself that differentiated enslaved people from working-class and poor white people, and attempted to erase the existence of free black people as part of the United States.⁸⁷

Ultimately, knowing more about the clothing of enslaved people in the antebellum South demonstrates how deeply entrenched race and racism were in the United States by the antebellum period. Even something as trivialized as the fashion system was used by white people to exclude African Americans from participating in American culture, from expressing themselves individually and collectively, and from being recognized as contributors to mainstream society. Patches became tools for resistance when enslaved people used them to throw off the "badge of slavery" as Harriet Jacobs called it, that came with the wearing of negro cloth. Meanwhile, enslavers used their cultural capital in the race-based fashion system to dismiss enslaved peoples' efforts at collective and self-expression.

Every moment of life became a contest between enslaving and enslaved people in a power system as uneven as the antebellum US South. The ruling class attempted to control their human property by various avenues, including the physical appearance of enslaved bodies. Enslavers gained cultural capital by defining a visual representation of the enslaved body as only property, monochrome and monotonous, one person virtually indistinguishable from the next, and a tool to display their own wealth and social standing. Enslaved people resisted this valuation by individualizing their everyday appearance in subtle ways that went undetected by enslavers.[88] Enslaved people dyed and embellished cloth given as an allowance, and reused and reworked cast-off, gifted, or trashed clothing to supplement their work wardrobes. Sources reveal a visualization of slavery that demonstrates the everyday wear of enslaved southerners in the antebellum period was highly individualized and comprised a multitude of fabrics, colors, and styles.

Enslaved people were on the front lines of production and were the indirect consumers of negro cloth, a product that marked the first step in defining black bodies as unfashionable. They acted as producers and consumers, though they did not legally own their labor or their moveable property. Yet their economic power as consumers within the southern economy helped to undermine their legal status as property. Enslaved southerners continually used their position as consumers of goods to resist their situation as consumed goods by insisting on their own fashionability. They struggled against a racist culture that attempted to exclude them as valid participants in and creators of American fashion culture. Understanding how they defined space for their bodies when clothed in negro cloth, the product of a new and fast-growing racist global capitalism, centers enslaved people in this historical moment and within the longer history of the modern textile and fashion industries.

Notes

1. Harriet Jacobs, *Incidents in the Life of a Slave Girl*, edited by Jean Fagan Yellin (Cambridge: Harvard University Press, 2000), 11.

2. Robert S. DuPlessis, "Cloth and the Emergence of the Atlantic Economy," in Peter A.

Coclanis, ed. *The Atlantic Economy during the Seventeenth and Eighteenth Centuries: Organization, Operation, Practice, and Personnel* (Columbia: University of South Carolina Press, 1999), 72–94 (quotation page 83). See also Robert S. DuPlessis, *The Material Atlantic: Clothing, Commerce, and Colonization in the Atlantic World, 1650–1800* (Cambridge: Cambridge University Press, 2016) and Joseph E. Inikori and Stanley L. Engerman, eds., *The Atlantic Slave Trade: Effects on Economies, Societies, and Peoples in Africa, the Americas, and Europe* (Durham: Duke University Press, 1992).

3. The term negro cloth encompassed a variety of fabrics throughout the late eighteenth and early nineteenth centuries made from linen, cotton, wool, or mixed combinations of these fibers. These fabrics went by other names, including plains, woolen, kersey, Lowells, and linsey-woolsey.

4. Recent publications on the global economies of cotton and slavery include Edward E. Baptist, *The Half Has Never Been Told: Slavery and the Making of American Capitalism* (New York: Basic Books, 2014); Sven Beckert, *Empire of Cotton: A Global History* (New York: Alfred A. Knopf, 2015); Sven Beckert and Seth Rockman, eds., *Slavery's Capitalism: A New History of America's Economic Development* (Philadelphia: University of Pennsylvania Press, 2016); Walter Johnson, *River of Dark Dreams: Slavery and Empire in the Cotton Kingdom* (Boston: Belknap Press, 2013).

5. I use the phrase "Africanisms in American culture" in reference to a collection of essays edited by Joseph E. Holloway, *Africanisms in American Culture* (Bloomington and Indianapolis: Indiana University Press, 1990). For an assessment of the earliest scholarship on African Americans and American material culture, see the introduction in Holloway and Theodore C. Landmark, "Comments on African American Contributions to American Material Life," *Winterthur Portfolio* 33: 4 (Winter 1998), 261–282. For a more recent collection of scholarship on this topic see Jacob U. Gordon, ed., *The African Presence in Black America* (Trenton: Africa World Press, 2004).

6. My primary data source for newspapers was the digital archive "America's Historical Newspapers." I used the query terms "runaway" and "negro," and limited my search to only advertisements for the period 1830–1865. This provided a sample of several hundred runaway advertisements and dozens of merchant's advertisements for textile and clothing goods.

7. There have been many arguments for and against the use of the WPA narratives as a reliable source given that the people interviewed were far removed from the time of enslavement, most were children during slavery, and many were interviewed in the rural South by white interviewers in the midst of Jim Crow segregation and racial violence. I have chosen to rely on these sources as valid because of the commonalities across so many interviews and the agreements of the statements with other kinds of sources that date more closely to the antebellum period. For other views regarding the WPA narratives as a source, see Stephanie M. H. Camp, *Closer to Freedom: Enslaved Women and Everyday Resistance in the Plantation South* (Chapel Hill: University of North Carolina Press, 2004), 8; Walter Johnson, *Soul by Soul: Life Inside the Antebellum Slave Market* (Cambridge, MA: Harvard University Press, 1999), 9–11, 226n24; C. Vann Woodward, "History from Slave Sources: A Review Article," *American Historical Review* 79 (April 1974), 470–81. The amount and quality of clothing of enslaved people was a standard question on the list given to interviewers, though some did not stick to this script.

8. During research for my dissertation I located approximately thirty items of clothing, shoes, and apparel accessories. This list is evolving as I locate new pieces or learn more about the provenance of those already brought to my attention. See a table in the Introduction of Katie Knowles, "Fashioning Slavery: Slaves and Clothing in the U.S. South, 1830–1865," doctoral thesis, Rice University, 2014.

9. Malcolm Barnard, *Fashion as Communication* (2nd edition; London and New York, 2002). 12. For more on theories of fashion and dress as methods of communication, see Alison Lurie, *The Language of Clothes* (New York: Henry Holt and Company, 2000); Tim Edwards, *Fashion in Focus: Concepts, Practices, and Politics* (London and New York: Routledge, 2011); Elizabeth Wilson, *Adorned in Dreams* (New Brunswick: Rutgers University Press, 2003). Roland Barthes is credited with originating this theory in his work *The Fashion System* (New York: Hill and Wang, 1983).

10. Barnard, *Fashion as Communication*. 95; Edwards, *Fashion in Focus*. 2; Ruth P. Rubenstein, *Dress Codes: Meanings and Messages in American Culture* (Boulder, CO: Westview Press, 2001), 150.

11. When thinking about enslavers' motivations, cultural dominance cannot be separated totally from their capitalist desires to spend as little as possible. The goal of saving money by purchasing poor quality fabrics for enslaved people paired well with the additional result of enslaved bodies appearing unfashionable. Conceptualizing fashion as a power relationship also assists in understanding how it became an important method of resistance against racism for enslaved and free black people in the antebellum United States.

12. Marisa J. Fuentes, *Dispossessed Lives: Enslaved Women, Violence, and the Archive* (Philadelphia: University of Pennsylvania Press, 2016), 7.

13. Fuentes, *Dispossessed Lives*, 77–78. Fuentes also discusses the violence of archival sources in the perpetuation of silences and prejudices, which can be expanded to include the violence of the material archive, as the surviving clothing of enslaved people is nominal and was primarily saved by white people who were enslavers or were descended from enslavers.

14. See for example Baptist, *The Half Has Never Been Told*; Beckert, *Empire of Cotton*; Beckert and Rockman, eds., *Slavery's Capitalism*; Giorgio Riello, *Cotton: The Fabric That Made the Modern World* (Cambridge: Cambridge University Press, 2013). Seth Rockman is currently researching the connections between products made in the North for sale to plantations in the South. I am grateful to him for sharing his work with me and for assisting me with my own research.

15. *Oxford English Dictionary Online*. www.oed.com. Accessed July 18, 2017.

16. Florence M. Montgomery, *Textiles in America, 1650–1870* (New York: W. W. Norton & Company, 2007), 309.

17. Phyllis G. Tortora and Robert S. Merkel, *Fairchild's Dictionary of Textiles* (New York: Fairchild Publications, 2007), 382–383.

18. The earliest mention of negro cloth listed in the Oxford entry is 1653.

19. In his research of northern textile factories, specifically the Peacedale Manufactory in Rhode Island, Seth Rockman reached similar conclusions about negro cloth being ascribed a racial or racist connection.

20. Keri Leigh Merritt, *Masterless Men: Poor Whites and Slavery in the Antebellum South* (Cambridge: Cambridge University Press, 2017), 118; Tyler Rudd Putman, "The Slop Shop

and the Almshouse: Ready-made Menswear in Philadelphia, 1790–1820," master's thesis, University of Delaware, 2011.

21. Katie Knowles, "The Fabric of the Frontier: How Textiles Help Us Understand the American West," on "O Say Can You See," blog of the Smithsonian National Museum of American History, posted November 3, 2014, http://americanhistory.si.edu/blog/fabric-frontier-how-textiles-help-us-understand-american-west.

22. Advertisement. *New Orleans Times-Picayune*, April 3, 1839.

23. Advertisement. *Macon Weekly Telegraph*, September 8, 1846.

24. See Linda K. Baumgarten, "Plains, Plaid, and Cotton: Woolens for Slave Clothing," *Ars Textrina* 15 (1991), 203–222; Linda K. Baumgarten, "'Clothes for the People': Slave Clothing in Early Virginia," *Journal of Early Southern Decorative Arts* 14: 2 (November 1988), 26–70. My thanks as well to Andrew Johnson for sharing his findings in eighteenth-century runaway advertisements in South Carolina newspapers.

25. Kathleen M. Brown, *Foul Bodies: Cleanliness in Early America* (New Haven: Yale University Press, 2009), chapter 12; Camp, *Closer to Freedom*, chapter 3; Joan Entwistle, *The Fashioned Body: Fashion, Dress, and Modern Social Theory* (Malden, MA: Polity Press, 2000); Johnson, *River of Dark Dreams*, 207.

26. George P. Rawick, ed., *The American Slave: A Composite Autobiography*, supplement 2, vol. 1.16 (1941, Westport, CT: Greenwood Publishing Company, reprint ed., 1972), 402.

27. Beckert, *Empire of Cotton*; T. H. Breen, "Baubles of Britain," *Past and Present* 119 (1988), 73–102; T. H. Breen, "An Empire of Goods" *Journal of British Studies* (October 1986); T. H. Breen, *The Marketplace of Revolution* (2004); Johnson, *River of Dark Dreams*, 12, 480n15.

28. Barbara M. Tucker, *Industrializing Antebellum America: The Rise of Manufacturing Entrepreneurs in the Early Republic* (New York: Palgrave Macmillan, 2008). The establishment and development of the textile industry in the United States in the late colonial and early national periods is a fascinating yet incredibly understudied topic. The most useful surveys date back several decades, including Rolla Milton Tryon, *Household Manufactures in the United States, 1640–1860: A Study in Industrial History* (Chicago: University of Chicago Press, 1917); Harold Woodman, *King Cotton and His Retainers: Financing and Marketing the Cotton Crop of the South, 1800–1925* (Columbia: University of South Carolina Press, 1968); Thomas H. O'Connor, *Lords of the Loom: The Cotton Whigs and the Coming of the Civil War* (New York: Charles Scribner's Sons, 1968); Caroline Ware, *The Early New England Cotton Manufacture: A Study in Industrial Beginnings* (New York: Russell and Russell, 1966). One notable exception is Tucker, *Industrializing Antebellum America*. Economic historians have returned to this topic in more recent years, including Giorgio Riello, *Cotton: The Fabric That Made the Modern World* (Cambridge: Cambridge University Press, 2013); Sven Beckert, "Emancipation and Empire: Reconstructing the Worldwide Web of Cotton Production in the Age of the American Civil War," *American Historical Review* (December, 2004), 1405–1438; Beckert, *Empire of Cotton*; Joseph E. Inikori, *Africans and the Industrial Revolution in England: A Study in International Trade and Economic Development* (Cambridge: Cambridge University Press, 2002). However, these works take a global focus that often neglects the US textile industry in the nineteenth century for the dominant manufacturing powerhouses in Britain. For a good case study of one manufactory in Rhode Island, see Susan Oba, "'Mostly Made, Especially for This Purpose, in Providence, R.I.': The Rhode Island Negro Cloth In-

dustry," bachelor's thesis, Brown University, 2006. Seth Rockman's current research focuses on the same Rhode Island manufacturer as Oba's thesis.

29. John Devereux in account with M. Furrall, September 4, 1848, Devereux Family Papers, Duke University Special Collections.

30. Blanket List for 1853, Slave Blanket Book 1853–1860, South Carolina Historical Society.

31. William Newton Mercer papers, Manuscripts Collection 64, Louisiana Research Collection, Howard-Tilton Memorial Library, Tulane University, New Orleans, Louisiana; William Newton Mercer papers, Mss. 292, 1051, 1233, Louisiana and Lower Mississippi Valley Collections, LSU Libraries, Baton Rouge, Louisiana. By 1851 or 1852, Mercer was living in New Orleans rather than at one of his four plantations. He hired a man to manage them along with his four hundred slaves, while he lived in the city and invested in stocks, financing, and real estate. Throughout the 1850s Mercer traveled to New York in late May, placed orders to be sent south, and then traveled around the Northeast. He spent a significant amount of his time in Newport, Rhode Island, where he may have owned a house. Around late October or early November, he would return to New York and see off the goods he had ordered in May, then travel inland by river back to New Orleans, where he would arrive in time to receive the goods and have them settled into his New Orleans properties or sent to his plantations. It appears that he traveled with enslaved personal servants, but hired paid servants in Newport and stayed in hotels or with friends in other locations while traveling. Mercer's papers are available in the microfilm collection "Records of Ante-bellum Southern Plantations from the Revolution through the Civil War."

32. "Our Heritage" on Brooks Brothers company website, accessed July 23, 2017, http://www.brooksbrothers.com/about-us/about-us,default,pg.html. This fits with the style of the frock coat being from the 1850s. They also had a storefront at the corner of Grand Street and Broadway during these years, which is the location indicated on the label.

33. Object file, 2013.0138, Historic New Orleans Collection, New Orleans, Louisiana. This coat was passed down through the white family until it was purchased by the Historic New Orleans Collection in 2013. The family identified it as a great coat, not a frock coat, and family tradition held that Dr. Mercer himself wore this coat. While the Brooks Brothers label would signal high fashion and expense to modern sensibilities, in the early years the firm catered to all classes who could purchase tailored menswear of a variety of qualities and styles. It would have been very strange and unfashionable for a wealthy white man to go about in a frock coat that was nearly identical to the livery coat worn by his enslaved servant.

34. For work on the early southern textile industry, see: Tom Downey, *Planting a Capitalist South: Masters, Merchants, and Manufacturers in the Southern Interior, 1790–1860* (Baton Rouge: Louisiana State University Press, 2009); Michele Gillespie, "Building Networks of Knowledge: Henry Merrell and Textile Manufacturing in the Antebellum South," in *Technology, Innovation, and Southern Industrialization: From the Antebellum Era to the Computer Age*, edited by Susanna Delfino and Michele Gillespie (Columbia: University of Missouri Press, 2008), 97–124; Michele Gillespie, "To Harden a Lady's Hand: Gender Politics, Racial Realities, and Women Millworkers in Antebellum Georgia," in Susanna Delfino and Michele Gillespie, eds. *Neither Lady Nor Slave: Working Women of the Old South* (Chapel Hill: University of North Carolina Press, 2002), 261–284; Bess Beatty, "I Can't Get My Bored on Them Old Lomes: Female Textile Workers in the Antebellum South" in *Neither Lady Nor Slave: Work-*

ing Women of the Old South, 249–260; John Killick, "The Cotton Operations of Alexander Brown and Sons in the Deep South," *Journal of Southern History* 43: 2 (May 1977), 169–194. It should be remembered that textile production included other kinds of mechanization such as ginning factories, and in large measure the making and selling of gins. Angela Lakwete points to this aspect of antebellum southern industrialization in chapter five, "The Saw Gin Industry, 1830–1865," in *Inventing the Cotton Gin: Machine and Myth in Antebellum America* (Baltimore: Johns Hopkins University Press, 2003).

35. Interestingly, historians of the Piedmont and northern Georgia have noted a decline in home textile production during the 1840s and especially the 1850s. This decline coincides with the rapid rise in the number of small textile mills that sprouted up in these same regions. More research needs to be done in areas of the South that did not see concentrations of textile factories in order to determine how much correlation there is between locally available cheap textiles as replacements for homemade goods. See Lacy Ford, *Origins of Southern Radicalism: The South Carolina Upcountry, 1800–1860* (New York: Oxford University Press, 1988); Stephanie McCurry, *Masters of Small Worlds* (New York: Oxford University Press, 1997); Steven C. Hahn, *The Roots of Southern Populism: Yeoman Farmers and the Transformation of the Georgia Upcountry, 1850–1890* (New York: Oxford University Press, 1983).

36. Rawick, *American Slave*, vol. 12.2, 317.

37. Rawick, *American Slave*, vol. 12.1, 186–187.

38. The view that factory-made goods were better-quality than homemade goods is probably partially a reflection of the cultural assumptions of the Great Depression since Jewel and Claibourn were both interviewed about their experiences in slavery in 1937. However, similar views are expressed in records that do date to the antebellum period, indicating that there was a shift occurring in the valuation of factory goods as more prestigious than handmade items.

39. Rawick, *American Slave*, vol. 13.4, 183.

40. Plantation book for Magnolia Plantation, November 23, 1848, Rice C. Ballard Papers, Southern Historical Collection, University of North Carolina at Chapel Hill. There are several other similar entries in this plantation journal by the same overseer.

41. Recent scholarship examining the capitalist slavery system perpetuates this perception of certain kinds of labor as "non-work." For example, in Baptist's *The Half Has Never Been Told*, he explains in detail how the labor of enslaved people was defined and valued by enslavers on cotton plantations. His narrow focus on the time and type of labor done by enslaved people serves to relegate other kinds of labor, defined often by enslavers as free time or enslaved people performing work for their own benefits, into an unimportant status. In reality, clothing, housing, and eating were necessities of their survival so that they could return each day to the fields to perform what enslavers interpreted as real work. See Baptist, 118–119.

42. Rawick, *American Slave*, vol. 11.7, 85 (interview with John Wells); supplement 2, vol. 6.5, 2128 (interview with Lottie Jones).

43. Rawick, *American Slave*, supplement 1, vol. 5.1, 14.

44. Rawick, *American Slave*, vol. 2.1, 72.

45. Rawick, *American Slave*, supplement 1, vol. 12.1, 17. Banks also noted that the sheep were sheared in May. This was a common practice as it left the animals cooler during the hot summer months, but allowed enough time for them to regrow a full coat before the next winter.

46. Rawick, *American Slave*, vol. 13.3, 28.

47. Rawick, *American Slave*, supplement 1, vol. 12.1, 18.

48. For more on home production of flax and wool see Adrienne D. Hood, *The Weaver's Craft: Cloth, Commerce, and Industry in Early Pennsylvania* (Philadelphia: University of Pennsylvania Press, 2003), chapter 3.

49. Rawick, *American Slave*, supplement 2, vol. 10.9, 4125.

50. Rawick, *American Slave*, supplement 1, vol. 2.4, 232.

51. A useful table of the dyestuffs and mordants mentioned in the WPA slave narratives is "Appendix III" in Helen Bradley Foster, *"New Raiments of Self": African American Clothing in the Antebellum South* (Oxford: Berg, 1997).

52. Colleen E. Kriger, *Cloth in West African History* (Lanham, MD.: AltaMira Press, 2006), 43 and 124. In areas of West and Northeast Africa where the narrow treadle loom was used (known for producing the strip cloths popular as currency in African trade routes), men were the primary weavers. See Kriger, *Cloth in West Africa*, 70; Judith Perani and Norma Hackelman Wolff, *Cloth, Dress, and Art Patronage in West Africa* (Oxford and New York: Berg, 1999), 120.

53. Adrienne D. Hood, *The Weaver's Craft: Cloth, Commerce, and Industry in Early Pennsylvania* (Philadelphia: University of Pennsylvania Press, 2003); Marla R. Miller, *The Needle's Eye: Women and Work in the Age of Revolution* (Amherst: University of Massachusetts Press, 2006); Laurel Thather Ulrich, *The Age of Homespun: Objects and Stories in the Creation of an American Myth* (New York: Knopf, 2001). All three of these studies focus on the Northeast. For work specifically on England, see "Industry, Idleness, and Protest: The Spitalfields Weaver as Guild Member and Cultural Symbol," in Zara Anishanslin, *Portrait of a Woman in Silk: Hidden Histories of the British Atlantic World* (New Haven: Yale University Press, 2016), 124–139.

54. Drew Gilpin Faust, "Chapter Ten: If I Were Once Released: The Garb of Gender," in *Mothers of Invention: Women of the Slaveholding South in the American Civil War* (Chapel Hill: University of North Carolina Press, 1996), 220–233; Elizabeth Fox-Genovese, *Within the Plantation Household: Black and White Women of the Old South* (Chapel Hill: University of North Carolina Press, 1988).

55. James Heyward plantation book, 1852–1858, James Barnwell Heyward Papers, South Carolina Historical Society.

56. Entry for December 6, 1855. Comingtee Plantation Record Book. Duke University Special Collections. On this plantation the men received six yards of cloth and the women five yards, boys and girls listed as "second class" hands received between three-and-a-half and four yards of cloth. The number 150 for the total enslaved population comes from the individual entries for each person in this account entry, plus at least fifty children who were excluded from this list, but who numbered at least twenty-nine and whose mothers received from one to three yards per child. In 1856, the total number of children is listed at fifty-four in a separate entry. See also earlier record books for Ball family plantations, including Comingtee, at the South Carolina Historical Society; John Coming Ball Plantation Book. South Caroliniana Library at University of South Carolina; William James Ball Plantation Book. Southern Historical Collection, University of North Carolina at Chapel Hill.

57. Bill for A. North Jr. from David Hopkins, May 2, 1833, Hopkins Family Papers, South Carolina Historical Society. French muslin purchased in 1833 was a thin, almost gauze, fabric of high-quality cotton from India that was bleached white and sometimes printed or embroidered with small floral decorations. Six or seven yards would be enough to make a

woman's gown. Likely, this purchaser bought the muslin as a gift for a wife or daughter when he placed his seasonal order of clothing for the plantation. For another example of a detailed price list of different items for clothing, including several fabrics, buttons, needles, thread, etc., see the entry titled "Plantation Expenses" in the Weehaw Plantation Journal, 1855–1861. Henry A. Middleton Jr. Papers, South Carolina Historical Society.

58. Heyward Plantation Book, South Carolina Historical Society. All of the numbers given here are taken from the entry for Rotterdam plantation on November 16, 1852. The number of total people and the yardage they received varies little over the six-year span of the plantation book. This is one of the most complete lists throughout the record. Not all of them include columns for entering caps, handkerchiefs, and great coats. This may be because Heyward did not give out these items every year, or it may be that he simply varied in how he kept his records. Record books were often filled out by plantation overseers rather than the owner. The changing of overseers happened more frequently than the changing of owners and may account for the discrepancy in record keeping as well.

59. For an example of such a trade system, see Jillian E. Galle, "Designing Women: Measuring Acquisition and Access at the Hermitage Plantation," in Jillian E. Galle, ed., *Engendering African American Archaeology: A Southern Perspective* (Knoxville: University of Tennessee Press, 2004). Galle and the other archeologists on a project at Andrew Jackson's Hermitage plantation discovered a high concentration of sewing implements near one living space, indicating it was where the enslaved seamstress Gracy resided. But they also located many pins, needles, and scissors in other areas around the plantation. They concluded that Gracy, who did not have time to grow extra food, likely bartered with other enslaved people on the plantation with the tools of her trade for foodstuffs from their gardens.

60. Rawick, *American Slave*, vol. 12.1, 300–301.

61. Rawick, *American Slave*, vol. 12.1, 300–301.

62. Object file, HT2902, Charleston Museum. Charleston, South Carolina.

63. Object file, HT2903, Charleston Museum. Charleston, South Carolina. Both aprons were donated to the museum by the same woman, Elizabeth F. Smith, in 1926. Smith was a white woman likely involved in the project of mythmaking and remembering fondly the Old South, which was a popular trope in the 1920s. These aprons are an example of how the object archive is as violent as the written archive as explored by Marisa Fuentes in her book *Dispossessed Lives*.

64. Daina Ramey Berry, *The Price for Their Pound of Flesh: The Value of the Enslaved, from Womb to Grave, in the Building of a Nation* (Boston, MA: Beacon Press, 2017). Berry lays out her concepts of valuation succinctly on pages 6–7.

65. Rawick, *American Slave*, supplement 2, vol. 2.1, 238.

66. Brown, *Foul Bodies*, chapter 12.

67. Rawick, *American Slave*, vol. 8.2, 194.

68. Rawick, *American Slave*, supplement 1, vol. 1.1, 452.

69. Rawick, *American Slave*, supplement 1, vol. 1.1, 452.

70. Rawick, *American Slave*, vol. 12.1, 266.

71. Rawick, *American Slave*, supplement 1, vol. 10.5, 2076.

72. Berry, *The Price for Their Pound of Flesh*, 6.

73. Camp, *Closer to Freedom*, 66–68.

74. Camp, *Closer to Freedom*, chapter 3.

75. Camp, *Closer to Freedom*, chapter 3; Foster, 'New Raiments of Self'; Elizabeth Fox-Genovese, *Within the Plantation Household: Black and White Women of the Old South* (Chapel Hill: University of North Carolina Press, 1988), 216–219; Tamara J. Walker, *Exquisite Slaves: Race, Clothing, and Status in Colonial Lima* (Cambridge: Cambridge University Press, 2017), especially chapters 2 and 3; Shane White and Graham White, *Stylin': African American Expressive Culture from Its Beginnings to the Zoot* Suit (Ithaca: Cornell University Press, 1998); Deborah Gray White, White, *Ar'n't I a Woman?: Female Slaves in the Plantation South* (New York: W. W. Norton and Company, 1999), 143.

76. As Walter Johnson notes, "When slaves went into the field, they took with them social connections and affective ties"; in other words, their time working could not be totally separated from their time not working. See Johnson, *River of Dark Dreams*, 9.

77. Beverly Lemire, *Dress, Culture and Commerce: The English Clothing Trade before the Factory, 1660–1800*. (Basingstoke, UK: Macmillan/Palgrave, 1997); Miller, "Clothing and Consumers in Rural New England, 1760–1810," in *The Needle's Eye*, 25–55; John Styles, *The Dress of the People: Everyday Fashion in Eighteenth-Century England* (New Haven: Yale University Press, 2008).

78. Advertisement, *Austin City Gazette*, May 26, 1840.

79. Rawick, *American Slave*, vol. 2.1, 189.

80. Rawick, *American Slave*, vol. 6.2, 26.

81. Rawick, *American Slave*, vol. 12.2, 258.

82. R. Turner Wilcox, *The Dictionary of Costume* (New York: Charles Scribner's Sons, 1969), 16.

83. Rawick, *American Slave*, supplement 2, vol. 4.3, 1127.

84. Merritt, *Masterless Men*, 118.

85. Advertisement, *Richmond Enquirer*, May 11, 1838.

86. There are also documented cases of enslaved people with very light skin, such as the advertisement for a "White Negro Boy" who ran away and would "pass for a poor white boy" in his outfit of "a black coat, checked vest, blue striped pants, straw hat and a coarse pair of shoes." Advertisement, *Daily Columbus Enquirer*, August 2, 1859.

87. For more on free people of color, particularly those of the middle and upper classes, see Jasmine Nichole Cobb, *Picture Freedom: Remaking Black Visuality in the Early Nineteenth Century* (New York: New York University Press, 2015) and Whitney Nell Stewart, "Fashioning Frenchness: *Gens de Couleur Libres* and the Cultural Struggle for Power in Antebellum New Orleans," *Journal of Social History* 51: 2 (Winter 2017), 1–31.

88. Patricia K. Hunt makes a similar conclusion regarding the individualized nature of enslaved women's clothing, but she does not connect this practice to resistance. See Hunt, "'Round Homespun Coat & Pantaloons of the Same': Slave Clothing as Reflected in Fugitive Slave Advertisements in Antebellum Georgia," *Georgia Historical Quarterly* 83: 4 (Winter 1999), 727–740; Patricia K. Hunt, "The Struggle to Achieve Individual Expression through Clothing and Adornment: African American Women Under and After Slavery," in Patricia Morton, ed. *Discovering the Women in Slavery* (Athens: University of Georgia Press, 1996), 227–40. The debate about the agency of enslaved people has been going on since the first history of slavery was written. For an excellent breakdown and analysis of this historiogra-

phy and an idea toward a new approach, see Walter Johnson, "On Agency," *Journal of Social History* 37: 1 (Fall 2003), 113–124. Johnson also draws on his new theory of agency in his monograph *River of Dark Dreams*, especially pages 9, 207–208, and 217. Even more recently, Marisa J. Fuentes offers ways of working through violence and silence in the archive while honoring and studying enslaved people in *Dispossessed Lives*, 10–11.

CONFEDERATE CULTURES OF MILITARY CLOTHING PRODUCTION

SARAH JONES WEICKSEL

In 1861, Susan Bradford sat for a photographer so that she might be included in a composite photograph of the members of the Ladies' Soldier's Friend Sewing Society, to which she and her mother belonged, near Tallahassee, Florida. The photograph celebrated and commemorated the members' contributions to the Confederate cause, depicting elite white women alongside textile and sewing-related imagery—the cards necessary for processing wool and cotton fiber; sewing machines; and finished bundles of clothing, ready to be sent to soldiers at the battlefront. The society, Bradford noted in her diary, met "first at one house and then at another, and all of us sew steadily all day long."[1] The provision of clothing by soldiers' aid societies like Bradford's was celebrated both during and after the war. There was just one problem: in 1861, at the outbreak of the American Civil War, Susan Bradford did not know *how* to sew a soldier's shirt—or any kind of shirt for that matter.[2]

Susan Bradford was not alone in lacking plain sewing skills, those required to piece together, hem, and stitch ordinary clothing. Indeed, many elite white southern women admitted to being at a loss when it came to the process and skill of sewing the shirts, drawers, pants, and coats that were so central to outfitting soldiers for war. Yet it was *their* work and that of *their* sewing societies that garnered the greatest cultural value in the Confederate and post-war South. Although women's sewing circles dominated postwar reminiscences throughout the nation and have subsequently garnered the greatest attention in Civil War historiography, the vast majority of military garments were produced through an outwork system based out of army clothing depots that employed cutters, tailors, seamstresses, and inspectors.

The Confederate uniform is usually situated in the context of the high-level provisioning of the army, the celebrated efforts of women's patriotic sewing circles and families supplying clothing for their husbands, sons, and

Photo collage, Ladies Soldiers Friends Sewing Society, Tallahassee, Florida, 1861. Courtesy, State Archives of Florida, Florida Memory. Accessed May 8, 2017, https://www.floridamemory.com/items/show/25906.

brothers. Sewing societies with a membership of women, like Bradford, who could not sew efficiently do not fit with the accepted narrative of those societies' initial contributions to the war effort or the framework historians have constructed to explain women's roles in producing military clothing in the Confederate South. Nor does the work of enslaved, poor, and working-class seamstresses.

This essay focuses on women who sewed soldiers' clothing, recapturing the complexity of the labor required to supply the Confederate army, the experience of sewing in the context of war, and the changing nature of white women's relationships with the Confederate and state governments that were tied to their sewing work. Sewing, of course, was but one facet of the process of making and provisioning soldiers with cloth and clothes. Focusing on women who sewed, however, allows us to not only revisit and revise a well-worn narrative of ladies' sewing societies, but also to consider the consequences of that narrative—consequences that had lasting effects for ordinary sewing women.[3] Drawing together textual, visual, and material sources, this essay challenges our understanding of how elite southern women defined their contribution to the war effort and the consequences of those contributions for women more widely, simultaneously broadening the cast of characters who were involved in wartime clothing production.

Admiration for ladies' sewing societies and the women who contributed to them was by no means a Confederate phenomenon—the patriotic sock knitter was also culturally significant for the Union. Whether or not a woman's sewing was categorized as patriotic was largely based on remuneration or lack thereof. When performed by middle- and upper-class women as donations to aid societies or for family members, sewing was considered a womanly sacrifice. At the same time as this emphasis on the patriotic nature of white Union and Confederate women's sewing was growing, enslaved women's work as seamstresses was becoming more invisible. Working-class women who labored in textile mills or with needle and thread over piecework obtained from clothing depots, on the other hand, were given little credence about their patriotic intentions and were even looked on with suspicion.

Wartime praise of women's patriotic sewing circles in both the Union and Confederate context, and the post-war effort to document their "sacrifices," overshadowed the labor of the thousands of working-class women who supplied the armies through contract and depot-based labor. Literate women—throughout the nation—who possessed the leisure time to write and publish their reminiscences seized control of the narrative of wartime clothing production, diminishing and even erasing the memory of the work performed by the seamstresses and newly freedwomen who continued to sew, mend, and knit in support of themselves and their families. Such accounts were bolstered by the publication of celebratory histories sporting titles such as "Women of the War: Their Heroism and Self-Sacrifice," which directly tied women's sewing skills to patriotic fervor.[4] The resulting narrative that tied together patriotism and sewing was potent—so potent, in fact, that it directed the way in which generations of historians understood women's wartime work. However, this post-war narrative also had tangible consequences for those southern women who had sewn and knitted.

Making Clothes

Modern museum visitors encounter Civil War-era military uniforms displayed on mannequins behind Plexiglas cases, presented as either representative examples of what someone would have worn or as relics owned by famous generals or local heroes. More frequently, those uniforms are encountered as two-dimensional illustrations. In photographs or mounted on dress forms, buttoned up and stuffed with padding, it is difficult to comprehend the many layers of clothing that were worn and the various steps that went into making them. But when we lay out the pants, unbutton the coat, and turn back the coat flaps, we see the seams, the patches, and the individual pieces of cloth from which a uniform is constructed. From there, we can begin to extrapolate the work, the hands, and the implements and machines that went into making that uniform.

The production of large quantities of clothing was facilitated by developments in the emerging ready-made clothing industry. In the 1840s and 1850s tailors working at the US Office of Army Clothing and Equipage at Philadelphia's Schuylkill Arsenal developed a standardized sizing system for clothing based on their determination that men with a certain chest measurement were likely to have a corresponding waist size, shoulder width, and length of leg, arm, and torso. The implementation of this sizing system meant that when war erupted in 1861, army clothing depots and private clothing manufacturers could work towards producing a range of common sizes.[5] The majority of soldiers, then, did not wear clothing that was specifically fitted to their bodies. Indeed, as one tailoring manual noted, specificity was required to obtain a proper fit: "Our diagrams are calculated for proportionate or common forms of any size. The deviations are, the very erect, very stooping, high and low-shouldered, the round and the flat-backed forms, which require a little variation from the diagrams to fit them perfectly."[6] Clothing produced to fit a series of common sizes could not account for such variations in body type.

Although male government officials determined the boundaries of military uniform culture, male cutters and tailors worked alongside women, who were primarily responsible for its implementation in both the North and South, whether as government-employed seamstresses, textile workers for private manufacturing firms, slave laborers, or wives and mothers sewing at home. In both northern and southern post-war reminiscences, elite and middle-class women prided themselves on their "sacrifices" for their respective causes, highlighting their role in the formation of soldiers' aid societies, sewing uniforms and battle flags, and picking lint for wound dressings. However, although they were memorialized in song and poetry, the efforts of these elite and middle-class women represented only one subset of the textile work in which women engaged. Enslaved women were ordered to weave and sew for both the Confederate government and private use. Work that some women considered a patriotic contribution, others relied on for financial support. Seamstresses were paid by families to sew uniforms for their husbands, sons, and fathers. Women living near quartermaster depots took up piecework for the government, sewing together fabric cut out by male cutters.[7] Wage-earning women in both the North and South were employed by privately owned clothing and textile manufacturing firms, as well as by state-run clothing bureaus and warehouses. Occasionally, impoverished soldiers' wives and widows were employed by soldiers' aid societies as a form of relief.[8]

The tasks related to clothing production performed by a person depended on geographical location, economic status, rank of the soldier for whom the uniform was being made, and whether or not the maker was employed by the government, self-employed, or volunteering their labor. Women from all social classes throughout the nation engaged in sewing clothing for soldiers; most fell into one of six, at times overlapping, categories: 1) seamstresses working for government contractors; 2) quartermaster-depot seamstresses employed directly by the government; 3) soldiers' aid society members; 4) enslaved women forced to sew; 5) family members providing for individual soldiers; and 6) women who were seamstresses or engaged in business ventures. Some women undertook year-round sewing for the duration of the war, while others sewed for a few weeks or months as necessity or opportunity dictated.

The fact that both Union and Confederate officers were required to provide their own uniforms had important consequences for the people who sewed clothing, contributing to a gendered division of labor. Dress uniforms worn by high-ranking officers were generally made by professional tailors using a man's individual body measurements. The Petersburg, Virginia, tailoring firm of Gruter and Gerecke, for example, supplied Confederate officers with frock coats, gold braid, and tailored pants well into 1864. There were no specific military-service exemptions granted to tailors, and indeed, many served in the Confederate army. Some who remained on the home front may have been older than the conscription age, while others worked directly for the government in a role that was seen as critical. Male tailors and cutters provided the precision of professional patternmaking, the skill of cutting cloth in ways that would leave the fewest remnants, thereby reducing waste and maintaining a sizing system, however imprecise. The number of seamstresses would have far outweighed the number of tailors and cutters, in part because the task of sewing a uniform was much more arduous and time consuming than cutting it from a pattern. The Atlanta Depot for instance, employed three thousand seamstresses, but only twenty-seven male cutters.[9] Women typically made uniforms that were worn by lower-ranking soldiers, along with undergarments, including drawers, shirts, and socks, worn by men in all ranks. This was a continuation of antebellum practices, as women frequently produced such garments for their families, relying upon tailors for pants and coats when they could afford to do so.[10]

Rethinking Patriotic Sewing Societies

Throughout the nation, women learned of soldiers' needs through family members' letters, word-of-mouth, newspapers, and printed circulars published by aid societies. Yet the need for clothing ultimately necessitated communication between the government and those who could assist in supplying clothing, including both organizations and individuals. This frequently took the form of issuing circulars to sewing aid societies that were reprinted in newspapers. In South Carolina, for instance, the quartermaster general explained that depots were being established in Charleston and Columbia to receive donations and distribute clothing. The department would "receive all donations of clothing, say frock coats and pantaloons, of heavy worsted goods, shirts and drawers of heavy homespun or flannel, wool, or heavy cotton socks, blankets, new or second hand, also heavy shoes."[11]

In a May 1861 letter to "The People of Georgia," Governor Joseph E. Brown called on the inhabitants of the state to provide "material aid," to volunteer soldiers. In lieu of greater taxation or the state taking on "heavy debt," he urged Georgians to "show to the world . . . that we have the ability and the will, by private subscription, to clothe and feed our glorious and gallant troops in the field and their families at home." "The soldiers," he directed, "must have clothing." Brown's first appeal was "to the ladies, whose fervant patriotism, burning zeal, and energetic action in our glorious struggle, rekindle in our minds the memories of the immortal women of the Revolution of 1776."[12] Here, Brown drew on the rhetoric of patriotism that characterized much of the discourse surrounding women's work sewing uniforms for soldiers, simultaneously conjuring up imagery of the American Revolution.

This recurring image of the daughters of Revolutionary women plying their needles for the cause of freedom was deployed in both Northern and Southern patriotic propaganda. Such rhetoric evidenced a shared, national culture rooted in the memory of the Revolutionary experience that celebrated elite white women's relationship to wartime support, both in their material contributions and in sending men to war. Women were urged to "look to the example of their revolutionary foremothers, to make the family and domestic sacrifices that the country required."[13] Young women also emphasized their personal connections to women who had lived through the American Revolution. One Charleston woman, writing anonymously for the *Weekly News and Courier*, recalled her grandmother picking lint during the Civil War, while she told "many a story of the days of '76 when she was a 'wee one.'"[14]

In Georgia, Governor Brown asserted that women's actions in 1861 proved that these daughters of the Revolutionary generation "have improved upon their intelligence and refinement, and have more pecuniary ability to act, they have abated nothing of their patriotism and their devotion to the cause of freedom."[15] He both lauded women for exhibiting a patriotic zeal equal to that of their Revolutionary mothers, and asserted that these women had exceeded the Revolutionary generation in social and cultural refinement. In so doing, he suggested, however subtly, that in 1861 Georgia women were superior to those of the Revolutionary generation.

Wartime need for soldiers' clothing increased the frequency of women's contact with government officials throughout the Union and Confederacy. However, circumstances of Confederate supply meant that southern women generally found themselves in more direct contact than their northern counterparts. As a circular issued by the governor of North Carolina explained, "The scarcity of material for sale in this State, and the uncertainty of procuring supplies from abroad, force us to rely on our domestic resources."[16] Similarly, in his effort to confront the cost of fabric goods, the quartermaster general of South Carolina issued a circular to the Soldiers' Aid Societies on behalf of the governor, noting that "these laudable 'Associations' of ladies and gentlemen, are cordially welcome as coadjutors in this noble work" of supplying clothing.[17]

Brown went further in his attempt to persuade women to participate in the outfitting of Georgia's soldiers. He also offered and promised women the potential for a different kind of relationship with the government based on their work sewing uniforms. While public rhetoric often declared that women's work would be rewarded with eternal gratitude, Brown offered a more tangible form of acknowledgment in the state's records. Laying out a system through which donations would be received and recorded by the County Clerks of the Superior Court, Brown promised that each donor would have her name and contribution entered into a book that would be sent to the Executive Office of the State of Georgia, where it would "be deposited among the permanent records of the State."[18] By sewing uniforms, then, women could receive state recognition as individuals, offering them an opportunity to have a relationship with the state—however tenable—that was based on their own identities and contributions and entirely unrelated to their husbands or fathers. Furthermore, such recognition was not class-based—whether a woman donated ten complete uniforms or a few pairs of socks, her contribution would be preserved in the official state records.

While all female contributors were promised name recognition, Brown also offered women the chance to receive additional commendation from the executive for their efforts:

> To the lady making the most valuable contribution of clothing before the first day of August next, to be judged by the Quarter Master General, the Treasurer, and the Comptroller General I will present a beautiful golden cup, and will cause her name to be enrolled on a blank leaf of the Book of Minutes of the Executive Department, with a statement of the reasons why it is so enrolled.

The next nine women making the most valuable donations would also have their names "enrolled, each, on a separate leaf, in like manner in the order in which the honor is awarded to each." Notably this was the same award for the men who donated the largest amount of money.[19] At a moment in which the state of Georgia was embarking on a new, rebellious experiment in governance, Brown sought ways to encourage the support of, and sense of belonging among, not only male, but also female, residents of the state.

Brown's letter was published in newspapers throughout Georgia. Some of the women who read and responded to Brown's call viewed the letter as inviting them into a collaborative effort with the governor, writing directly to him to report their communities' efforts and to request assistance in procuring or paying for materials. Within one week of the publication of Brown's letter, one woman wrote to the governor to say that she had read his address and to "assure" him "that as a native Georgian I feel grateful to you for the suggestions therein contained. I shall endeavor to do my whole duty in this good work." As evidence of her efforts, she offered a report on her community's work: "Our sex have been busily engaged in getting ready for the conflict the 'Barnesville Blues' who will soon be on a war footing and ready to march wherever duty calls."[20] Sarah Bugg, president of a Soldiers' Aid Society in Oglethorpe County, confirmed having "read with pleasure [Brown's] feeling and patriotic letter," and wrote to inform the governor that her society had "500 yards of Janes, which we propose to cut and make up for the Oglethorp Rifles now at Manassas." But Bugg was either unable or unwilling to donate the cloth, informing him that the society would proceed to cut and sew only if Brown was willing to purchase the fabric for them.[21] Women's expectations that the governor would work with them in their effort to aid soldiers continued. Julia Fisher, for instance, wrote to Brown in 1862 to "beg" his "kind assistance and co-operation in our plans for the relief" of Georgia soldiers fighting in Virginia.[22]

As suggested by Bugg's request that Brown provide her society with cloth, women's clothing manufacturing skills were perceived as being of the greatest importance; cloth could be obtained by men, but—male tailors aside—the sewing of that cloth into uniforms required the skills of women. Skills were also at the center of plans for broadening support for Georgia's soldiers. As one anonymous man noted in a letter to the *Macon Telegraph*, Brown's published appeal was more likely to reach women living closer to towns who were engaged in forming sewing societies. There were, the writer noted, "*in the back woods*, if you please, thousands of as noble hearts and willing hands for the work, if the appeal could reach them"—a task that he believed could be best carried out by family physicians traveling throughout the countryside. Physicians could request contributions of clothing, cloth, "*or of anything else, which can be bartered for material for proper uniforms*." He suggested calling all citizens to a meeting, then distributing material to the ladies to sew.[23] Doing so would overcome the problem of distance between homesteads of yeoman and poor whites, and make it possible for women who could not contribute cloth to instead donate their time and skills.

While plans to supply sewing societies and individual citizens with cloth were well-intentioned, such efforts were quickly abandoned because of the expense. In North Carolina, Governor Henry T. Clark believed that it was critical to engage people across all classes in the effort to supply winter clothing for troops and in 1861 published a circular directed to the "great body of the people" in the state. Reprinted in the *Fayetteville Observer*, this circular asserted, "Every family can spare one or more Blankets without personal inconvenience, or a pair of Woolen Socks, and it is believed that for such a purpose a call would be responded to with alacrity." County sheriffs were instructed to "act as agents of the State," circulate the notice and "employ agents in every district" to solicit contributions and record the names of donors.[24] In Alabama, one woman wrote that she was "knitting socks for the volunteers; every lady in the state is requested by the Governor to knit one pair of socks."[25] Through such requests and instructions, state officials were drawing women of all classes into a more direct relationship with the government.

In both Confederate and Union political discourses, women's contributions to the cause centered on their ability to sew and knit. But not all possessed those skills. Northern women, particularly those living in the Northeast, seem to have had a broader range of basic sewing skills, along with lower-class southern women and enslaved women. Elite women in both northern and southern regions, however, seem to have been most well-versed in needlework, not "plain sewing." In the context of war, many women throughout the nation learned to sew, while others struggled with the task. White southern women from the slave-owning class in particular frequently admitted in letters, diaries, and memoirs that they themselves did not possess the necessary skills to perform what was considered a traditional female chore. Even those women who were skilled seamstresses and knitters were not necessarily aware of the items that were most needed by soldiers in the field and learned how to sew and knit new, or redesigned, clothing items. At first glance, the sewing machine would seem to have offered a ready solution to women's sewing problems. But using these machines required another set of skills, and the machines were capable of producing only the most basic of stitches—much of the work of finishing a garment required sewing by hand.[26] Supplying men at war, then, was a learning process in which women throughout the nation, both Union and Confederate, were engaged.

While many women learned how to outfit men for war, the manner in which elite Confederate women conveyed that experience departed significantly from their northern peers. While Northern women did not write about their sewing with any less frequency, the process of acquiring the skills required for knitting, sewing, mending, weaving, and spinning appear in many Confederate women's diaries, letters, and memoirs at a more frequent rate than those of women who sewed for Union soldiers. This was especially true for women whose social position allowed them to pay for, or compel, the work of others who were more skilled in sewing and mending. Elite Confederate women seem to have taken pride in conveying a narrative of helplessness when it came to the process of making clothing. But in the course of the war, sewing reemerged as a mark of pride for elite women;

not the intricate sewing associated with embroidery—that female art had retained its social power. Instead, it was a willingness to learn and engage in the practical tasks of marking patterns, cutting fabric, and plain sewing that became a mark of patriotic expression.

Elite Confederate women's narratives often began with an admission of ignorance about sewing, knitting, weaving, or spinning, then expressed a willingness to accept the challenge, followed by failure at their first attempt to sew a shirt or knit a sock, and ultimately mastery of the ability to productively contribute to soldiers' provisioning. As Susan Bradford wrote,

> The women of the South had never known what it was to work with their own hands but now nothing, which could contribute to the welfare of the soldiers, was too hard for them to do. Dainty fingers sewed on uniforms and flannel shirts, and later on, when no cloth could be had from which to make these needed garments, they learned to spin and weave and knit and sew, that their loved ones might be clothed.[27]

Such narratives are so common—in both wartime and postwar accounts—that they are a trope of southern women's writing.

The physicality of sewing and the materials themselves were central to these narratives. Women described their work as "rough," and the materials with which they worked, "coarse." In some instances, women were challenged by not only the process of sewing or knitting, but also by the quality of the materials with which they were working. One Charleston woman wrote about knitting with wool that had not been thoroughly carded to remove burrs and sticks before being spun into yarn:

> My first pair of socks were of coarse woollen yarn, most uneven thread, with stick snag burrs throughout. Diligently I set to work to remove all flaws, but before I had gone very far, being naturally indolent, and like most girls fond of commencing but not finishing work, I got very tired and thought the sticks and burrs knit in would help to "fill up."

She never forgot her mother's reproof: "'And did you never think of the poor, bleeding feet?" The young woman "was conscience stricken" at the realization that her laziness would have caused the soldier-recipient pain.[28]

Women experienced their own physical discomfort as their knitting needles clicked and their fingers were pricked and became more calloused.

The cloth-related work in which women engaged varied widely, from carding cotton to preparing fibers for spinning, to deconstructing old garments, and "picking lint" to make wound dressings. The demands of sewing flannel shirts with coarse cotton thread contrasted with the delicateness of silk embroidery. Where once these women might have sewn only when applying lace or other finishing details to a dress, they were now presumably responsible for sewing whole garments. Over the course of the war, some women found themselves engaged in not only sewing coarse cloth, but also preparing raw materials for production into that cloth. "Cotton cards," one woman explained, "were handled by hands that had known no heavier toll than to thrum the strings of the guitar, harp and other musical instruments. Home-woven garments were made by fingers never accustomed to heavier work than that of silken embroidery."[29] They emphasized the experience of their "smooth, dainty fingers" becoming accustomed to the practice of sewing quickly, rather than as a pleasant, social pastime. Kentuckian Florida Saxon wrote, "Dainty fingers that had never known rougher work than the hemming of cambric ruffles or the manufacture of delicate lace, were busily making the coarse cotton yarn into socks."[30] One Charleston woman described her grandmother's commitment to working to the point of misshapenness: "So diligent was she about it that I remember her having corns on her fingers from the constant picking [of lint]."[31]

It is easy to dismiss these women's recollections as exaggerations or as the lore of postwar reminiscences, but the materials themselves lend credence to women's emphasis on the physicality of processing cotton and wool, and sewing uniforms in contrast to embroidery or even working on their own clothing.[32] Much of the fabric used for soldiers' clothing would have felt different in their hands, especially as coarser fabrics became the norm. Similarly, while muscle memory allows experienced knitters to work quickly, holding knitting needles, casting on, and counting and memorizing stitches is a challenge for beginners. The labor associated with processing raw materials, spinning, and weaving, however, required the most time and energy. Processing wool, for instance, requires washing, carding, combing, and spinning before yarn is ready to be woven or knitted. Carding wool by hand was a very physical process—the wool was drawn between two wire-toothed paddles until the tangles and bits of sticks or burrs were removed and the fibers aligned in one direction. The wool itself had an odor and was greasy to the touch because of the lanolin secreted by the sebaceous glands of the sheep. The sensory experience—the smells, touch, and physical motions—associated with carding wool was far removed from not only silk embroidery, but also sewing finished cloth. The disconcerted feeling expressed by white women undertaking these tasks for the first time, then, was not without grounds.

Despite the fact that it took months of practice for many women involved in sewing societies to become efficient at plain sewing, thousands of uniforms were quickly available to and worn by Confederate soldiers. This was in part due to the work of tailors and women who were seamstresses by trade who were employed by individual families to sew men's uniforms and by those working for state-run clothing depots. Textual evidence, however, shows that elite women were immediately active in "fitting up" companies of soldiers. What, then, did women of the slaveholding classes, who made up the majority of Confederate sewing societies, consider within the purview of their own "sewing"? When women wrote about making uniforms what did that actually entail? Certainly many white women were themselves sewing soldiers' shirts, pants, and coats. But "making" uniforms was also defined as supervising enslaved women while *they* did the sewing.

Female enslavers possessed a range of sewing skills—but so did the enslaved women they owned. Many articles of clothing worn by both enslaved people and slave owners were purchased from ready-made retailers. Frequently, enslaved tailors and dressmakers fit dresses and suits to white customers. Furthermore, evidence suggests that enslaved women sewed not only clothing for themselves and their families, but also some of the clothing worn by their enslavers. In the course of a WPA interview, for instance, William Branch reflected on clothing production on the Texas plantation where he was raised:

> How'd us slaves git de clothes? We carded de cotton, den de women spin it on a spinnin' wheel. Afte dat day sew de gahment togeddah on a sewin' machine. Yahsur, we's got sewin' machine, wid a big wheel and a handle. One woman t'un de handle and de yuther woman do de sewin'. Dat's how we git de clothes for de 75 slaves. . . . Over nigh Richmond a fren' of Marster Woodson has 300 slaves. Dey makes all de clothes for dem.

When asked about his masters' clothing, he replied, "Marster's clothes? We makes dem for de whole family. De missis send de pattren and de slaves makes de clothes."[33] As Branch's recollections suggest, white mistresses and enslaved women frequently collaborated to varying degrees in the production of clothing. In some instances, white mistresses taught enslaved women how to make clothing. Formerly enslaved woman Rosa Maddox noted it was

"Mis' Fannie" who taught her to knit, sew and spin.[34] However, in wartime, many white women found themselves learning those same skills from enslaved women.

The experiences of Kate Stone and the women enslaved on her family's Louisiana plantation, Brokenburn, offer an example of the complexity of black and white women's interactions related to clothing production. Clothing, she noted, was generally cut and made by enslaved seamstresses under the supervision of mistresses or, occasionally, an overseer's wife. In her diary, it is clear that Stone and her mother did the most basic work related to sewing and relied on enslaved seamstresses to actually sew garments. On various occasions, Stone's mother chalked patterns on uncut cloth, which were then cut out by the seamstresses. She also "basted for the seamstress," taking the cloth that had been cut into a pattern and tacking it with loose stitches for sewing. Similarly, Stone did the machine work on some chemises but had the seamstress finish them.[35] Still, Stone considered chalking out patterns and supervising the cutting to be hard work. "After a day or so of this work," she noted, "Mamma would go to bed quite broken down and Aunt Lucy, the colored housekeeper, would finish the superintending."[36]

How, then, did this system of supervision and joint clothing production translate from sewing plantation clothing to sewing soldiers' clothing? Specific sewing tasks are not frequently mentioned in diaries—women usually note that they "sewed" with the society. However, we can extrapolate from those that *do* detail what was being done. In some instances, the work of the Stones' sewing society involved gathering to cut out the pieces of cloth and giving them out to the members to be made which was, in terms of depot production, the appropriation of male labor. Those same sewing society members took cut fabric home for enslaved women to sew into uniforms. As a former plantation mistress recalled, "We had no sewing machines and the work was done by ourselves and our [enslaved] seamstresses. Mine made fourteen pairs of drawers in a week for that [patriot sewing] association, and never seemed hurried."[37] Formerly enslaved people also recalled the critical role enslaved seamstresses played in clothing the Confederate Army. Nancy Johnson, for instance, recalled that she was "nearly frostbitten" because "my old Missus made me weave to make clothes for the soldiers till 12 o'clock at night."[38] A man noted that his master in Texas "had de womenfolks on de plantation to make up lots of clothes for de soldiers. I has seen several wagonloads of clothes hauled off from dar at one time."[39]

The reminiscences and diary excerpts of Susan Bradford Eppes help to piece together the relationships between white women's sewing societies and the work of enslaved African Americans. When war broke out, Susan Bradford was fifteen or sixteen years old. She readily acknowledged her lack of sewing skills at the beginning of the war. "I did not know much sewing at first; at the beginning I made Charley Hopkins two flannel shirts but I am ashamed to say Lulu did most of the sewing." Watching Lulu, an enslaved nurse, sew the flannel shirts that Bradford then presented as a gift to Charley Hopkins likely helped Bradford improve her own sewing skills. By April 1862 she claimed, "Now I can take any kind of a garment and make it entire, even the buttonholes, though Sister Mag says my button holes 'gape.' I mean to improve on them."[40] Bradford devoted three days of each week to sewing for soldiers.[41] Enslaved African Americans on the Bradford plantation did more than sew—they also facilitated the packing and transportation of soldiers' clothing. Two enslaved carpenters owned by the Bradfords—Peter and Mack—worked to "make packing cases and it is astonishing how many garments go forward from the Bradford neighborhood."[42]

Photographs of twenty-eight members of the Ladies' Soldier's Friend Sewing Society, including Bradford, were combined in a composite photograph that tied together the women's sewing and their patriotism. At the center of the photograph is a woman with a cotton card in her hand flanked by two women seated at sewing machines with pieces of cloth. Surrounding the women is an image of neatly stacked piles of bound clothing or blankets beside an elegant chair and sewing-machine table, across which a piece of fabric is draped. Below the women is a hand-written, now faded key to the names of the members of the society, preserving the women's claims to their contributions to the society. Together, the composite photograph visually asserts that these women were central to the war effort at multiple stages of clothing production. From the cotton card used to work raw materials, to the sewing machines, to the finished piles of goods stretching into the distance, the collage asserts that these women were crucial to supplying soldiers. No evidence suggests that anyone other than these white women themselves performed all of the work involved in producing clothing from raw cotton to packages ready to be shipped. Indeed, the work performed by Mac, Peter, and Lulu that enabled the Bradfords to contribute to the society has been erased.

If we take into consideration the circumstances of enslaved women's work in clothing Confederate soldiers, the relationship between the government and elite sewing women and their societies looks quite different. When Georgia's governor offered women the possibility of having their names recorded in the official state records, they were to be rewarded for not only their sewing skills, but also their ability to command the work of enslaved women. Indeed, the women who wrote to the governor attempting to establish a collaborative relationship were all small slaveholders. Confederate women's patriotism, then, was tied not only to the sewing they performed with their own hands, but also that which they commanded from enslaved women.

Consequences

The link between sewing, patriotism, and loyalty that emerged in relation to elite women pervaded understandings of women's wartime sewing work. To sew or knit clothing that would ultimately be worn by a soldier became deeply politicized, whether or not a woman was motivated by love of the Confederacy or economic necessity. This pervasive narrative had significant consequences for women during the postwar years. Between 1871 and 1873, southerners submitted paperwork to the Southern Claims Commission, a US federal government organization through which southerners filed claims for reimbursement of personal-property losses due to the Civil War.[43] Only southerners who could provide evidence of their loyalty to the United States throughout the war were eligible for such reimbursement. The cultural association between women, sewing uniforms, and loyalty that pervaded both northern and southern discourses was critical to the success or rejection of women's claims. Female claimants were explicitly asked:

> Did you ever belong to any sewing society organized to make clothing for Confederate soldiers or their families, or did you assist in making any such clothing, or making flags or other military equipments, or preparing or furnishing delicacies or supplies for Confederate hospitals or soldiers?[44]

Whereas northern women's work sewing uniforms for soldiers was portrayed in not only patriotic terms but as a duty to male members of her family, the Southern Claims commissioners, exercising a victor's justice, took a narrow view of southern women's work as seamstresses: if a woman had sewn clothing that ultimately ended up on the back of a Confederate soldier, her claims were rejected.

Sewing and semiskilled textile work were inherently problematic occupations for southern women because federal officials interpreted their wage labor and piecework as evidence of complicity with and support of the Confederate cause. Women's motivations for engaging in wartime clothing production were immaterial to the Claims Commissioners. Some of these women were seamstresses by trade before the war, while others took up sewing uniforms for private families or the quartermaster's office as a means of supporting themselves during wartime. While a number of women were indeed Confederate soldiers' wives and widows, others were single women or widowed before the war who were attempting to eke out a living in a war-torn economy. They claimed that they did not support the Confederate cause.

Regardless of their loyalties, these predominantly poor white and yeomen women were faced with wartime struggles and shortages that left them with little recourse and few opportunities to earn a living. Many women took advantage of living near the quartermasters' depots that were responsible for supplying the army. One woman recalled, "This pay work was given to the wives of poor soldiers many of whom would walk into town to get it long distances from the neighboring sandhills."[45] They picked up bundles of cloth cut by male cutters in the quartermaster's clothing warehouses, which they then sewed for pay. Regardless of whether they took part in the outwork system of the Quartermaster's Department, or what their motivations for sewing uniforms were, working as seamstresses disproved these women's claims to loyalty to the United States. Directly, or indirectly, they had supported the Confederacy.

Both Elizabeth Grubb and Lusana Muselwhite, for instance, were, by occupation, seamstresses before the war. Grubb's claims of property loss were officially denied because she "was employed at times in making clothing for the rebel Quartermaster's Dept," even though she "did very little of this."[46] Muselwhite, on the other hand, "sometimes made clothing for soldiers, but it was for private families & to make a living."[47] Although the commissioners viewed both Grubb and Muselwhite's sewing work as evidence of their support of the rebels, the women's motivations were likely more complicated. In 1860 Grubb was a thirty-six-year-old widow, living alone with her nine-year-old son in Atlanta, in a neighborhood where other Atlantans who were employed in the clothing trade also lived. Both she and Muselwhite sewed for a living, and in the context of the war and the redirection of resources to army supply, much of the work available to seamstresses was intended for army consumption.

One of the most illustrative examples of the ways in which sewing uniforms trumped all other evidence for claims of loyalty is the story of Carrie Hambrick, who petitioned the US government for reimbursement of livestock and other property requisitioned by the US army totaling $429.75. The final report rejecting her claim asserted that the "Claimant admits that she was employed in the Rebel Q.M. Department at Atlanta sewing on soldiers clothing." The significance of this employment was made clear: "This is voluntary aid and comfort to the Rebels for which Claimant received compensation, and for which she has no excuse. It was as much as a woman of her circumstances had opportunity to do for aid of the Rebellion." The commissioners admitted that Hambrick had some redeeming qualities, including "a very commendable act of humanity towards a Union officer," but ultimately asserted that they could not "find in view of her employment in the Q.M. Department that she was loyal from the opening to the close of the war."[48] Her claim was rejected.

The "commendable act of humanity" towards a Union officer that was dismissed by the commissioners was later recorded in that officer's wartime memoirs, where he recounted being shot and taken prisoner before he escaped and stumbled on Hambrick's house in the woods outside Atlanta.[49] More tellingly, that officer also testified in front of the Claims Commission in regard to not only Hambrick's role in saving his life—taking him into her home, nursing him back to health, and helping him to escape back to Union lines—but also to her loyalty to the United States. He asserted that she believed that "the south commenced the war against the government without just cause. That she had nothing to complain of against the government that it was good enough for her." The officer also relayed Hambrick's reflections on her husband's death, which left her a widow with two toddler-aged children: "She told me that her husband was 'conscripted' into the rebel army but died at the hospital . . . and that she was glad that she could say that her husband died before he had fired a gun against the flag of his country."[50] Despite the compelling testimony of a former Union soldier, the Claims Commissioners rejected Hambrick's claims, solely based on her answer to the question of whether or not she had ever been employed by the Confederacy; a question to which she truthfully replied that she "had nothing to do with the soldier part of the war," but "was employed by the rebel Quartermaster's Department at Atlanta Ga to sew on some clothing for the army" and "was thus employed for two months." Hambrick's two months of piecework outweighed any claims to support of the Union that were illustrated by her actions in saving and hiding a Union officer from Confederate forces.

Carrie Hambrick experienced acutely the repercussions of the wartime redefinition of the relationship between gender and clothing-related work. Defining gender in relationship to clothing production at first seems unremarkable. Sewing and knitting were widely considered domestic activities suitable for women throughout the nineteenth century. However, the clothing production that took place during wartime was *not* the same type of production that took place on a daily basis in a typical domestic setting. This was not daily mending, fancy sewing and embroidery, or sewing a new shirt for one's husband. Instead, women were engaged in the harder labor of plain sewing and knitting in vast quantities; the kind of sewing that aggravated arthritic hands, hardened calluses, and strained one's eyes. The productive capacity of many women was stretched to its limits; they were engaged in making clothing as part of a war machine.

Clothing production was typically understood as a domestic chore that took place within the confines of the household or a respectable occupation for poor women, but it took on complex political meanings in the context of governmental need to supply clothing to armies. Governments on both sides were invested in similar ways in this industrial-like scale of production. In the process, gender was being defined in relationship to the government. Political implications were re-enforced and expanded as elite and middling women embraced the opportunity to see their contributions elevated to and praised on the national stage.

In the context of wartime clothing production, some women were invited into and embraced a new, cooperative relationship with government authorities, including military officials and governors. Others found themselves embroiled in conflict with these same authorities. Wartime demands for military supply created opportunities for women to labor while simultaneously heightening the political implications of that labor. These various interactions and the importance the government placed on women's textile skills had important implications for not only women's wartime experiences but also how their work was valued by society and remembered in popular culture. Evolving governmental attitudes towards women's work resulted in the public elevation of some women's experiences and the simultaneous erasure of others. In the case of white southern women of all classes, the United States government and its officials viewed women's work producing cloth and sewing uniforms not as private, feminine pursuits, but as public—and in some cases treasonous—activities.

Notes

1. Susan Bradford Eppes, "Diary of Susan Bradford Eppes," in *Through Some Eventful Years* (Macon, GA: Press of the J.W. Burke Co., 1926), 183.

2. Susan Bradford Eppes was the daughter of Dr. Edward Bradford, owner of the Pine Hill plantation near Tallahassee. According to the 1850 census, Bradford owned over one hundred enslaved people. The family lost their wealth as a result of the war. Bradford married Nicholas Ware Eppes in 1866 at the age twenty. After her husband was murdered in 1904,

Eppes lost her home. A member of the United Daughters of the Confederacy, she began to write her memoirs at the age of seventy-nine. Her books included *The Negro in the Old South* (1925), *Through Some Eventful Years* (1926), and *Verses from Florida* (1938). As Tracey Revels has noted, "All were heavily soaked in moonlight and magnolias." Tracy J. Revels, *Grander in Her Daughters: Florida's Women during the Civil War* (Columbia: University of South Carolina Press, 2004), 142.

3. References to women's work sewing army uniforms appear in nearly every scholarly work on women and the war, although there is no sustained study of these efforts. In the twentieth century historians' questions were largely directed by Civil War era women's own reminiscent interpretations of their involvement with clothing production. Women's work sewing uniforms has generally been viewed as expressions of patriotism and is firmly situated in what Drew Faust has referred to as "politics of sacrifice." However, such patriotic contributions of elite and middle-class women were only one part of women's involvement with the much broader system of supply—one to which laboring women were central, and for whom necessity could easily overshadow patriotic fervor. Two notable exceptions include recent work by Judith Giesberg and Stephanie McCurry, both of whom address working-class and yeomen women. Stephanie McCurry has offered another interpretive framework through which to understand women's wartime actions—a "politics of subsistence" firmly grounded in women's self-identification as soldiers' wives who believed themselves to be entitled to the support and protection of the government that their husbands, fathers, and brothers served. In the context of clothing we see at work both Faust's politics of sacrifice and McCurry's politics of subsistence. Drew Gilpin Faust, *Mothers of Invention: Women of the Slaveholding South in the American Civil War* (Chapel Hill: University of North Carolina Press, 1996); Stephanie McCurry, *Confederate Reckoning: The Political Transformation of the Civil War South* (Cambridge, MA: Harvard University Press, 2010); Elizabeth Leonard, *Yankee Women: Gender Battles in the Civil War* (New York: W. W. Norton, 1994); Nina Silber, *Daughters of the Union: Northern Women Fight the Civil War* (Cambridge, MA: Harvard University Press, 2005); Judith Giesberg, *Army at Home: Women and the Civil War on the Northern Home Front* (Chapel Hill: University of North Carolina Press, 2009).

4. For examples of women's reminiscences of wartime work, see: L. P. Brockett and Mary C. Vaughan, *Woman's Work in the Civil War: A Record of Heroism, Patriotism, and Patience* (Philadelphia: Zeigler and McCurdy, 1867); Frank Moore, *Women of the War: Their Heroism and Self-Sacrifice* (Hartford: S.S. Scranton & Co., 1866).

5. Gordon L. Jones, *Confederate Odyssey: The George W. Wray Jr. Civil War Collection at the Atlanta History Center* (Athens: University of Georgia Press, 2014), 359.

6. Asahel F. Ward, *The Philadelphia Fashions & Tailors' Archetypes for Spring and Summer 1864* (Philadelphia: 1864), 3.

7. Important Confederate quartermaster depots were located in Richmond, Charleston, Atlanta, Columbus, Savannah, New Orleans, Nashville, and Memphis.

8. Madelyn Shaw and Lynne Z. Bassett, *Homefront & Battlefield: Quilts and Context in the Civil War* (Lowell: American Textile Museum, 2012), 78.

9. Harold S. Wilson, *Confederate Industry: Manufacturers and Quartermasters in the Civil War* (Jackson: University Press of Mississippi, 2002).

10. For studies of women sewing within the home, see: Barbara Burman, ed. *The Culture of*

Sewing: Gender, Consumption and Home Dressmaking (Oxford: Berg, 1999); Jeanne Boydston, *Home and Work: Housework, Wages, and the Ideology of Labor in the Early Republic* (New York: Oxford University Press, 1990).

11. S. S. Glover, "Circular: To the Soldiers' Aid Societies of S.C.," *Camden Confederate* (Camden, SC). March 28, 1862, p. 4.

12. "Gov. Brown to the People of Georgia," *Macon Daily Telegraph*. May 23, 1861, p.3.

13. Silber, *Daughters of the Union*, 18.

14. Anonymous, "In the Cradle of the War," in *"Our Women in the War": The Lives They Lived; the Deaths They Died* (Charleston: The News and Courier Book Presses, 1885), 281.

15. "Gov. Brown to the People of Georgia," *Macon Daily Telegraph*. May 23, 1861, p.3.

16. Henry T. Clark, Governor of North Carolina, "To the Sherffs of the Several Counties of North Carolina," *Fayetteville Observer*, September 26, 1861, p. 4.

17. S. S. Glover, "Circular: To the Soldiers' Aid Societies of S.C.," *Camden Confederate* (Camden, SC), February 21, 1862, p. 4.

18. "Gov. Brown to the People of Georgia," *Macon Daily Telegraph*. May 23, 1861, p.3.

19. "Gov. Brown to the People of Georgia."

20. Mrs. J. C. C. Blackburn to Joseph E. Brown, May 24, 1861. Joseph Emerson Brown Governor's Incoming Correspondence, Georgia State Archives, Atlanta, Georgia.

21. Mrs. Sarah T. Bugg to Joseph E. Brown, September 9, 1861, Brown Correspondence.

22. Julia M. Fisher to Joseph E. Brown, October 6, 1862, Brown Correspondence.

23. "Patriotism and the Practice of Physic. A Word to Country Physicians," *Macon Daily Telegraph*, May 31, 1861, p. 1.

24. "To the Sherffs of the Several Counties of North Carolina."

25. Diary Entry, 27 August 1861, Diary of Sarah Rousseau Espy, Alabama Department of Archives and History, Montgomery, Alabama, http://digital.archives.alabama.gov/cdm/ref/collection/voices/id/3607.

26. For more on the role of the sewing machine, see Amy Breakwell, "A Nation in Extremity: Sewing Machines and the American Civil War," *Textile History* 41, sup. 1: 98–107.

27. Eppes, *Through Some Eventful Years*, 147.

28. Anonymous, in *Our Women in the War*, 281.

29. A. C. Cooper, "Days That are Dead," in *Our Women in the War*, 437.

30. Florida Saxon, "Unto the Bitter End," in *Our Women in the War*, 71.

31. "In the Cradle of the War," in *Our Women in the War*, 281.

32. As Constance Classen, Sander Gilman, and Mark Smith have noted, touch was a critical part of historical experience, but the historical study of touch and tactility is difficult. Mark Michael Smith, *Sensing the Past: Seeing, Hearing, Smelling, Tasting, and Touching in History* (Berkeley: University of California Press, 2007), 93.

33. William Branch, in Works Progress Administration, *Slave Narratives: A Folk History of Slavery in the United States from Interviews with Former Slaves*, Texas Narratives, Volume XVI, Part 1 (Washington, DC: 1941), 143–144.

34. Rosa Maddox in *Bullwhip Days: The Slaves Remember, An Oral History*, ed. James Mellon (New York: Grove/Atlantic, 1988), 120.

35. Kate Stone, in *Brokenburn: The Journal of Kate Stone, 1861–1868*, ed. John Q. Anderson (1955; 1972; Baton Rouge: Louisiana State University Press, 1995) 7; 32; 58.

36. Stone, 7.

37. This woman also implied that slaves' compulsory work on these drawers for Confederate soldiers was evidence of their support of their masters. She wrote, "The negroes were faithful and kind. They did not believe our troops would ever be beaten." Mrs. Thomas Taylor, et al, eds. *South Carolina Women in the Confederacy* (Columbia, SC: The State Company, 1903), 79.

38. For a broader study of enslaved women's wartime work and experience, see Thavolia Glymph, *Out of the House of Bondage: The Transformation of the Plantation Household* (Cambridge: Cambridge University Press, 2008). Testimony of Nancy Johnson, March 22, 1873, Southern Claims Commission, in Ira Berlin, Barbara J. Fields, Thavolia Glymph, Joseph P. Reidy, and Leslie S. Rowland, eds. *Freedom: A Documentary History of Emancipation, 1861–1867*, ser. I, vol. I, *The Destruction of Slavery* (Cambridge: Cambridge University Press, 1985), 151.

39. Calvin Moye, in Mellon, 167.

40. Eppes, *Through Some Eventful Years*, 179.

41. Eppes, *Through Some Eventful Years*, 183.

42. Eppes, *Through Some Eventful Years*, 179; Eppes, *Negro of the Old South*, 108.

43. For studies addressing the Southern Claims Commission, see: Susanna Michele Lee, *Claiming the Union: Citizenship in the Post-Civil War South* (Cambridge: Cambridge University Press, 2014); Dylan C. Penningroth, *The Claims of Kinfolk: African American Property and Community in the Nineteenth-Century South* (Chapel Hill: University of North Carolina Press, 2003); Frank W. Klingberg, *The Southern Claims Commission* (Berkeley: University of California Press, 1955).

44. Martha Ledbetter Claim, List of "Standing Interrogatories," Southern Claims Commission Records, 1871–1873, M1470, National Archives and Records Administration (Washington, DC).

45. "Women's Activities at the Capital," in Taylor, 79.

46. Elizabeth W. Grubb Claim, Fulton County, Georgia, Southern Claims Commission Records, M1470, NARA.

47. Lusana Muselwhite, Georgia, Southern Claims Commission Records, M1470, NARA.

48. Carrie Hambrick, DeKalb County, Georgia. Southern Claims Commission Records, NARA M1470.

49. George Bailey, *A Private Chapter of the War (1861–1865)* (St. Louis: G. I. Jones and Company, 1880).

50. George Bailey, Testimony on behalf of Mrs. Carrie Hambrick, Decatur, Georgia. Southern Claims Commission Records, NARA M1470.

WPA SEWING PROJECTS

A Case Study in Southern Encounters with the New Deal Welfare State

SUSANNAH WALKER

The September 1936 issue of the Louisiana Works Progress Administration's monthly bulletin described the state's sewing projects, active in fifty parishes, as "'bee-hives'... humming with activity" in which "3,000 women are happily at work making clothing and household articles for the needy of their communities." The article noted that "the sewing units make garments as nearly as possible to fit the individuals for whom they are intended," emphasizing that the women on the project not only earned a living, and learned "the arts of sewing," but also attended lectures each week in homemaking, childcare, and personal hygiene.[1] The piece was typical of promotional writing about sewing rooms in the South and the nation, a message often echoed in the local press. The Works Progress Administration (WPA) and its predecessor program under the Federal Emergency Relief Administration (FERA) were conceived by their administrator, Harry Hopkins, as a way to provide breadwinners with employment rather than the dole—"work relief" instead of "direct relief." Hopkins also imagined WPA projects as a way to keep sharp, and improve, workers' skills. The director of women's work for FERA and for the Women's and Professional Projects (WPP) division of the WPA was Mississippi native Ellen Woodward. Woodward fought, with variable success, to ensure women eligible for work relief found opportunities in the WPP that matched their skills, and she supported the idea that projects like the sewing rooms, set up primarily for women without work experience, should provide training to make these women more employable in the private sector. In practice, however, most local sewing-room administrators emphasized the points in the Louisiana article: the usefulness to needy families of the items produced, the wages sewing-room workers earned, and training that emphasized female domesticity.

Women, on average, made up 15 percent of WPA workers between 1935 and 1942, reaching a peak of over four hundred thousand in 1938. More than half of the women who held WPA jobs worked in sewing-rooms, repairing and manufacturing clothing and household linens for families on relief. Sewing projects were also the largest category of nonconstruction WPA projects, both in terms of cost and numbers employed.[2] Sewing projects were a highly visible part of the WPA work-relief programs in all the southern states.[3] Writing about the development of the welfare state in southern history, Elna C. Green points out that the New Deal era represented a time when southern states were playing catch-up with the nation to build their social welfare infrastructures. At the same time, because of its disproportionate power in the Democratic Party, the region played a decisive role in shaping what the American welfare system would be like, a situation that resulted in a decentralized structure that allowed, among other things, for state and local governments to control how the system would (or would not) work for their poor populations, and more specifically, how it would (or would not) work for African Americans.[4]

The work-relief sewing projects illuminate these and other aspects of implementing the New Deal welfare state in the South. Women's project administrators throughout the region promoted the sewing rooms, with some success, as more than just a source of income for needy women, but as providers of attractive and functional clothes for people on the welfare rolls. In the context of a national narrative and New Deal rhetoric that portrayed the South as the ultimate example of Depression-era American destitution, supporters noted that garments made in sewing rooms helped people on relief to not look as though they were. This helped to promote a positive image for sewing projects, but it did not ensure their untroubled existence. The federal government did not operate projects directly; state WPA offices did that, and projects required partial funding from local sponsors, usually state, county, or municipal governments. In the South, many counties and states built their welfare infrastructures virtually from scratch in the 1930s, often in places with few resources and limited commitment to building them.[5] Newspaper records suggest that sewing rooms in the region were constantly in danger of being shut down, even where they were popular, because city and county welfare boards (usually the sponsors of sewing projects) could not secure adequate funding from local governments. Furthermore, federal goals for the sewing rooms, as places to rehabilitate and train unskilled women for jobs that would make them economically independent, were unevenly implemented, in part due to lack of adequate resources, and in part due to the competing perception from local governments that the sewing rooms were only supposed to be a temporary source of income for needy female-headed households.

The role of states in administering the WPA, and of local governments in funding them, also facilitated racial discrimination, and impeded African Americans' efforts to seek redress. All southern sewing projects were segregated, and the WPA's Washington office routinely rerouted discrimination complaints it received to state WPA administrators to investigate. Such investigations usually exonerated sewing-room supervisors and local welfare boards of any wrongdoing.

WPA Clothes and Combating the "Look" of Poverty

Because the garments and other articles made in WPA sewing rooms were distributed to families on local relief rolls, the look and quality of the clothes was important to administrators, sewing-room supervisors, and sewing-room workers. The clothes were supposed to be attractive and up-to-date, a goal that reflected the New Deal emphasis on WPA projects that did not just employ people, but were useful to, and appreciated by, the communities that benefitted from them. As a magazine published by the Department of Agriculture observed in a 1939 profile of the sewing projects, "Realizing that badly made clothes that stamp their wearers as welfare recipients would not build the morale of people already hard put keeping up spirits, WPA sewing projects have placed particular emphasis on making good clothes from attractive patterns."[6] Reports and press releases from state WPA offices in the South indicate that sewing projects, even in the smallest and poorest communities, strove to meet these ideals.

In 1938, Franklin Roosevelt famously characterized the South as "the nation's No. 1 economic problem."[7] This assessment was not necessarily welcomed in the South, where some continued to deny or romanticize rural poverty.[8] And yet, the South was, for many New Deal administrators, a primary example of the kinds of social and economic deprivation, exacerbated by neglect and outmoded ways of doing things, that were fixable by modern government programs and interventions. One of the most visible examples of this was the Photography Division of the Farm Security Administration (FSA), whose director, Roy Striker, sent photographers across the country to take pictures of New Deal aid recipients. The Photography Division exhibited photos, and made them available to the press with the goal of documenting poverty, arguing for the necessity of New Deal programs, and invoking public sympathy for the poor. In the South, much of the Division's task involved photographing the rural poor (most of them recipients, specifically, of FSA aid), as a way of critiquing the tenant farming and sharecropping systems the agency was working to reform.[9] The photographers who took these iconic pictures, and the FSA who publicized them, have provoked criticism, then and since, for exploiting and embarrassing their subjects.[10] Thus reports on the attractive clothing made in WPA sewing rooms offer an interesting, if not explicitly articulated, dialogue with the rhetoric of southern poverty such as that expressed in poignant images of ragged families in FSA photographs.

Many internal WPA reports and newspaper articles from southern communities praised local sewing projects for making garments that looked as though they were store-bought. "The overalls and pants we make can hardly be distinguished from ready made ones," said one narrative report from a rural area in North Carolina in 1938.[11] A reporter for the *New Orleans Times-Picayune*, writing in 1938 about clothing made on a New Orleans sewing project in a factory-like operation, observed that the clothing was professionally made without looking generic: "Not only is each piece finished in such a way that it cannot be told from a 'store bought' article but there is such variety of treatment and material that standardization is eliminated." Dozens of sewing projects hosted open houses, participated in exhibitions, and put on fashion shows to proudly show off the garments they had created. At the same time, most of the projects in southern states did not really operate under factory conditions or use factory equipment. Even in large cities, most sewing rooms employed a mix of sewing machines and hand sewing, and many used patterns produced for home sewing. So, it is not clear that the majority of the clothing made on the sewing projects looked "factory made" or "store bought," but it seems that project administrators almost considered it more important that it looked as good as store bought, and that it not make the wearers look like they were on relief.

Many proud descriptions of the clothing in state reports actually emphasized uniqueness and handcrafted details. A North Carolina WPP Report from 1938 observed, in describing a sewing room's work on school clothes for local children, that "we have had an unusually varied supply of material for girl's clothing and no two dresses have been made alike of any one material in any one county." The same report remarked on boys' clothing as well, emphasizing the importance of boys not having to wear the same clothes to school as they might wear to do chores at home: "We are making an effort to get enough pants and knickers made for boys so that we will do away with little fellows having to go to school in overalls. Our slogan is, 'No overalls at school for children of relief families.'"[12] Projects consistently emphasized making school clothes for children, and project reports often made references to parents who had kept their children out of school for lack of decent clothes, before receiving WPA garments. "It is in the manufacture of children's clothing that the sewing centers produce their most impressive results," reported one Maryland newspaper. "The gayer-colored textiles are made into charming dresses that any little girl would be proud to wear."[13] In St. Louis, Missouri, the School Relief Fund, a charitable organization funded from the contributions of teachers and Board of Education employees, sponsored WPA sewing workers to produce clothing to be distributed directly to schoolchildren.[14] A report from the South Carolina WPA was among many from other states in its assertion that their sewing projects had "supplied clothing for a large number of school children in acute need of it," and that the children who previously were kept home from school for lack of decent clothes were now able to attend."[15] A 1939 report from North Carolina claimed that, according to school attendance officers, the sewing program had "increased school attendance by forty per cent (40%) and that children who wear garments made on WPA sewing projects are the best dressed children in school."[16]

There is also evidence that local sewing rooms, rather than solely adhering to the latest factory-made, store-bought fashions, adjusted their production for local tastes. Many, many reports described embroider, smocking, and other handwork on children's and infant clothing that reflected the individual skills and aesthetics of the maker. Several reports noted making clothes specifically to fit the intended wearers. A sewing room in Assumption Parish, Louisiana, reported in 1936 that it had completed over two thousand garments of different types made especially to fit the needs and tastes of various recipients: "For instance style was disregarded in garments made for the old country women who, in spite of more modern examples brought forth for their approval, insistently preferred the old fashioned, loose-wasted, full-skirted, ground-length top garment and long, full chemise with round, built-up neckline for an underslip."[17] Some sewing projects in western Virginia, perhaps taking a cue from some of the folkways-preservation projects in other sections of the WPA, experimented with local dyes, and enthusiastically reported on them to Ellen Woodward.[18] A Louisville newspaper reported in 1937 about a sewing project in southeastern Kentucky making buttons using native materials. In this case, the motive was initially financial: the sewing room did not have the funding to supply store-bought buttons and turned to cross-sections of hickory nuts and corn cobs, as well as covered bottle caps, to serve the purpose.[19] Necessity may have driven these material choices, just as the lack of industrial sewing machines surely affected the look of the clothes. Still, it seems that the net result of this effort was often clothes that were unique, made to order, and that sometimes featured fine handiwork, regional techniques, and local materials—clothes, in other words, that looked not like they came from a store or the Sears and Roebuck catalog, but rather, that looked like they came from where they were made.

WPA Sewing Rooms and Implementing a Welfare State in the South

In order to participate in New Deal programs, many southern states had to establish welfare infrastructures and bureaucracies where few or none had existed before. In communities across the South, newly formed county welfare bureaus sought to sponsor sewing rooms, first under FERA between 1933 and 1935, and then under the WPA.[20] Sewing rooms offered a number of benefits to underfunded local welfare offices that were often hard-pressed to meet clients' needs. On WPA projects, sponsors paid for materials and equipment, and provided locations, while the WPA paid workers' wages. In the case of sewing rooms, the WPA also provided textiles and occasionally, but less consistently, equipment, such as sewing machines. Welfare agency-sponsored sewing projects created jobs for women on relief rolls that paid more than they could receive in direct relief, and these wages were paid for entirely with federal dollars. The finished clothes would be distributed to relief families. The cost of all this to the sponsors was relatively small: rent on the necessary buildings (though this could be free if public buildings were used, or spaces were donated), and the cost of "findings" such as thread, pins, scissors, buttons, and the like.[21] Nevertheless, even though they were relatively cheap, sewing rooms were vulnerable in communities with minimal welfare structures and resources. Small as they were, the sticking point was material costs. Unlike more high-profile WPA infrastructure projects in which city and county investment in materials (to build roads, bridges, public buildings, etc.) ostensibly served the entire population, the sewing rooms provided clothes only to families on relief.[22] The fact that the WPA paid for materials used in sewing rooms, when it did not do so on most WPA projects, may point to a lack of local commitment to fully sponsoring sewing projects. However, this proved controversial in Washington. As Ellen Woodward pointed out in a 1936 memo to Harry Hopkins, sewing rooms received criticism for spending too much federal money on materials.[23] In the memo, she acknowledged the need for sponsors to contribute more, but when the WPA set new policies requiring this, it tended to lead to sewing-room closures and layoffs.

Sewing projects across the South appear to have been constantly on the brink of being shut down. Many were established on short-term timelines and welfare agencies had to reapply every few months to keep them open. Almost always the problem was limited funding. The sponsor's share of expenses for most sewing-room projects was 7 percent in 1936, but county welfare agencies consistently found getting that funding difficult.[24] Following broad cutbacks in New Deal programs in 1937, the WPA mandated that the federal government would pay only 10 percent of what it paid out in wages for materials on any project, a policy that cut federal contributions to sewing-room materials by more than half.[25] A couple of years later, local sponsors were required to fund 25 percent of the cost of sewing rooms, a policy that caused a new round of threatened closings and layoffs.[26] In most cases where the issue was covered in the press, it seems county and city governments were unwilling or unable to put up the extra money.

In October of 1937 a dispute ensued in Jacksonville, Florida, over the additional $500 a month needed to keep the local sewing-room project going. According to the *Jacksonville Times-Union*, the Duval County Welfare Board cited its need to fund existing direct relief programs, while the County Board of Commissioners said that they would not appropriate more money for the Welfare Board. WPA-funded salaries for the 500 women working in the sewing room amounted to about $16,000 a month, which supported those women, and some 1,100 other people in the country, the women's dependents. That same year a sewing project in Savannah employing 300 people had to close because the city said it "could not afford the cost of materials."[27] In these and similar cases, the amount needed to keep the sewing projects open dwarfed the WPA-funded salaries to the workers, all women eligible for relief, whose salaries contributed to the local economy, and who might have to go back on county-funded direct relief if the sewing rooms closed.

Since the sewing rooms seemed to offer a good deal to local governments, why did any hesitate to keep them funded? Some evidence indicates that the need for women's work relief was not always taken seriously. In interoffice correspondence at Georgia FERA in 1935, a women's project administrator expressed frustration with local officials who, she thought, viewed sewing projects as less important that the construction projects that primarily employed men. "Public officials must be convinced," she wrote, that funding sewing rooms was "as important as furnishing construction materials," and that "this program is not extraneous to business recovery."[28] Press releases and statements from federal and state WPP administrators repeatedly emphasized the need to provide work relief for unemployed female breadwinners, which suggests they felt the need to convince the public and government officials of this point.

It seems local authorities supported the sewing projects when they did not have to pay much for them. In Memphis in the summer of 1937, 352 women were dropped from local WPA roles and told to apply to the state for old-age, widow, or dependent-children benefits under Social Security. This meant, as a local newspaper pointed out, that these women would have a lower income than under the WPA, but it lowered overall welfare costs for the county.[29] Other governments cited legal constraints for funding sewing rooms; once the county had set its budget, local laws barred them from appropriating or reallocating more money. In Macon, Georgia, in October of 1937, for instance, a sewing project employing three hundred women closed because the city and county could not come up with $900 a month. The *Atlanta Constitution* quoted the county chairman saying that he saw "no legal way in which the county could put up its share" of the money.[30] In Atlanta, the local WPA asked Fulton County for $3000 a month to keep a sewing project employing a thousand women (and receiving wages worth $57,000/month) open through the end of 1938. The county responded that they had already exceeded their relief-work budget.[31] Sewing rooms continued to operate in these places, which suggests that funding eventually came through, but not without pressure from the media and the public, and not before a period of layoffs and deeper hardship for relief families.

News of sewing-room closures drew criticism in the press, and sometimes provoked protests from sewing-room workers. In Mobile, Alabama, conflicts over local funding for sewing rooms cropped up between the spring of 1938 and the winter of 1939, when the county refused to fund its share of the local sewing room—$1,350 a month in materials—putting 350 women, earning $18,000 a month in wages, out of work.[32] About half of the women ended up organizing and demonstrating at the county commission offices. A local paper blamed the county government for lack of foresight in budgeting, and went so far as to editorialize that "there is some evidence now that the board did not simply forget to include the sewing-room project in its budget, but was hopeful that the project might die a quiet death if no provision were made for it in the annual allotment of funds." It went on to assert that "as it is now, the public naturally imagines that the sewing-room project is a useful and deserved form of relief. If the board doesn't think so, let it say why."[33] This public support might have been limited. Eventually Mobile county commissioners appropriated funds to keep the sewing rooms open for another few months, but by January, 1939, the sewing rooms again faced layoffs when the county could not maintain needed sponsor contributions of a few hundred dollars a month. "My heart bleeds for these women," said one county commissioner after the body managed to squeeze enough money out of the budget to put 40 of 213 women back to work, "but you can't take any more money out of a hat than you can put into it. . . . Go out and ask the taxpayers to increase their payments. And if you do, you won't get a dime more."[34]

In her article examining a 1937 WPA sewing-room sit-down strike in Tampa, where women fought (unsuccessfully) to reverse layoffs from the project in the wake of federal cuts to relief programs, Elna C. Green argues that the strikers used the "language and tactics of the labor movement," but were asserting a "right to relief" that was rooted in their responsibilities as mothers even though it was not yet articulated as a "right to welfare."[35] The rhetoric of the Mobile sewing-room women and their supporters corroborates this. "I've made a visit into the homes of these women and have seen conditions," a spokesperson for the 1938 protestors told the *Mobile Press*. "Babies are going hungry and must have relief."[36] One protestor reportedly shouted, "Next time we'll bring our kids along [to the demonstration]. Then we'll show them."[37] A little over a year later representatives for laid-off sewing-room workers in Mobile accused the county government of "breaking down the morale of some good women" who "are in dire need," including "widows with five children."[38] In 1936, WPA administrators in Georgia collected a number of stories in response to a request from the regional director for information on how women on WPA projects were being helped. In one case, a woman with four children who "was deserted by her husband" found work in a sewing room and remarked that the job was "a means of providing food, shelter, and education for my children," adding that the training she received on the job would allow her to provide for her family in the future." Another woman, a widow, reported supporting seven children, aged three to sixteen, on her WPA sewing-room wages.[39] In a letter to Harry Hopkins reporting racial discrimination in WPA projects in Whiteville, North Carolina, a group of African American women asserted that they were "unable to make a meager living for our selves and our dependents,"[40] Need, and the imperative to care for children, shaped women's claims for work on the WPA sewing projects.

Women's Work Relief/Women's Welfare: Training and Skill on the WPA Sewing Projects

Assertions that women deserved jobs in WPA sewing rooms so that they could provide adequately for their children fits, but not completely, with what previous scholars have seen as the "maternalist" intentions of New Deal welfare programs. According to this scholarship, New Deal administrators geared work relief primarily to men. Needy women with young children were ideally not supposed to work for wages. Women's work-relief jobs were ostensibly for husbandless women who were childless or had grown children.[41] In reality, many women with school-age (and younger) children sought and got jobs in WPA sewing rooms.[42] WPA wages, even at the unskilled level, were higher than widow and ADC benefits.[43] Ellen Woodward, herself a widow with a school-aged child in the 1930s, felt women who had access to childcare should be eligible for WPA jobs.[44] Government studies of the unemployment problem revealed a significant number of women who needed to work, and would continue to work after the depression was over. Woodward believed the purpose of the women's projects of the WPA should not be different from that of all WPA projects: to provide employment to the unemployed, *and* to preserve and develop workers' skills. Sewing rooms were initially set up under FERA with the rationale that most needy women had no employment experience and no skills, but that, at the very least, almost any women could sew.[45] However, this assumption did not always prove to be correct, certainly if one of the other goals of the projects was to produce well-made clothes people on relief would be proud to wear. By the time the WPA replaced FERA work-relief in 1935, Woodward was emphasizing that sewing projects should train women in professional methods for making clothes so that they might be eligible for sewing jobs in private industry. The WPA encouraged states to make sure that sewing projects maintained quality and efficiency standards and, where possible, that they used modern methods and technology. However, this happened inconsistently on sewing projects throughout the South. Only in cities with established garment industries could women expect to get training in industrial sewing methods. While there were some other instances where women gained sufficient training to work as home dressmakers or doing alterations in department stores, most southern sewing projects had neither the equipment nor, it seems, the goal to train women as professional seamstresses. The majority of training programs in sewing rooms focused on helping women become better home sewers, and better homemakers. Many of the women themselves resisted implementation of skill and efficiency tests, seeming to emphasize "relief" over "work" in work-relief programs, and suggesting that these jobs were for women in need who should not be expected to uphold professional standards.

Women's work-relief project administrators recognized early on that a significant portion of the women they served were heads of households who needed to support families. One FERA official for women's work relief in Mobile, Alabama, wrote to Woodward that "practically all of the women are the sole support of dependent families" and "will have to continue as wage earners after the present crisis is over. . . . Simply to give the women temporary work to tide them over is not enough." Explaining that she strove to make sure women in Mobile sewing rooms received training for work in private industry as seamstresses, this official explained that she was resigning because the local FERA branch did not support her efforts.[46] WPA sewing-room supervisors in cities like Baltimore, Atlanta, and New Orleans consistently told the press that their aim was to train women for work in factories or other businesses that employed seamstresses. In a 1936 memo to Harry Hopkins titled "Justification of Sewing Projects," Ellen Woodward cited the necessity of providing work relief for female heads of households and for single women that would provide "rehabilitation, . . . training and retraining of such women as are qualified and of suitable age for private employment."[47] Woodward and Eleanor Roosevelt encouraged Hopkins to include women in work relief on an equal basis with men, and to make sure that local WPA administrators did as well, a goal he facilitated by requiring that all state directors of Women's and Professional Projects were female.[48] As Roosevelt wrote to Hopkins in 1935, "I hope in some way you will impress on state administrators that the women's programs are as important as the men's. They are so apt to forget us!"[49]

Hopkins supported women's relief work, but he and many other administrators felt that that women's work created special problems for the WPA. While construction projects could employ large numbers of unskilled male workers, women's projects (sewing, canning, and the like) created more diverse types of work that required more training and closer supervision.[50] Although sewing was seen as the perfect solution for employing women with no previous work experience, even women who knew how to sew needed to learn techniques and protocols required in WPA sewing rooms. Some women needed to learn the most basic hand sewing techniques, and others needed to learn how to operate sewing machines. Put simply, although the WPA labeled hand sewers and foot pedal sewing machine operators, along with ditch diggers and other manual laborers, as "unskilled," in practice, sewing required quite a bit of skill and supervision to ensure consistency and quality control for the clothing produced.⁵¹ Thus, all the sewing projects implemented training programs for new sewers, and continuing education for everyone else, and federal guidelines encouraged sewing rooms to provide one to two hours of instruction per week. While Woodward, Roosevelt, and others were focused on the kind of training that would prepare women for future employment, implementation of this, and its success in getting women off the WPA and into private industry, was uneven at best.⁵²

In 1935, Woodward, growing interested in knowing about reemployment of sewing-room workers, wrote to WPP directors across the country for reports on women who had left WPA sewing projects for jobs in the private sector. One reason she wanted this information was for public relations purposes. "I am eager to know as much as possible about these cases so I may refer to them in talks over the radio and in various parts of the country," she wrote in a letter to Florida's director of women's work in 1935.⁵³ Supporters of work relief for women strove to keep success stories in the news. Writing of a visit to a sewing room in Knoxville, Tennessee, in her nationally syndicated column, "My Day," Eleanor Roosevelt remarked that, based on the finished garments she had seen, the project "must be turning out really skilled workers," who, she concluded, could make a good living from their sewing.⁵⁴ In newspaper articles and internal reports, WPA officials and sewing-room supervisors bragged about their workers finding jobs and leaving the relief rolls. In the South, larger cities that already had garment industries before the depression hit boasted of some success in industrial employment.⁵⁵ In smaller cities and towns, a few women found work doing alterations in department stores, as private dressmakers, and the like.⁵⁶ But overall, as long as the Depression continued, and the garment industry was stagnant, such opportunities were limited. As one New Deal official put it, "Until industry provides *opportunities* for employment, the field of sewing would seem to me to be a rather vain undertaking."⁵⁷ This situation was compounded in the South by the fact that the garment industry was still relatively small, even in urban areas, and opportunities were scarcer still in the countryside.⁵⁸ A woman who worked in a sewing room near Macon, Georgia, observed to WPA interviewers that, while her sewing skills had improved to the point where "I am in a better position to do my home sewing, and if there were people who wanted to hire their sewing done, I could do it," and that she might be eligible for an industrial job if the family moved to the city. Commercial employment would not be realistic "as long as it is necessary for us to live in the country." Another woman from the same area "seemed fearful at the thought of finding adequate income by private industry." A woman in Marion County, Georgia, had her doubts even about making money doing sewing for her neighbors, telling interviewers that she "would like to take in some sewing, but nobody is able to pay for sewing to be done. There just ain't any work in our town to be done."[59]

Perhaps because local administrators recognized these limitations, and perhaps because they had different priorities, little of the training in most sewing rooms of the South seemed geared toward training women to be factory operatives in the garment industry. Even at a large sewing project in New Orleans, one that employed 1,600 workers in 1938 and used industrial equipment, the workers did no piecework, but made complete garments from start to finish. In fact, while a few sewing rooms segmented the process, the majority taught women to make whole garments of several types. These were useful skills in home sewing or a small sewing business, but they were unlikely to be used in a garment factory. Furthermore, few sewing rooms had a sewing machine for every worker. Most employed groups of women in hand sewing. This work was also reserved for inexperienced sewers who were supposed to "graduate" to machines, but many sewing rooms in the South simply did not have enough machines. One narrative report from a WPA district in North Carolina mentioned that sewing rooms there had only one machine for every four workers.[60] In other places, women brought machines from home, or used home machines lent and donated to the sewing projects. Thus, very few women gained experience on industrial power machines like those used in factories. Sewing Consultant Julia Shackleton traveled throughout the country in 1939 assessing the quality of work and training programs in sewing rooms, and her reports from Virginia noted that many sewing rooms there did not train women to a professional standard.[61] In an essay about the WPA sewing rooms in Atlanta, historian Georgiana Hickey examines the work of local Democratic club women who tirelessly complained to state and federal officials about the poor quality of sewing training given, particularly to African American women.[62] Local WPA officials and sewing-room supervisors themselves sometimes said that few of the women working in them were likely to be ready for factory work. More frequently, they explained that working in the sewing rooms would allow women to make clothes for their families, and perhaps make a living mending and producing garments for individual clients.[63]

WPA sewing rooms offered frequent training seminars. Some were aimed at improving workers' sewing, such as the well-documented workshops conducted in Louisiana with titles such as "Making of Seams and Where to Use Them," "Demonstration on Buttonhole Attachment," "Methods of Taking Measurements," and "Knowledge Required in Cutting Garments."[64] Still, these could just as well have aimed at helping women to become better home sewers. In fact, many of the courses offered in the Louisiana sewing rooms concerned homemaking, as well as personal and social hygiene, with titles such as "Home and Community Life," "Food for Body Building," "Meal Planning," "Removal of Stains," "Control of Weight by Dieting," and "First Aid."[65] The North Carolina WPA reported in 1939 that, in addition to having "learned to sew well," women on the sewing projects had "learned rules of sanitation and hygiene" and "have become conscious of the meaning of good personal appearance for themselves and their families."[66] The Maryland WPA noted that in Baltimore, women with no previous sewing experience had not only learned to complete all sorts of garments, but had also gotten training in "personal hygiene and health."[67] A South Carolina report asserted that the sewing training women received made them able to "carry on the vocation of seamstresses" but also to "make clothes for themselves and their children" and to be "better and more economical homemakers."[68] The Georgia WPA reported that sewing-room workers received an hour per day of "homemaking instruction," and at least one worker from a Georgia sewing room commented that "during homemaking hour, I have learned a lot about saving and making my home a better place to live and raise my children."[69] The main focus of training in many sewing rooms appears to have been basic competency in making the clothes and improving the home lives of the women on the project.[70]

Washington asked all sewing projects to assess workers' skills and to use a consistent system of evaluation to decide whether a sewing-room operator should get a promotion or a change in skill classification. This policy provoked resentment from some workers. In 1937, Georgia sewing-room supervisors reported a variety of skill- and efficiency-monitoring policies to regional WPP director Blanche Ralston, who had asked for the reports, in part, to assess complaints she had received about such tests.[71] That same year, Annie Smith, a sewing-room worker in Spartanburg, South Carolina, wrote to a local WPA labor-policies board (the complaint eventually reached Ellen Woodward) challenging "these neveracking [sic] rigid tests that women in the sewing room have to go through with every 2 or 3 months. With the threat that if we fail we will lose our jobs or a cut in salary." Smith also argued that the tests were not in keeping with the purpose of work relief: "We all understood when President Roosevelt set up this work there was no red tape attached to it in any way," and that it was for "needy people" like her (she was an older woman who felt she was unlikely to ever find work in private industry).[72] In 1936, a group of sewing project workers in New Bern, North Carolina, wrote to President Roosevelt, Hopkins, their congressman, and the state WPA director in a similar vein, complaining that they had to complete "2 shirts or dresses in the course of a day" in order to get paid at the semiskilled salary, a standard that, they asserted, put them "at the point of hysteria," and which "only one woman who was an expert seamstress for years was able to accomplish." The women blamed the supervisors in their sewing room for the situation, stating that they did not think the US government intended for the supervisors to behave as "a slave driver." Invoking gendered language that seems old fashioned even by 1930s standards, they added, "No task should be set for any woman that the average American woman could not readily accomplish without nervous prostration and hysteria."[73]

In fact, the WPA mandated such standards. In a response to the New Bern women, the state director for the WPP pointed out that standards were necessary to assess women's "skill as seamstresses," adding that standards were also necessary because the WPA sewing project was "a production and construction program" and needed to avoid "criticism from private industries and communities" so that the program could continue.[74] Ellen Woodward seconded this, explaining to the New Bern women in another letter that all the states felt "standards in the sewing room should be gradually raised" as they gained "training and experience" on the projects.[75] In a second letter to WPA officials, South Carolinian Annie Smith complained about her skill classification being adjusted from semiskilled to unskilled (with a corresponding decrease in salary). Woodward responded, explaining that Smith and other foot-pedal-machine operators had been misclassified as semiskilled (a designation reserved for power machine operators) and pointing out that skills tests were WPA policy.[76] Another letter, this time from a woman in Columbia, South Carolina, echoed Smith's complaints, mentioning tests requiring workers to "complete two garments a day, from now on," decreases in wages for those who did not, and unnecessary employment of nurses (at "professional" wage level) in the sewing rooms at the expense of unskilled and semiskilled sewing positions: "In the beginning of this WPA work, I thought that it was created especially for the need of the poor, as was Roosevelt's intention. Now, the head workers are trying to make it seem otherwise, and they are getting larger wages than the humblest workers."[77] In fact, the WPA was expressly founded to employ experienced workers (including white-collar workers) in ways that would allow them to preserve and improve their skills, and unskilled workers in ways that would build skills they could use in a recovered economy. These facts did not, however, match the perception of many WPA sewing-room workers, who saw themselves as needy but desired work relief rather than direct relief.[78]

Racial Discrimination on the Sewing-Room Projects

Though they were almost always segregated, sewing rooms were established for black women in southern communities.[79] Federal policy officially forbade racial discrimination on the projects, but did not do enough to prevent it in practice.[80] Because state WPA officials administered projects, and because projects required local sponsorship, Washington had inadequate tools for addressing unequal funding for projects and racial discrimination when it came to sewing-room closures and layoffs. A report from one WPA district in North Carolina noted, for example, that the sponsors in their area "do not seem to want us to put the colored women in the sewing rooms," noting only two counties with sewing rooms for black women.[81] Before the New Deal, private charities, and what few government-aid agencies there were, provided little or no help to unemployed African Americans. During the New Deal, state governments sought to limit African Americans' access to relief. In the case of the work relief, African Americans were underrepresented on WPA projects, state officials expressed unwillingness to provide projects for African Americans as long as whites needed work, and in some cases, states refused to pay equal wages on its WPA projects. Southern officials seemed to particularly resent the fact that African Americans in WPA jobs might make more money than they could in private employment.[82] Civil rights leaders and the black press recognized that the WPA employed more African Americans and exhibited less discrimination than previous FERA and PWA work-relief programs, but they continued to work with black citizens to fight for equal access to WPA work.[83]

Discrimination persisted for black women in the South who hoped to work in WPA sewing rooms or similar projects.[84] There are many documented examples of African American women who were dropped from the WPA rolls altogether, or transferred to less desirable projects doing heavy landscaping work or cleaning public buildings. In many cases, women dropped from the rolls reported that they were told to take agricultural and domestic service jobs available in the private sector. In all cases, the women reported that white women on the sewing projects were either not laid off at all, or were laid off in smaller numbers. Some African American women claimed they were let go for insufficient sewing skills, while white women with the same or less skill were retained. Aggrieved sewing-room workers directed their complaints to Washington, presumably because they had gotten nowhere at the state level, or feared retaliation from state and local authorities for complaining.[85] Yet WPA policy was to send such complaints back to state WPA offices for investigation, a practice that hampered effective redress of racial discrimination charges.

In autumn of 1936, the *Birmingham World* reported that eight hundred African American women in Birmingham had been forced out of sewing rooms and onto outdoor manual labor projects beautifying the sides of local highways, building sidewalks, and providing landscaping in the city, "work that should be given to men," the *Birmingham World* opined, citing concrete mixing and ditch digging among the tasks assigned.[86] A later report called the local director of the WPA "a bitter enemy of the Negro" and accused his office of a number of abuses, including attempting to disguise the women in heavy clothes so they would not be recognized as female, not providing toilet facilities, ignoring instances of sexual harassment, and forcing women physically unable to do heavy work to quit their relief jobs.[87] By winter, a number of women who had protested these conditions were dropped from the WPA rolls. As of October of 1938, the African American sewing rooms in Birmingham had not been reopened. The WPA generally maintained gender segregation on its projects. Sewing rooms provided relief work for unskilled and untrained women, whereas outdoor manual labor projects usually employed men. In Birmingham and other places in the South, however, white administrators deemed manual labor often designated male (road work, janitorial duties in public buildings, etc.) as suitable for black (but not white) women.[88] Editorial pieces in the black press explicitly challenged this, asserting that assigning women to these jobs was an insult to their womanhood. As reporter H. D. Coke put it upon breaking the story, "I know Mr. Roosevelt, you must certainly not be aware of the things your Southern gentlemen make my women do."[89] A letter to the editor of the *Birmingham World* from the Homewood Colored Civic League likened putting women to work on the sides of highways to chain gangs, and called it "an attempt to degrade our women."[90]

In other cases, the excuse white officials gave for laying off African American sewing-room workers was the availability of private sector agricultural or domestic work. In October, 1937, the *Chicago Defender* described a formal protest from the NAACP national office to Harry Hopkins "against the forcing of Negro labor off the WPA rolls in southern states into jobs as cotton pickers," which cited a list of complaints the NAACP had received from a number of southern states over the past year.[91] One such letter, from Valdosta, Georgia, observed that sewing projects for black women there had been closed (those for white women continued) and that "the black women had been put to land clearing beside the men." The letter described cold weather and inadequate clothing, and workers who included "the aged (some great grandmothers), the undernourished, the delicate in health." Recognizing that local officials were responsible for this situation, the writers pointed out that the incident had national implications, because the "net result of it is to put the official stamp on the practice . . . and make the government program a party to a system of 'Collective peonage.'" A postscript noted that the African Americans of Valdosta dared not protest locally because "they are intimidated with threats of arrest, of being run out of town, and of bullets thru their heads."[92]

The disparity between WPA and private-sector wages and hours for African Americans in the South was considerable. At the lowest unskilled pay level, WPA workers made about $24 a month and commonly worked less than forty hours a week. The NAACP reported, for instance, that workers in North Carolina earned about fifty cents a day ($12–15 a month) for picking cotton (almost certainly working for more than eight hours a day).[93] The *Norfolk Journal and Guide* reported in 1936 that women in Louisiana got the same wages for WPA jobs as domestic service jobs, but, much to the chagrin of local white employers, preferred WPA because the hours were shorter.[94] A 1939 report from New Orleans found that African American women had been reduced to half-time in the sewing rooms "because many of them are said to have continuously refused private employment" especially in domestic service.[95] These examples suggest that WPA jobs offered an alternative, and a challenge, to the low wages and the long hours that African Americans in the South had faced for generations.[96] The last example also points to efforts by WPA administrators to keep this cheap labor supply intact for private employers.

A case in North Carolina illustrates this dynamic, as well as the limited response African Americans could expect from Washington. In February of 1937, a group of African American women in Whiteville, North Carolina, wrote Ellen Woodward complaining that they were not given a fair proportion of the WPA sewing-room jobs, and that the small number of women who had gotten jobs were recently laid off with no explanation. In the letter, the petitioners emphasized their right to WPA jobs as American citizens.

"We feel it was the intention of the Government that an equal distribution of work was to be made to all Counties and peoples in need of the same, alike, without prejudice or discrimination."[97] In a letter to the spokesperson of the group, Woodward explained that the state and district WPA was in charge of the WPA in their area, adding, rather unhelpfully, "It is fully intended by the Federal Administration that there be no discrimination in the administration of its program because of race or for any other reason," and informing the spokesperson that she was referring the case back to the North Carolina WPA for investigation.[98] The North Carolina WPA then asked local WPA officials to make a report responding to the charge of racial discrimination.

The unnamed local official making the report admitted to closing both white and African American sewing rooms and then reopening only the white sewing rooms seven months later. The official explained "that to reopen the colored sewing rooms would tend to increase the shortage of domestic labor in this country," adding, that, because "housewives in the South have never employed white domestic labor," unskilled white women needed the sewing-room work, while "there seems to be a scarcity, not only of domestic labor, but of field labor in the county, and there is no reason why any colored women cannot secure employment at a reasonable wage in domestic service." The report went on to further challenge these women's need for relief and fault them for seeking higher wages for fewer hours on the WPA:

> Most of the names signed to this petition are those colored women who are known personally by me, and there is not any doubt in my mind that these women could secure work if they so desired. Of course, it is natural that they would prefer working sixteen days a month at a wage of $22.12 [in WPA sewing rooms] to working full time for that same wage; and I believe that this accounts for the feeling that they have been discriminated against.[99]

Thus, this report challenged African American women's right to welfare, setting a different and more generous standard for white women.[100] Woodard acknowledged and accepted this report with no further comment, a pattern that repeated itself in Birmingham, Norfolk, Blackwell, Arkansas, Fayetteville, North Carolina, and other locations. The federal WPA rarely directly investigated complaints and invariably accepted reports by local authorities that found no discrimination had happened.

Racial discrimination also appears to have occurred in the application of WPA-established skill designations to workers on sewing projects. As mentioned earlier, the WPA designated sewing-room workers as unskilled if they did hand sewing or foot-pedal machines, and semiskilled if they could use power sewing machines. Pattern makers, forewomen, supervisors, and the like could get skilled or white-collar designations. The difference in wages between skill designations could be $10 or more a month. Workers in African American sewing rooms in the South seem to have been disproportionately designated as unskilled, and the sewing projects themselves often lacked the equipment and training programs that would have allowed them to improve their skill designation. Accusations of inadequate skill were among the justifications for African American sewing projects being discontinued, and their workers being laid off or put onto undesirable manual labor or janitorial projects.

Because the WPA counted previous work experience in assigning people to WPA projects and assessing skill levels, and because the majority of African American women in the South worked as domestics or agricultural workers before the Depression, almost all of those on the sewing projects entered their work as unskilled workers.[101] Admittedly, most of the sewing rooms were set up to employ women without previous work experience, and so most of their workers, regardless of race, were designated unskilled. Nevertheless, race (and class) could and did affect opportunities. For instance, some WPA districts in the South reported that they had too many educated women (who were disproportionately white) on sewing projects because of a lack of sponsor support for white-collar projects for women. Officials framed this a problem of women taking jobs that were beneath them; but looked at another way, these women were getting priority for available WPA jobs by virtue of their class and racial status, edging out unskilled white and African American women for this work.[102] Availability and distribution of sewing machines was also a factor. Few districts in the South had enough sewing machines for every sewing-room worker. In photographs of sewing rooms in Georgia, groups of hand sewers are found in both African American and white projects, but no African American women are shown using machines, and all are classified as "unskilled." White women using power machines and foot-pedal machines are both designated as "semi-skilled," even though WPA guidelines categorized foot-pedal-machine sewing as unskilled.[103]

In some cases, African American sewing-room workers believed they were removed from sewing-room jobs because of overt racial discrimination in the guise of maintaining skill standards. In a letter to the North Carolina WPA WPP director, Woodward alluded to transfers of African American women to custodial and manual labor projects: "In some of the letters and reports which we have received, there is an indication that some transfers are based on the assumption that no Negro woman can sew. If Negro women can prove themselves to be as efficient workers as the white women on a given project, they should receive equal consideration."[104] The director responded that women were only moved to cleaning projects when they were willing to do so, and that the sewing rooms' skills tests had "shown objectively a lack of ability to meet the standards set."[105] Still, in at least one of these North Carolina cases, African American women were transferred after two years of working in sewing rooms. In another instance in Portsmouth, Virginia, when sixty-six African American women were dismissed from sewing projects, the skills issue came up again. This time, a representative for the women wrote the district's congressman, claiming that many of the women were "real seamstresses" and that, before being laid off, all the black women on the project were employed at the same pay rate, regardless of skill.[106] In 1939, an African American sewing room in Jackson, Mississippi, was shut down entirely when the local Negro Chamber of Commerce requested that African American supervisors, who had lately been replaced by white supervisors, be put back in charge.[107] These cases of racial discrimination on the WPA sewing projects offer a close-up view of how the structure of WPA programs dovetailed with racial labor practices in the South to derail equal opportunity in work relief, but they also reveal cases of African Americans in the South who were quite willing to organize and advocate for themselves as American citizens and had the right to access New Deal programs on an equal basis with whites.

Conclusion

The WPA sewing rooms were part of a larger commitment by Ellen Woodward and Harry Hopkins to include unemployed women in work-relief programs. As this and previous studies show, the WPA, like other New Deal programs, reflected gendered assumptions about families and about women's versus men's work. The programs maintained gender segregation in the kinds of projects women could work on and excluded women from the kinds of industrial training that allowed many working-class men to qualify for skilled work once the Depression was over.[108] Only a few of the sewing rooms offered industrial training that qualified women for jobs in the garment industry, an occupation already dominated by women and not known for high pay or good working conditions.

Examining the sewing rooms in the southern states also illuminates other aspects of the New Deal that are important for historians of the South in the twentieth century and of the development of the welfare state in modern US history. Sewing rooms illustrate the control that state and local governments had over many New Deal programs, a model that southern lawmakers in Washington had a large part in creating, and one that had consequences in a region with a small social welfare infrastructure. This study focused on the WPA records in southern states, and it would be interesting to examine the records from other regions, particularly to see whether (and how) such things as opportunities for African Americans, the quality of training programs, and sponsor funding for women's might have differed in other parts of the United States.

Notes

1. "Sewing Projects Bee-hives of Activity," *Work* (Newsletter of the WPA of Louisiana), 1:2, (September 1936), 17, Box 2: Indiana–New York State, State WPA Publications, 1936–1940, Division of Information, Works Progress Administration (WPA), Records of the Works Progress Administration (WPA), Record Group 69 (RG 69), National Archives at College Park, MD (NACP).

2. For descriptions of the basics about the WPA sewing projects, and information on numbers and proportions of women employed on various WPA projects, see the following WPA publications: Corrington Gill and Emerson Ross, *An Analysis of Women on Works Progress Administration Projects, December 1935 through May 1935* (Washington, DC, 1936); Enid Baird with Hugh P. Brinton, *Average General Relief Benefits, 1933–1938* (Washington, DC: General Printing Office, 1940); "Work Pays America" (pamphlet) (Washington, DC: General Printing Office, n.d.), and the following secondary sources: Elna C. Green, "Relief from Relief: The Tampa Sewing-Room Strike of 1937 and the Right to Welfare," *Journal of American History* 95 (March 2009), 1018; Sara B. Marcketti, "The Sewing-Room Projects of the Works Progress Administration," *Textile History*, 41:1 (May 2010), 28–31; Martha Swain, *Ellen S. Woodward: New Deal Advocate for Women* (Jackson: University Press of Mississippi, 1995), 80.

3. Particularly in Georgia, North Carolina, Virginia, Maryland, Louisiana, and Florida. Recent scholarship on the sewing projects has a southern focus: Green, "Relief from Relief": 1012–37; Georgia Hickey, "The Lowest Form of Work Relief": Authority, Gender, and the State in Atlanta's Sewing Rooms," in *The New Deal and Beyond: Social Welfare in the South since 1930* (Athens: University of Georgia Press, 2003). For a general overview of the sewing rooms, see: Marcketti, 28–49.

4. Elna C. Green, ed., *The New Deal and Beyond: Social Welfare in the South since 1930* (Athens: University of Georgia Press, 2003), x–xi. For an interesting analysis of the southern influence over the New Deal, see Ira Katznelson, *Fear Itself: The New Deal and the Origins of Our Time* (New York: Liveright Publishing, 2013).

5. Green, *The New Deal and Beyond*, x; Ted Ownby, "Three Agrarianisms and the Idea of a South without Poverty," in Richard Godden and Martin Crawford, eds., *Reading Southern*

Poverty Between the Wars, 1918–1939 (Athens: The University of Georgia Press, 2006), 4.

6. "Haberdashers to the Needy." *Consumers' Guide* (Publication of the Department of Agriculture), VI:2 (May 1, 1939), 4, Box 85, Entry 678, folder: Sewing Projects, Information Service (Primary) File, Division of Information, WPA, RG 69, NACP.

7. Franklin D. Roosevelt: "Message to the Conference on Economic Conditions of the South," July 4, 1938. Online by Gerhard Peters and John T. Woolley, *The American Presidency Project.* http://www.presidency.ucsb.edu/ws/?pid=15670.

8. For more on this reaction and further discussion of southern reaction to FDR's statement, see Ownby, "Three Agrarianisms," 2.

9. See Cara Finnegan, *Picturing Poverty, Print Culture and FSA Photographs* (Washington: Smithsonian Books, 2003), 8, 33. Finnegan also discusses the use of FSA photographs in the progressive magazine *Survey Graphic*, explicitly to expose the evils of tenancy and sharecropping, and promote government efforts to combat poverty, see Chapter 2: "Social Engineering and Photographic Resistance: Social Science Rhetorics of Poverty in *Survey Graphic*," 57–119.

10. Finnegan, *Picturing Poverty*, 197–199, 218; and Stuart Kidd, "Dissonant Encounters: FSA Photographers and the Southern Underclass, 1935–1943," in Godden and Crawford, *Reading Southern Poverty*, 29–30, 31–36, 38–41.

11. Narrative Report, Women's and Professional Division (WPP), Eastern North Carolina, Area 5, September and October, 1938, "Sewing," Box 85, Entry 678, folder: Sewing Projects: Nebraska-Wyoming, Information Service (Primary) File, 1936–1942, Division of Information, WPA, RG 69, NACP.

12. Narrative Report, Women's and Professional Division (WPP), Eastern North Carolina, Areas 1 & 2, September and October, 1938, "Sewing," Box 85, Entry 678, folder: Sewing Projects: Nebraska-Wyoming, Information Service (Primary) File, 1936–1942, Division of Information, WPA, RG 69, NACP.

13. "Baltimore Will Take Over Two WPA Sewing Centers," *Baltimore Sun*, February 14, 1937, 2.

14. "School Funds Gives Clothes to Pupils," *Globe-Democrat* (St. Louis), November 25, 1937, 8-B, Box 190, folder: Sewing: August 1937–November 1937, Newspaper Clippings File, Division of Information, WPA, RG 69, NACP.

15. State Appraisal Committee, *United States Community Improvement Appraisal, State of South Carolina, March, 1938* (Colombia, SC: Works Progress Administration, 1938), Box 3, Entry 745, State WPA Publications, 1936–1940, Division of Information, WPA, RG 69, NACP.

16. "Narrative Report, North Carolina Works Progress Administration, Professional and Service Division, May 1, 1939, Box 2199, folder: North Carolina, 661, May, North Carolina 661–661.1, WPA Central Files: State, 1935–1944, RG 69, NACP.

17. "Excerpt from LA Narrative Report" June 20, 1936, 2, Box 85, Entry 678, folder: Sewing Projects: Alabama-Montana, Information Service (Primary) File, 1936–1942, Division of Information, WPA, RG 69, NACP.

18. Ella G. Agnew, Director of WPA Women's and Professional Projects for Virginia, sent recipes and sample swatches of natural dyes from Wise, Dickenson, and Scott counties to Ellen Woodward. "State of Virginia: Home Dyes," Box 2712, folder: 661, Virginia, January-December, 1937, WPA Central Files, State, 1935–1944, RG 69, NACP.

19. "Buttons, Buttons—WPA's Got Buttons," *Louisville Herald Post*, October 27, 1936, Box 190, folder: Sewing, November 5, 1935-October 31, 1936, Newspaper Clippings File, Division of Information, WPA, RG 69, NACP.

20. Some sewing rooms operated briefly as part of the Civil Works Administration, which operated briefly during the winter of 1933–1934 under the authority of the Interior Department's Public Works Administration (PWA). Swain, 38–45.

21. Sewing-machine availability was a perpetual problem on the projects. Sponsors sometimes purchased them, and there are some references to the WPA itself providing them. Often, people in the community donated sewing machines, or women working on the Sewing Projects provided their own.

22. This was true for other WPA projects set up for women, such as canning and the school lunch program.

23. She states that materials were 30 percent of sewing projects' cost, of which 23 percent came from the WPA, and 7 percent came from local sponsors. Typically sponsors of WPA projects paid the entire cost of materials. This memo was clearly distributed to state WPA women's project directors, perhaps for use in defending the sewing rooms from critics (the author found a copy in the Mississippi folder of the WPP WPA records). Ellen Woodward to Harry Hopkins, Memorandum: "Justification of Sewing Projects" (copy), December 23, 1936, Box 1: Sewing Project, Alabama-Maryland, folder: Mississippi, Records of the Division of Women's and Professional Projects, PC37–39, RG 69, NACP.

24. Ellen Woodward to Harry Hopkins, Memorandum: "Justification of Sewing Projects" (copy), December 23, 1936, Box 1: Sewing Project, Alabama-Maryland, folder: Mississippi, Records of the Division of Women's and Professional Projects, PC37–39, RG 69, NACP.

25. "City Asked for $2000 Monthly to Continue Sewing Project," *Baltimore Sun*, January 19, 1937, 22, Box 190, folder: Sewing, November 1, 1936–March 31, 1937, Newspaper Clippings File, Division of Information, WPA, RG 69, NACP.

26. "Needy Women Will Suffer If Sewing Rooms Close," *Tampa Times*, newspaper clipping, December 24, 1940, Box 85, Entry 678, folder: Sewing Projects, Alabama-Montana, Information Service (Primary) File, 1936–1942, 951A-953A, Division of Information, WPA, RG 69, NACP.

27. "600 Made Jobless as WPA Work Ends: Macon and Savannah Sewing Rooms Closed," *Atlanta Constitution*, October 2, 1937, 9.

28. Jane Van De Vrede to William Key, Interoffice Correspondence, Federal Emergency Recovery Administration Re: State Departmental Program, Women's Work, Atlanta, Georgia, August 3, 1935, Box 1156, folder: 661, Georgia, 1935–, Central Files: State, 1935–1944, WPA, RG 69, NACP.

29. As the paper reported, "WPA pay is $35 a month. Old age pensions will not be more than $25 monthly, and most of them will be less. Mothers of dependent children will receive $12 a month for one child and $8 for each additional child." "40 Mothers Present Demands for Relief," *Memphis Commercial Appeal*, July 17, 1937, 9, Box 190, folder: Sewing, April 1, 1937-July 31, 1937, Newspaper Clippings File, Division of Information, WPA, RG 69, NACP.

30. "600 Made Jobless as WPA Work Ends: Macon and Savannah Sewing Rooms Closed," *Atlanta Constitution*, October 2, 1937, 9.

31. "County Traffic Rules Drawn Up for Commission," *Atlanta Constitution*, October 10, 1937, 7.

32. In addition to the $1,800 in materials the federal WPA provided. "WPA Sewing Room Workers March on County Officials," *Mobile Press*, March 24, 1938. 1, Box 190, folder: Sewing, March 1938–April 1939, Newspaper Clippings File, Division of Information, WPA, RG 69, NACP.

33. "Hide and Seek" (editorial), *Mobile Press Register*, March 27, 1938, 8, Box 191, folder: Sewing, March 1938–April, 1939, Newspaper Clippings File, Division of Information, WPA, RG 69, NACP.

34. "County Board Provides Fund for Sewing Room; To Replace 83 Joints of WPA Road Pipe," *Mobile Press Register*, April 17, 1938, 1, Box 191, folder: Sewing, March 1938-April, 1939, Newspaper Clippings File, Division of Information, WPA, RG 69, NACP; "City Furnishes $200 Per Month for Sewing Room," *Mobile Press*, January 19, 1939, 1, Box 191, folder: Sewing, March 1938–April, 1939, Newspaper Clippings File, Division of Information, WPA, RG 69, NACP.

35. Green, "Relief from Relief," 1013, 1024. These women, and some of the others who organized protests, joined or were organized by the Workers Alliance of America, a left-leaning labor union that represented relief workers. Green, "Relief from Relief," 1019.

36. "WPA Sewing Room Workers March on County Officials."

37. "WPA Sewing Room Workers March on County Officials."

38. "City Furnishes $200 Per Month For Sewing Room."

39. Interview with "Mrs. L." of Bibb, County, GA. From a report based on interviews with Georgia sewing-room workers, sent with a cover letter from Jane Van De Vrede, Georgia WPP Director, to Ellen Woodward, August 10, 1936, Box 1157, folder: 661, Georgia, May 1936–July, 1936, WPA Central Files: State, 1935–1944, RG 69, NACP.

40. Hattie White to Harry Hopkins, February 10, 1937, Box 2198, folder: 660 (A-B) - - D, WPA Central Files: State, North Carolina, 652.36, (1939) 660, RG 69, NACP.

41. If married with children, their husbands should have WPA or other work-relief jobs; if single with children, they were eligible for widow and/or Aid to Dependent Children (ADC) benefits under Social Security. See Gwendolyn Mink, *The Wages of Motherhood: Inequality in the Welfare State 1917–1942* (Ithaca, NY: Cornell University Press, 1995), 7–8, 124–130. See also June Hopkins, *Harry Hopkins: Sudden Hero, Brash Reformer* (New York: St. Martin's Press, 1999), 165.

42. Many reports from state WPP WPA administrators, and newspaper articles about sewing rooms, mention workers with children who were school-age or younger.

43. Swain, 81. Not to mention the fact that, of course, unmarried women who were separated or divorced from their husbands could not get widow benefits, nor could women whose husbands were in the home but unable to work because of injury or illness.

44. She also thought married women should be able to work. Both ideas put her somewhat at odds with the maternalist view of the issue. Woodward's biographer emphasizes her desire to earn a middle-class living for herself after the death of her husband, as well as her interest in making sure the Women's and Professional division of the WPA encouraged states to found projects that could employ educated, white-collar female workers like herself. Swain, 12–13, 17, 43, 62–63.

45. Susan Ware notes that "In 1936, 56 percent of all women in the WPA worked in sewing rooms. One WPA official summarized the primary role of these sewing projects succinctly: 'For unskilled men we have the shovel. For unskilled women we have only the needle.'" Ware, 109.

46. Florence van Dickler, Director, Social Services Division, Mobile County Relief Division to Ellen Woodward, October 9, 1933, Box 6, Alabama, FERA Central Files, Work Relief Women's Projects, 453 Pc 10, RG 69, NACP.

47. Ellen Woodward to Harry Hopkins, Memorandum: "Justification of Sewing Projects."

48. Swain, 42, 59, 65; Ware, 108; Hopkins, 189–190.

49. Ware, 105.

50. Ware, 109; Swain, 44–45.

51. This is, of course, emblematic of gendered notions of skill that diminished the skill status of "women's work."

52. In her Tampa study, Green argues that the use of sewing rooms to employ unskilled women on the WPA "represented a profound lack of imagination by policy makers." While unskilled men on WPA projects got significant vocational training, gender segregation placing women into sewing rooms prepared them for low-paying jobs in the garment industry (if they could get them). WPA administrators expressed a sincere belief that despite this, women with no industrial skills would be more employable if they got good training and experience in the sewing rooms, but Ellen Woodward also worried that the garment industry might exploit women trained in the sewing rooms. At the local level, Georgia Hickey offer evidence that sewing rooms in Atlanta had quite poor training programs that offered little opportunities for workers. Green, "Relief from Relief," 1022; Swain, 88; Hickey, 10–12.

53. Woodward to Bella Southworth, Acting Director of Women's Activities, Jacksonville, Florida, October 1, 1935, Box 1115, folder: Florida 661, November 1935–December 1935, WPA Central Files: State, Florida, 1935–44, RG 69, NACP.

54. Eleanor Roosevelt, "My Day" (syndicated column), published in the *Atlanta Constitution*, March 27, 1937, 14.

55. For example, in Richmond: WRVA interview with Mrs. Henry Street of the Women's Club of Virginia, radio transcript, February 5, 1939, Box 2712, folder: 661 January 1938–1939, WPA Central Files: State, Virginia, 1934–1935. And also in Baltimore: "Baltimore Will Take Over Two WPA Sewing Centers"; "City Asked for $2000 Monthly to Continue Sewing Project."

56. For example: Sewing Room Inspection, Bristol, VA, March 27, 1936, State Files, Women's Work, 661, VA, January–March, 1936; Bella Southworth (Woman's Work Consultant, WPA) to Ellen Woodward, Jacksonville, Florida, October 21, 1935, Box 1115: Florida 661, June, 1935–May 1936, folder: Florida 661, November 1935–December, 1935, WPA Central Files: State, 1935–1944, RG 69, NACP.

57. Celia R. Case to Walter E. Brummett Jr., Executive Assistant to Florence Kerr, Assistant Administrator, (memorandum) "Mr. Myers' Memo on Retraining Women on Sewing Projects," March 27, 1939, Box 0555, folder: Sewing Projects A-Z, WPA General Subject Series 218.1, RG 69, NACP.

58. The garment industry began a shift from the Northeast to the South in the 1930s, but this move did not really gain momentum until after World War II. See Michelle Haberland,

Striking Beauties: Women Apparel Workers in the U.S. South, 1930–2000 (Athens: University of Georgia Press, 2015), 5–7.

59. "The Story of a Woman Who Lives in a Rural County and Works in a W.P.A. Sewing Room," interview with "Mrs. C" of Marion County, Georgia, July, 1936, from a report based on interviews with Georgia sewing-room workers, sent with a cover letter from Jane Van De Vrede, Georgia WPP Director, to Ellen Woodward, August 10, 1936, Box 1157, folder: 661, Georgia, May 1936–July 1936, WPA Central Files: State, 1935–1944, RG 69, NACP.

60. Narrative Report, Women's and Professional Projects, Area 11 & 12, Western North Carolina, September and October, 1938, 38, Areas 11 & 12 Report, Box 85, Entry 678, folder: Sewing Projects, Nebraska-Wyoming, Information Service, Primary_ File, 1936–1942, 951A-953A, WPA Division of Information, RG 69, NACP.

61. Julia Shackleton WPA Sewing Consultant to Florence Kerr, (memorandum) "Field Trip to Virginia, April 17–21, 1939," May 31, 1939, Box 0555, folder: Sewing Projects A-Z, WPA General Subject Series 218.1, RG 69, NACP.

62. Hickey, see especially pages 7–10.

63. There was some discussion of "retraining" women on sewing projects for jobs as domestic servants, but this seems not to have gone very far at the national level. See Howard Myers (Home Economics Division, Department of Agriculture) to Florence Kerr, (memorandum), "Your Memorandum of February 10 on Possibilities for Retraining Women on Sewing Projects," February 17, 1939, Box 0555, folder: Sewing Projects A-Z, WPA General Subject Series 218.1, RG 69, NACP. When sewing rooms reported the reemployment of women on projects, sometimes they mentioned that the African American women reemployed were working as domestic servants; however, they did not tend to make a connection to any training the women received by the WPA to get such jobs.

64. Narrative Report, Monroe District, Period Ending April 30, 1937, narrative report from Washington Parish, Box 1: Sewing Projects, Alabama-Maryland, folder: Louisiana, Records of the Women's and Professional Projects, 1934–1937, PC 37–29, RG 69, NACP.

65. Ibid. Many of these types of classes were taught by Department of Agriculture Home Demonstration Agents. "Excerpt from North Carolina Narrative Report," March 20, 1936, District #1, Box 85, Entry 678, folder: Sewing Projects Nebraska-Wyoming, Information Service (Primary) File, 1936–1942, 951A-953A, RG 69, NACP.

66. Narrative Report, North Carolina Works Progress Administration, Professional and Service Division, May 1, 1939, Box 2199, folder: North Carolina, 661, May, North Carolina 661-661.1, WPA Central Files: State, 1935–1944, RG 69, NACP. An earlier narrative report from a North Carolina district asserted, "Not only have the workers been trained in cutting and sewing and the economical utilization of materials, but the Supervisors have taken advantage of the opportunity to give instructions to the groups along other lines, such as sanitation, food values, and the recreational outlets." "Excerpt from North Carolina Narrative Report," March 20, 1936, District #1, Box 85, Entry 678, folder: Sewing Projects Nebraska-Wyoming, Information Service (Primary) File, 1936–1942, 951A-953A, RG 69, NACP.

67. "Report on Sewing Projects in Baltimore, Maryland," (memorandum), December 21, 1936, Box 1: Sewing Project, Alabama-Maryland, folder: Maryland, WPA Division of Women's and Professional Projects, 1934–1937, PC37–29, RG 69, NACP.

68. State Appraisal Committee, *United States Community Improvement Appraisal, State of South Carolina, March, 1938* (Colombia, SC: Works Progress Administration, 1938), Box 3, Entry 745, State WPA Publications, 1936–1940, Division of Information, WPA, RG 69, NACP.

69. Information Service, Division of Women's and Professional Projects, WPA. "Georgia," August 23, 1936 (Georgia Report found in in Tennessee file). Box 2595 Tennessee, 660–661, folder: Tennessee, 660, WPA Central Files: State, 1935–1944, RG 69, NACP; interview with Mrs. O, Marion County, July 1936, from a report based on interviews with Georgia sewing-room workers, sent with a cover letter from Jane Van De Vrede, Georgia WPP Director, to Ellen Woodward, August 10, 1936, Box 1157, folder: 661, Georgia, May 1936-July, 1936, WPA Central Files: State, 1935–1944, RG 69, NACP.

70. Several projects offered basic literacy instruction. Some mentioned homemaking training as beneficial to African American women in finding jobs as domestic servants, but this does not appear to have been a general trend. Martha Swain notes that WPA administrators found African American women uninterested in housekeeping training programs. Swain, 95.

71. Report on production standards attached to a letter from Blanch Ralston to Ellen Woodward, March 31, 1937, Box 1: Sewing Project, Alabama-Maryland, folder: Georgia, WPA Division of Women's and Professional Projects, 1934–37, PC 37–29, RG 69, NACP.

72. Annie Smith to Local Labor Policies Board, WPA, Spartanburg, South Carolina, January 22, 1937, Box 3, Sewing Projects Oklahoma-Wyoming, folder: South Carolina, WPA Women's and Professional Projects Division, PC 37–29, RG 69, NACP.

73. Ethel Casey (spokesperson for the New Bern, North Carolina, sewing-room women) to FDR, Harry Hopkins, George Coan (South Carolina WPA Director), and Congressman G. A. Barden, (letter signed by forty-six women from the sewing room), April 27, 1936, Box 2198, folder North Carolina 660, (A-B) - DD, WPA Central Files: State, North Carolina 652.36 (1939) 660, RG 69, NACP.

74. May E. Campbell Director of Women's and Professional Projects) to Casey, April 29, 1936, Box 2198, folder North Carolina 660, (A-B) - DD, WPA Central Files: State, North Carolina 652.36 (1939) 660, RG 69, NACP.

75. Woodward to Casey, April 30, 1936, Box 2198, folder North Carolina 660, (A-B) - DD, WPA Central Files: State, North Carolina 652.36 (1939) 660, RG 69, NACP.

76. Smith to Woodward, June 23, 1937; Woodward to Smith, June 30, 1937, both in Box 3, Sewing Projects Oklahoma-Wyoming, folder: South Carolina, WPA Women's and Professional Projects Division, PC 37–29, RG 69, NACP.

77. Anonymous letter to Eleanor Roosevelt, April 10, 1937, Columbia, SC, Box 3, Sewing Projects Oklahoma-Wyoming, folder: South Carolina, WPA Women's and Professional Projects Division, PC 37–29, RG 69, NACP.

78. A 1938 study found that 90 percent of Americans preferred work relief to cash relief. Finnegan, 18.

79. Martha Swain writes that this was mostly de facto segregation, as women got sewing-room assignments according to where they lived, but she also notes that whites complained when white and black women happened to be put into sewing rooms together. Swain, 95; Georgia Hickey mentions racial integration on three projects in Atlanta, although the photos in the WPA records show black and white women working separately and at different addresses, Hickey, 9.

80. For instance, Executive Order 7046 prohibited discrimination on FERA work projects "on any grounds whatsoever." Franklin Delano Roosevelt, Executive Order 7046, May 20, 1935.

81. NC Narrative Report, 1938, Area 8 Report.

82. And, indeed, more than working-class white workers could make in private industry. Harvard Sitkoff, *A New Deal For Blacks: The Emergence of Civil Rights as a National Issue* (New York: Oxford University Press, 2009, 1979), 37, 53.

83. This was particularly true outside the South (where, admittedly, only 25 percent of African Americans lived), but southern blacks were aware of this situation, and of the presence of "Black Cabinet" officials in Washington. Sitkoff, 37, 47–48, 59–60.

84. Swain, 92–93.

85. Letters were addressed to Hopkins, or sometimes to FDR or Eleanor Roosevelt. Some correspondents also wrote to Black Cabinet members such as Alfred E. Smith, who worked for the WPA in Washington. Some wrote to their Congressional Representatives. Some wrote to the NAACP headquarters in New York City.

86. "We Present the Facts" (editorial), *Atlanta Daily World*, November 9, 1936, 6.

87. "WPA Officers Insist on Insults," *Atlanta Daily World*, December 1, 1936, 1.

88. A practice that echoes white attitudes about black female workers that go back to the era of slavery. See examples in Jackson, Mississippi: "WPA Sewing Room Closed in Miss," *Norfolk Journal and Guide*, June 3, 1939, 3; Norfolk, Virginia: "State WPA Officials Investigate Relief Complaints," *Norfolk Journal and Guide*, February 12, 1938, 12; Fayetteville, North Carolina: "Take Women Off WPA to Pick Cotton," *Chicago Defender*, October 9, 1937, 2.

89. While pointing out that African American male workers "loaf around the gates and doors of the WPA daily looking for work" a reference to the lack of WPA jobs for African American men that seems to suggest that these manual labor jobs should have gone to them. H. D. Cole, "Writer Reports Finding Women Working on Project Digging Ditches, Similar Tasks," *Atlanta Daily World*, October 20, 1936, 1.

90. Homewood Colored Civic League, Birmingham, Alabama, "Road Slaves" (letter to the editor), *Atlanta Daily World*, October 27, 1936, 6.

91. "Take Women Off WPA to Pick Cotton."

92. The original letter was sent to the national office of the NAACP in New York City; Roy Wilkins sent it to Alfred Smith, WPA administrator and member of the Black Cabinet. Anonymous letter to Secretary, NAACP, New York, January 31, 1936, Box 1156, Georgia 651.386–661, January 1935–October, 1939, folder: 660 Georgia, January, 1939, WPA Central Files: State, 1935–1944, RG 69, NACP.

93. "Take Women Off WPA to Pick Cotton."

94. The article cited a lack of available domestic servants, and the greater desirability of WPA jobs over domestic service jobs to unemployed black women as the excuse local white officials gave for not having more WPA sewing projects set up for black women. The article pointed out that "from this it is easy to deduce that pay for domestic workers in New Orleans is extremely low as neither the FERA nor WPA pays large salaries on work-relief projects. "Despite Small Percentage of Pelican State Negroes on Relief, Race Fares Badly, Figures Show," *Norfolk Journal and Guide*, February 1, 1936, 19.

95. "Pay Differential for Race in WPA Probed," *Atlanta Daily World*, August 6, 1939, 1.

96. Of course, the 1938 Fair Labor Standards Act, which set minimum-wage and maximum-hours standards nationwide, did not initially apply to domestic and farm labor, in large part because of pressure from southern lawmakers.

97. Hattie White to Harry Hopkins (the letter was signed by seventeen women), February 10, 1937, Box 2198, folder: 660 (A-B) - - D, WPA Central Files: State, North Carolina, 652.36, (1939) 660, RG 69, NACP.

98. Woodward to White, March 24, 1937, Box 2198, folder: 660 (A-B) - - D, WPA Central Files: State, North Carolina, 652.36, (1939) 660, RG 69, NACP.

99. The report also stated, "Some of these women who signed this petition have employable men in the family. There is a large amount of building going on in and about Whiteville at the present time and I see no reason why these men could not secure private employment." Excerpts from the report quoted in May E. Campbell, Director, Women's and Professional Projects, North Carolina WPA to Ellen Woodward, April 15, 1937, Box 2198, folder: 660 (A-B) - - D, WPA Central Files: State, North Carolina, 652.36, (1939) 660, RG 69, NACP.

100. Using language and arguments familiar to historians of African American women's relationship to the welfare state in this and later eras. For the development of racial discrimination in the early years of the New Deal welfare state, Mink, 138–149. For the period after WWII, see Felicia Kornbluh, *The Battle for Welfare Rights, Politics and Poverty in Modern America* (Philadelphia: University of Pennsylvania Press, 2007).

101. 79.5 percent of all women on work relief in 1935 were skilled or semiskilled, and 90 percent of African American women on work relief were considered unskilled and had no previous waged work experience beyond domestic service. Swain, 80, 94.

102. May E. Campbell, Director Women's and Professional Projects, North Carolina WPA, "Monthly Progress Report," November 15, 1935–October 15, 1935, Box 2199, North Carolina 66–661.1, folder: 661 North Carolina, December 1935–January 1936, WPA Central Files: State, 1935–1944, RG 69, NACP.

103. Photographs of Atlanta (Fulton, County), and DeKalb County, Georgia, sewing rooms, Box 1, Sewing Project, Alabama-Maryland, folder: Georgia, Division of Women's and Professional Projects, 1934–1937, RG 69, NACP.

104. Woodward to G. W. Coan, Administrator, North Carolina WPA (cc'd to May E. Campbell, Director, Women's and Professional Projects, North Carolina WPA), April 28, 1937, Box 2198, folder: 660 (A-B) - - D, WPA Central Files: State, North Carolina, 652.36, (1939) 660, RG 69, NACP.

105. Campbell to Woodward, May 26, 1937, Box 2198, folder: 660 (A-B) - - D, WPA Central Files: State, North Carolina, 652.36, (1939) 660, RG 69, NACP.

106. David N. Harrell, Vice President, Sons and Daughters of Virginia to Congressman Norman R. Hamilton, Virginia, 2nd District, March 24, 1937, Box 2711, Virginia, 651.361–660, folder: Virginia 660 A-Z, WPA Central Files: State 1935–1944, RG 69, NACP.

107. "Protest Closure of WPA Sewing Rooms for Race Women," *Atlanta Daily World*, June 2, 1939, 1.

108. Green, "Relief from Relief," 1022.

"THINKING OF YOU EVERY MINUTE (AND EVERY STITCH)"

Sewing, Clothing, and Identity at the Mississippi State Penitentiary at Parchman, 1950–1969

BECCA WALTON

> Our thread hasn't arrived yet but we are expecting it most any day now. Our dry goods are getting low, but don't worry cats . . . we chicks are not going to let you get raggedy—smiles. . . . We still have enough wearing apparel to supply you poor little helpless boys for quite a long time.
> —THELMA HUSTON, News from Forbidden City, *Inside World*
> February 1953, 20.

In 1964 artist Albert Lee drew an illustration for *Inside World* featuring four glamorous women in striped, form-fitting pencil skirts and fashionable tops.[1] In this inmate-published magazine, Lee's drawing, titled "Parchman Fall Fashions," is a striking depiction of inmates at the notorious Mississippi State Penitentiary at Parchman. Lee captured a sense of humor, pride in appearance, and interest in style that subverted and remade both the material form of the prison uniform and the image that most have of life at Parchman historically and in the present. In the cultural imagination, we see the mid-twentieth-century Mississippi State Penitentiary at Parchman through a haze of Delta heat, with men picking cotton in the long lines, guns trained on them to prevent escape from the fenceless prison, their voices raised in the work songs that made the blues.[2] But beyond those images, we know little of how people incarcerated there experienced the world. We can easily understand, even expect, that people suffered and died at Parchman. But how did they live?

Albert Lee's cartoon depiction of women at Parchman in glamorously styled uniforms. Albert Lee, "Parchman Fall Fashions," Inside World, November 1954, 31.

Even more unknowable is the experience of the women incarcerated there from the first years of the twentieth century to 1986, so outnumbered by men that historians have largely dismissed their experience.³ Photographs of women at Parchman, taken in the 1930s by nurse and photographer Martha Alice Stewart, show them in the penitentiary sewing room, seated at sewing machines or standing at cutting tables, surrounded by bolts of fabric.⁴ Women at Parchman sewed all uniforms and bed linens for the vast plantation. Clothing, a necessity that is intimately experienced, can reveal much about daily life. How was clothing meaningful for women incarcerated at Parchman?

Prison clothing, worn for heavy labor, rarely survives, and is even less likely to be regarded as valuable enough to preserve in an archive.⁵ Knowing that women at Parchman sewed, I searched to find sources that might reveal what, if anything, clothing and sewing meant to them and the other inmates. What in the archive could reveal the stories of how the most marginalized in society engaged with clothing and fashion? The inmate-published magazine *Inside World*, rarely examined by scholars, contained countless conversations about clothing, with many cartoons and drawings depicting and reimagining uniforms.[6] *Inside World* was a monthly magazine that ran from 1950 to the early 1980s. It contained reports from the individual camps of the penitentiary, news from the prison baseball league, devotional writings from the prison chaplain, and reprints of other "penal press" publications on subjects like rehabilitation and recidivism. It also contained artwork, cartoons, and poetry. The camp reporters discussed everyday details and often included messages to other inmates or units.

Inside World and other penal-press publications are problematic because of administrative censorship, and for Parchman especially, the ability to communicate in writing was a privilege in a space where many could not read. But the magazine also revealed mundane details that would have been beneath the notice of the administration, and the inmates found some freedom in recounting the details of daily life. Camp reporters almost never mentioned the crimes for which they were imprisoned, choosing to focus on other defining characteristics and life experiences. Both men and women wrote continually of sewing and clothing, discussing their work in camp reports, sending messages related to clothing to inmates across the penitentiary, and drawing cartoons that featured fashion as a defining element. By discussing sewing-machine mishaps and ill-fitting pants, the men and women of Parchman formed relationships and maintained identities beyond and apart from their status as criminals.

Recognizing, in Elaine Scarry's words, that the "enduring and monumental reside in the daily," this essay examines the clothing worn, sewn, and imagined by men and women incarcerated at Parchman in the 1950s and 1960s, using *Inside World* as a primary source and drawing on both scholarship about incarceration and fashion studies. In violent conditions intended to break people, clothing reveals how people at Parchman remade a world that they could survive.[7] This world was imaginative and generative, a space of humor and kindness in which incarcerated people could experience a range of emotions, not just suffering. Studying an essential and everyday item like clothing allows us to see incarcerated people as they imagined themselves: creative, loving, funny, and stylish.

Parchman since its founding has had a majority-black population. With some exceptions, the men and women who speak in this study are African

American, though there are also a significant number of remarks from white women, a very small group that historians have studied even less than they have African American women. Being a white woman incarcerated at Parchman defied norms of gender and respectability to such an extent that their presence there is elided, and they are invisible in the archive. Parchman was racially segregated until court-ordered desegregation in 1972, and black inmates vastly outnumbered white inmates; there were on average 50–70 black women to 0–12 white women during the mid-twentieth century, with the population of male inmates around 2,000.

Despite segregated housing, white and black women worked under the supervision of the same sergeant, and parallel accounts in camp reports seem to indicate that they attended the same church services, musical performances, and holiday celebrations. In April 1957, Pam of the White Women's Camp wrote that white and "colored" women attended a church service with baptisms together.[8] The women worked in two separate sewing rooms, but they seemed to adjoin each other, and they often wrote of the same work projects. One can imagine the built space through a note by Nita Kelly, writing in the White Women's Camp Report in April 1958. She mentioned Rosie Page, who was part of the camp for African American women. "Rosie Page and I are the coolest, maybe after this, the hottest, egg snatchers on Parchman. Rosie sits in one sewing room and I in the other, watching the nest. That poor chicken doesn't have a chance. We don't even give her a chance to catch her breath or cackle before the egg is gone."[9]

It was rare for white and black women to send each other messages in *Inside World*, but it seems likely that they had in-person contact, making written messages unnecessary. Mississippians at the mid-twentieth century would have expected the units to be segregated, but it is uncertain how complete the spatial and social separation was. In official communications, administrators noted that black women canned and white women sewed. But the camp reports contradict this; both black and white women sewed, canned, picked vegetables, and picked cotton.[10] In April 1966, Ora Lee Adams noted that different groups of women were making mattresses, cleaning ditches, and "some [were] on the saw, cutting wood."[11]

Scholar Juliet Ash notes that prison clothing "regulates and incarnates the punishment of the wearer."[12] Because women at Parchman sewed their own and other inmates' uniforms, it was also a visual representation of their labor. Historically, prison dress has embodied contemporary attitudes about incarceration. Uniforms were either used to criminalize, humiliate, and marginalize the incarcerated, or during periods of reform, to rehabilitate prisoners through the wearing of clothing similar to that worn "outside," implying that they would again live in the free world.[13]

Throughout most of the United States, prison officials abolished the wearing of black and white stripes by 1914.[14] In 1951, the United Nations Standard Minimum Rules for the Treatment of Prisoners declared that clothing should not be "degrading or humiliating."[15] Parchman, several decades behind other prisons in terms of security, use of corporal punishment, and mechanization of agricultural practices, continued to dress inmates in stripes until Christmas Day in 1966. By the 1990s, with the rise of incarceration, many correctional facilities, Parchman included, returned to the "extreme form of embodied criminalization" of striped uniforms.[16]

Striped uniforms were intrinsically meaningful as garments of marginalization, but incarcerated people created further layers of meaning depending on their context. Talitha LeFlouria writes of women convict laborers in Georgia in the early twentieth century who burned their striped uniforms in protest of the extremely brutal conditions of convict labor camps.[17] Clothing arson "allowed some female convicts to openly express their inner discontents" and to resist the uniforms' forcible "defeminization" of the women, who were dressed in the same uniforms as men in a "public affront to black womanhood."[18] Mary Ellen Curtin notes that black women prisoners at Coalburg mining camp in Alabama refused to wear prison clothing when hired out to work as servants, angering prison administrators when they saw the women wearing nice clothing in town on Sundays.[19]

In prison, identity is dress. One is "in stripes"; freedom is the moment when one "changes their linen."[20] Men and women at Parchman thought about clothing in several ways, the first being the expected dislike for the "distinctive embodied punishment" of the uniforms.[21] They wrote often about how uniforms broadcasted their crimes and defined them in the gaze of onlookers. In November 1955, Albert Lee wrote of how the uniforms affected new inmates—"We see a rapid change in the new man after he donned the garments of stripes and settles into a routine."[22] Mary Marshall, writing in February of 1964, noted that a new inmate would "find your reality in a suit of stripes."[23] Like Bukka White in the blues song "When Can I Change My Clothes?" men and women incarcerated at Parchman longed to remove their stripes and put on freedom.[24]

In 1961, Mississippi State Penitentiary inmate James Hendricks was allowed to attend the Mississippi State Fair in Jackson in order to sell Parchman-made leather-goods and other crafts. "To say I was a little timid about all the people I was going to have to face wearing my large black and white stripes, would be the understatement of the century." But to his surprise, "The people of Jackson accepted us with open arms. We were made to feel at home, everyone speaking to us pleasantly, seeming to bend over backwards to ignore the obvious, the fact that we were convicts and clothed in stripes." He did, however, overhear one woman saying derogatory things about incarcerated people. He told her that he was sorry she felt that way, lifting his apron and "showing her my stripes." The embarrassed woman defensively told Hendricks she did not mean him when she spoke about the depravity of those in prison. "We are all the same, Ma'am," he replied, "Your son could accidently run over someone while driving, and could conceivably be sent to the penitentiary for negligence. When he donned these striped trousers, he would be a convict then."[25] Hendricks reminded the woman that there were many reasons outside of rape and murder that led to incarceration.

Inside World editor Jessie F. Durham wrote an editorial in June 1955 noting that, "It is apparent that the large majority of the public has the ingrown idea that once a man is convicted and set out in stripes he doesn't have one—not even one—good point about him."[26] Hendricks responded to disparaging remarks about the incarcerated by unequivocally stating that those in prison were not so different from those outside. Despite their incarceration, they were still capable of kindness. In the 1950s and 1960s, they frequently noted that even incarcerated people could be charitable and loving—they often wrote of willingly participating in blood drives, and they would collect money for staff members who were grieving the loss of a child or spouse. They enthusiastically donated to Easter Seals and the March of Dimes, and some were quite proud of their selfless willingness to participate in medical experiments.[27]

Parchman administrators understood the power of stripes to diminish inmates and used this sensitivity to reward and punish, establishing hierarchical uniform design. Trustees wore vertical stripes, or "up-and-downs" and all other inmates, who were called "gunmen" because they labored under the supervision of armed trustees, wore horizontal stripes or "ring-a-rounds."[28] The different classes of uniforms indicated status grounded in the threat of violence. Though presented as humorous, the following account from a woman at the "White Women's Camp" demonstrates how clothing at Parchman could be a marker of vulnerability to brutality and even death:

> Now for a little nonsense! The other day we were performing a duty that called for a long sleeve shirt, one of our trusties accidently put on a gun shirt. One of the girls asked her to go out in the yard for

something, and she got to thinking about it, and said, "Do you think I'll get shot with this shirt on?" So to make the story short, she went and didn't get shot.[29]

Gunmen occasionally expressed distaste for uniform hierarchy. In 1960, Ferita of the "Colored Women's Unit" responded to an *Inside World* editorial about the fair treatment of all inmates with the question, "Is there so much difference in ring-a-rounds than vertical stripes?"[30] At several points throughout the history of the penitentiary, the administration established "honor camps" with specially designed uniforms indicating status.[31]

In a May 1960 interview with Superintendent Fred Jones, *Inside World* editor James Hendricks asked him about the need for striped pants and jackets, explaining that they were humiliating. Jones responded that they were a security measure, because escapees could be easily identified.[32] Hendricks argued that once off the penitentiary grounds, an escapee "became a menace immediately in his search for unstriped pants." Jones conceded the point, but said that a change to uniforms would have to come from the legislature.[33] In 1961, the executive director of a correctional reform organization visited the prison. *Inside World* reported that he "advocated the abolishment of stripes and is all for the discontinued use of bullhide."[34] Inmates thought of the striped uniforms in the same terms as the dreaded whip used at Parchman long after other institutions had abandoned corporal punishment of incarcerated people.

In May 1966, an editorial from R. Harris announced the possibility that the administration was replacing striped uniforms with "gunman" blues and white trustee uniforms—"If this is to be true, I must say that this alone is a great step forward in our living conditions. Slowly but surely we are advancing in time. Four years ago when I first stepped into the confines of the Penitentiary, I thought I had stepped into the confines of hell."[35] In a January 1967 editorial, Joe Bumgarten noted that they had been the last institution in the nation wearing stripes: "We feel that blue denim pants and skirts, with the ordinary blouses and shirts the men and women have always been permitted to wear, will be better both from a practical and psychological standpoint than the loudly conspicuous black and white stripes."[36]

While striped uniforms were universally hated by Parchman inmates in the 1950s and 1960s, the women's assigned prison labor of sewing did play a surprising role in their own identity formation. When Jessie Lee Carter received parole in 1954, the camp reporter noted that she had been an "excellent sewing room girl" and that men receiving pants she had made were "very appreciative of her talents."[37] Women arrived at Parchman with varying levels of experience sewing, and some had none. Women occasionally wrote of themselves as seamstresses, though in most cases they did so humorously. "A group of ladies came through the other day, while asking questions, one asked Nita if she was a seamstress before she entered prison. 'No!' Nita said, 'I was an outlaw!'"[38] Women mentioned others who were talented seamstresses, having gained skills before or during their period of incarceration.

> We've just lost two of our best seamstresses: Helen (a member of our Women's Trio), and Ann. We miss them and wish them both the best of luck. One vacancy has already been filled by a petite brunette by the name of Beverly Barlow of Biloxi, and she gets along with her sewing machine quite well (#$%&?!@#).[39]

Sewing at Parchman was difficult. The women often noted mechanical issues with the sewing machines, which some gave nicknames, like "the Mare."

> Can anyone explain this? We are in the sewing room making shirts and pants. All of a sudden THE MARE just ups and quits, or the thread starts breaking, or she sews very badly. Try as we may, we can't do anything with her. So we call on the Sergeant. (Now picture this) In walks the Sergeant. We are setting there idle, you know like doing nothing. The Sarge goes over to the machine and we explain to him all our troubles, then proceed to demonstrate by taking a piece of cloth and starting to sew. BINGO!!! Never have you saw such a beautiful row of stitches. Any comments?[40]

In the same report, Ferita noted that the unit had several new women who "can do anything with a machine, including tearing them up. I have to run to aid them pronto, like crazy man crazy." Multiple camp reports in the spring of 1958 heralded the advent of zippers in the pants.[41] In 1960, they received new machines with the capability of making button holes, cutting, and bar-tacking.[42] The women faced the challenge of working with limited resources, frequently mentioning being out of material. In 1957, the Camp 10 reporter asked the women's camps why their new pants had a pocket directly in the center, "mak[ing] one feel somewhat like a kangaroo—backward."[43] In the following issue of *Inside World*, Joe Evelyn of the White Women's Unit explained that the pockets were sewn that way because they were cut down from larger pants.[44]

Prison officials strove to make the penitentiary as self-sufficient as possible, and bragged about only spending, for example, in January 1963, $1.27 per inmate per day.[45] It seems likely that they were parsimonious about the purchase of outside goods like fabric. In 1958, James Williams in the Camp 3 report wrote, "Say! Does anybody know why we can't get any clothes? I have run out of all my pants. Seems like that there is a shortage of cloth around here. Can you imagine that? And we raise cotton!"[46] The men and women were conscious of the incongruity of lacking cotton goods on a cotton plantation, with *Inside World* editor James Hendricks writing in February 1960,

> Why not a cotton mill? Other institutions have them and I should imagine, operate them at a profit for they have been running day and night for years and years. We raise the cotton so why not take it all the way to a finished product? It would take money, but again, think of the years ahead, the good it would do here, not to mention paying for itself quickly.[47]

Various superintendents tried different industries, from book binding to making ketchup, but superintendent's reports to the Mississippi State Legislature in the 1950s and 1960s never mention a textile mill as a viable option.

When the administration finally changed the uniforms from striped to solid denim, it required a tremendous effort by the women in the fall of 1966.

> As you all know we have a new style . . . a new thread. It's been a long time coming but like all things it is well worth waiting for. The color this season is navy blue and white. . . . this improvement is well beyond words and we're sure you'll all agree when you see what is happening. Our thanks to Mr. Breazeale [the Superintendent], Sgt. Van Landingham, and all others who are responsible for this newest and long-awaited improvement. . . . Xmas should find a pair or three in each of your stockings. Needless to say everything is wide open in preparation for this gala event. . . . Just for the record . . . we've a new pattern and it is guaranteed to fit.

She went on to say that Helen Mitchell, the inmate who repaired their sewing machines, worked feverishly to ensure they finished the six thousand pairs of pants by Christmas.[48]

The administration at times so emphasized the agricultural output of the farm that they did not acknowledge the women's labor. The women demanded credit for their contribution to the life of the farm, which was prodigious and hard to fathom in its scale. In 1951, Parchman incarcerated eighty women, and they used statistics to describe their productivity.

> Canning season [in which they canned 409,114 gallons of produce] closed November 15, and we began sewing in earnest. Some of the girls sew all year but the majority of us do not start until canning season is over. We made a total of 137 quilts from scraps which were left over from other items. These other items included 9879 pair of gunmen's pants, 2528 trusty pants, 6019 gunmen's jumpers and 199 trusty jumpers. We made 2939 pillow cases, 707 bed sheets, 495 mattress covers, 351 pillows, besides all the sewing for the Women's Camp and all the patching of thousands of pairs of torn pants and jumpers.[49]

The women's source of pride seemed to have much more to do with their hard work and skill than their contribution to the state's coffers. If there was going to be recognition of accomplishment, the administration should acknowledge them. In August 1961, Reba Morgan notes,

> No one ever seems to mention the importance of the Women's Camp to the farm. There are always reports of how the farm is going, how and what each camp participates in but there is never an outstanding illumination of the part we play. First of all, we furnish every camp with uniforms, sheets, pillow cases, towels, thread, pillows, mattresses, cotton sacks, cotton sheets, and one of the most important items: canned goods. There are many gallons of canned goods going out to each camp every week. Not only do the girls here can the food, some go out and help gather it. Besides all the things that go out to the camps, we also furnish other state institutions, county farms and counties with food and clothes. Even though the Women's Camp is never mentioned when credit is given for outstanding work, I wonder where the farm would be without "Forgotten City."[50]

More significant than their desire for recognition for their productivity were their repeated descriptions of their labor as a form of caretaking for the male inmates. Thelma Huston said that the women "sometimes wonder what you men would do without the Women's Camp to keep you looking nifty and well-fed all the time. It's quite a job to can enough food and make clothes for 2200 people, I can assure you."[51] Away from their loved ones and stripped of domestic roles, women at Parchman imagined themselves caretakers of the men, transforming what was backbreaking and tedious labor into an act of love.[52] In a particularly evocative note, Louise Smith wrote that, in addition to canning, they were "also making something for you . . . to keep warm and get some rest on these cold winter nights."[53] In October 1965, the Forbidden City reporter noted how the sewing rooms had been "buzzing" for weeks—"There is one thing about it, whether or not anyone else does anything for you, us gals look out for you guys. Just ask Mary and Sue, they double-teamed it while the rest of us took a powder."[54] Men at Parchman, who picked cotton in the late summer and early fall, did not write of their labor as anything besides drudgery. Their work benefited the administration, not fellow inmates. The women through their labor formed relationships with other inmates that were far more meaningful to them than generating revenue for the state of Mississippi.

Following the decision to change the uniforms in 1966, the men expressed gratitude to the administration. But more striking were their enthusiastic and heartfelt messages of thanks to the women in the January and February 1967 issues of *Inside World*.

> You girls will have to know that we know little or nothing about the services you all performed, in making our new clothes, it is even harder to visualize your repairing, cleaning, replacing buttons, washing, assorting, etc. but we want you to know that we appreciate all you have done in making our clothes a reality. I'm sure that some of us don't realize that you have a year-around work-load plus your own personal work, but, anyway, I want you to know that Camp Five is really appreciative for all you have accomplished, and we will be looking forward to wearing this type of uniform every day.[55]

These expressions of gratitude were common in *Inside World* throughout the 1950s and 1960s, and speak to the bonds formed between the men and women, many of whom had never and would never meet. Richard Lott of Camp 5 in April 1963 said, "I would like to mention that the ladies do all the canning, make all the clothes for the men, and perform many other jobs, vital to the well-being of the farm. I sincerely think that we should give them more thanks, than we do. 'Forgive us, for our neglect girls.'"[56] In a prison labor setting, this gratitude was meaningful. In December 1967, Carolyn Crowder noted that, "Working at the sewing room is pretty hard work, but we all enjoy it very much. For reasons that we are doing something for people who appreciate it and second, it helps pass our time."⁵⁷ While it is unlikely that many or all of the women laboring with Crowder did "enjoy" the experience, in the context of caretaking, it became more manageable.

There is a romantic element to many of the exchanges about clothing, and it is striking how sewing provided a discourse of intimacy for people who likely never met. James Lewis of Camp 8 sent greetings to "all you sweet wonderful girls at CWC [Colored Women's Camp]. All our pants are okay. Just keep up the good work. You make us very proud of you. Tell all the girls from Greenville if any that James said hello and he sent a big kiss to all of them."⁵⁸ The women noted that "we're thinking of you every minute (and every stitch)"⁵⁹ and in a passage that emphasized the female body,

> The house is rocking . . . stimulating vibrations from the musical system, inspires one's desire for demonstrating movement. The possessed foot presses heavily. The delicate hands push forward, eyes alert, supervising every man's heart's desire . . . thousands of striped pants, smile.⁶⁰

In the 1950s and 1960s, the men's camps often chose a "Queen" or "Sweetheart" from the women's camps—"To Ora Lee at C. W. C. you are still the pride of 'B.' Leadfield Dillion says he has eyes for you, and he wishes it possible for him to do all your sewing."⁶¹ In August 1968 Nathaniel Richardson thanked the "girls" for all the "time and love that was put into making our new clothes," and in September of the same year, James Edwards thanked the "lassies at the Women's Camp for your efforts at making our lives pleasant while we are here. Our thoughts are with you always."⁶² This discourse of caretaking defied what Kali Gross calls "black women's exclusion from notions of protection."⁶³ While the men's support was not material, it had imaginative force in the lives of women at Parchman, many of whom arrived at Parchman with histories of poverty and violence that underscored their lack of protection in Jim Crow Mississippi.

Clothing also provided an opportunity for humorous exchanges. Men frequently wrote playfully to the women's camp about their pants not fitting. In April 1964, the "Forbidden City" reporter responded to a complaint, teasing that "we have to do them completely from memory, as we haven't a model. . . . Now in the event one of you guys would like a modeling career, we need one badly."⁶⁴ John Keith, in the Camp 10 Report in May 1964, joked with the African American women's unit, "C.W.C, what's wrong? Why oh why, can't a guy get the size pants he ask for? I am a (244 pounder). I asked for size 42

Conversations between men and women about clothing often had a romantic element. Albert Lee, "Loading Can Goods," Inside World, July 1954, 30.

pants, what did I get, 32's for a fact I did. The pants had M.B. King, C.W.C. on one of the pockets. Just for that we are going to sit out an extra five acres of tomatoes for you to can. That will teach you, ha ha."[65]

Until late 1966, the women had inadequate patterns for the uniform shirts and pants, so fit for the men was often an issue. For the women, their knowledge of sewing and proximity to the sewing room would make it easier for them to alter their own clothing. While they do speak often about clothing, they do not talk of the fit of their own. They rarely mention their own uniforms, emphasizing their work sewing for others. Talking about their labor was meaningful when bound up in human relationships, but was far less so as coerced labor of unattractive and likely uncomfortable garments.

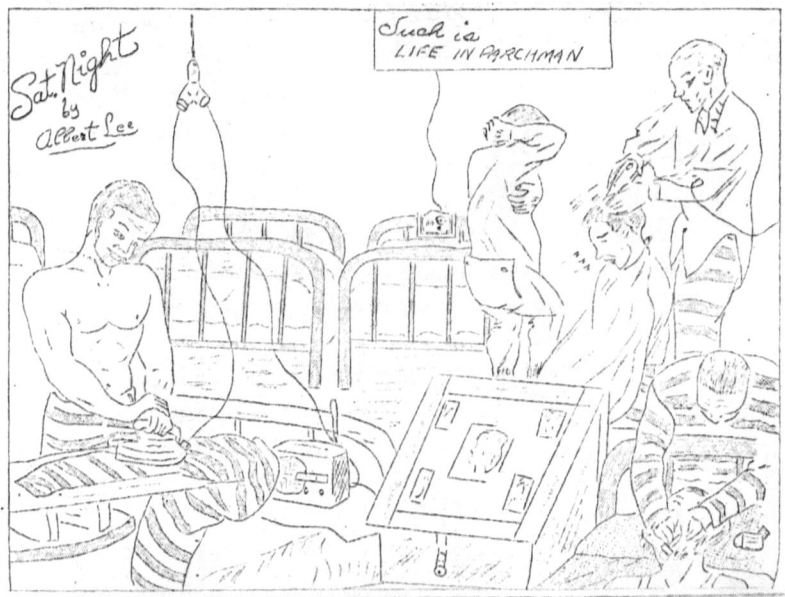

Men iron clothing and trim hair on Saturday night before Visiting Day. Albert Lee, "Such Is Life in Parchman: Saturday Night," cartoon, Inside World, March 1952, 17.

In addition to the construction of identities as caretakers and the cared-for, inmates frequently wrote of the two occasions when they were allowed to wear at least some their own clothing: visiting Sundays and the day when they would receive parole and leave the farm. For visiting days, it seems that inmates may have worn striped uniform pants or skirts, with their own shirts, though regulations often changed. Whether or not they wore stripes, the days were opportunities for them to look as nice as possible for visitors from the "outside."

Both men and women wrote of the anticipation for visiting day, typically the third Sunday of the month in the 1950s and 1960s.

> When the great day dawns at last, everyone, breathlessly and in great flurrees, carefully dolls and spruces himself in his Sunday best—bought and borrowed. Mirrors are brought out by the dozens and every whisker is closely shaved, . . . every bald-head is carefully shined, shoes are made to glitter, pants are creased to the sharpness of a razor, shirts are starched and ironed, ties are flying in the breeze, hearts are fluttering and every guy feels the excitement of expectancy swell within him.[66]

In the same issue of *Inside World*, Thelma Huston and Lulu Berry described "heartbroken" women who spent "hours Saturday night washing her hair, ironing her best skirt and blouse" only to not welcome a visitor after all. "It is about this time that you can see some unexpected soft spots show up in some of the 'heartless' women. You can bet your life that she will share someone's goodies that night."[67] The inmates' accounts of ironing, trimming hair, and in some cases applying make-up show a drive to appear well for their families, to look as close as possible to how would they would look in the free world. Their adornment was hopeful, and spoke to a sense of self undiminished by stripes.

Historian Mary Ellen Curtin notes that through "daily acts of self-assertion that reclaimed personal and social space," incarcerated men and women were able to "resist the dehumanizing effects of prison life."[68] For some Parchman inmates, neatness was an act of self-assertion. Especially on visiting days, inmates noted the importance of cleanliness. In 1959, George Golden of Camp B wrote defensively that a group of visitors had expressed surprise at how neat and clean the men were: "I answered that we had plenty of clothing and a free laundry, to wash our clothes. There is no reason for any of us not to be neat and clean."[69] The women were particularly concerned about clothing being properly ironed, both their everyday uniforms and visiting day clothing. Throughout the history of Parchman, white men of the "Disability Unit," worked in the laundry. Their work in caring for the clothing made by the women was a month-to-month source of conversation in the camp reports.

> We'll look, they said, like bloobs, on visiting Sundays! Please, take our good time and deny us parole, but don't do us thattta way, fellers. We promise to do a better job on the pants and jumpers from now on. We'll even put you two back pockets on your pants, and add a watch pocket besides. If we don't look our very best on visiting days "Josephine the Grinder" is sure to beat our time! Please, fellers![70]

Clothing played a central role in imagined and actual departures from the penitentiary. The December 1964 "Forbidden City" report described one woman's fashionable exit from Parchman: "Billie . . . left this month. She looked like something out of *Vogue*." Earlier, a woman named Frances left, "with tears and raindrops mingled with mascara and lipstick."[71] Mittie Waters, a North Carolina-based prison-reform activist who frequently visited the prison, donated sewing machines for the women's "cage" for their personal use, especially to make departure outfits.[72]

Greeting visitors wearing their best clothes. Albert Lee, "Such Is Life in Parchman: Sunday Visitors," Inside World, April 1952, 13.

Men at Parchman experienced departure differently. Upon release, the administration gave the men a cheap khaki suit, or a "sport shirt" with khaki pants, and a pair of shoes.[73] They were expected to make their way in the world with $10. *Inside World* editor Joe L. Bumgarner wrote an editorial in 1967 about a man's prospects upon release and the likelihood of recidivism. Bumgarner told the story of a man named John, who departed in "clothes that made him look like a scarecrow," and were easily identifiable as those of a released convict. John desperately sought work, "ashamed of his clothes and his past," and eventually stole food and ended up back in Parchman.[74] The khaki suits served a similar function as the stripes, casting the men as recently incarcerated and thus unemployable.

Inmate artwork and cartoons often reimagined prison attire that was attractive and flattering. Drawings of uniforms in *Inside World* were rarely an exact representation; they were stylish, glamorous representations of clothing made from striped cloth, cut in attractive ways. Cartoons by inmates Albert Lee in the 1950s and Ron Harris in the 1960s depict uniforms transformed to reflect fashion and individuality, often with an emphasis on sexualized forms. They paired tight-fighting striped pencil skirts with off-the-shoulder blouses and tops with plunging necklines. Almost all of the cartoonists for the magazine showed attractive men and women who rose above the experience

12

GARDEN of EDEN

Ora Lee Adams

Well readers, this is your news reporter; Ora Lee Adams here at C.W.C. to let you all in on the happenings. We all have been home and on those wonderful days. Well they were wonderful to those who made them that way, but me, myself had a little difficulty on mine. It seems as though the Bus Driver got twisted on the time.

We had both bands over this month and they really rocked us.

C-1: I hope this will do you guys some good. Dannie Jones sends Hello to her home boy, John Dixon, Willie Mason, Willie Thomas, says good things come to those who wait.

C-2: S.L. Tillman, Dannie Lee Jones, says thanks for wonderful Christmas gift and your kindness will never be forgotten.

C-3: I must take time out to say hello and Joe L. Wiggen I tried but it just failed. I missed my bus and I want you to know that your not the only one with a broken heart, because i have one too. I have learned not to put off today, for tomorrow. Your Queen, Gloria; says hello and have a good year.

C-8: Hattie Mae Brown to J.T. Thomas.

Camp 10: John Keith, Elnora Taylor, got your Buzz, but she is sorry that she hadn't arrived on the scene at the time. You should have left your number and the buzz, would have been returned. She says Hello to Robert Lee Smith. Rufus Williams, Gloria, says glad you haven't forgotten her and hopes she will still be remembered in March. Ruthie Reed Hi's a Special to W.D. Durrah.

C-11: Your Queen says hello and hurry up with the gifts, so be cool Man. Hattie Brown, sends a "L" Hello to Lester Patterson.

C-12: Your Queen says hello to all you guys and to her King of Kings, "Kenneth" She also says thanks and it seems as though you have your eyes on another Queen, but you just remember because she is an easy going girl doesn't mean that she's a fool. She knows whats going on, so she will just keep her cool. The same goes for you; Ed Stowers, from Taylor. Alonzo, Janice says thanks for present. Joe Kimmons, Lucille B. would very much like to say thanks for letting Santa drop in on her. C.E. Martin, Lennie R. Battles and Hattie Brown say hello and hurry back.

Dairy: Well boys the reason why we dont ever say anything, is because everytime we go the gate, some of you guys are always on the scene...so why waste time writing (SMILE) HillBilly, Jackie says the pie was delicious. I want to thank my home boy for the gift he sent me. A Sweet Hello to James E. Young, from Elnora Taylor.

Camp "B" I would like to say Hello to you all and especially to my King, if I have one still. To you John W. Jackson keep Cool!

So I guess this is all until next month and before I close, I am going to leave this thought with you; Be sweet and most of all be yourself and luck and happiness will follow.

The Dextrose Philosopher

INSIDE WORLD-FEBRUARY, 1966

Prison uniforms re-imagined as fashionable and attractive. Ron Harris, Illustration for the "Garden of Eden" camp report, Inside World, February 1966, 12.

The women's choir depicted in A-line skirts. Paula Berry, "Women's Camp Choir" cartoon, Inside World, April 1951, 30.

of incarceration, through pride in their appearance and their awareness of free-world fashions.

A cartoon by Paula Berry depicting the women's camp chorus from 1951 brings to mind Dior's New Look, with feminine A-line skirts and nipped-in waists.[75] A cartoon of a May 1952 radio broadcast of a performance by a quartet from Camp 11 shows the men dressed in striped pants, with dress shirts, natty coats with pocket squares, and ties.[76] This seems to be an imaginative rendering of the musical group, considering that they were singing for the radio.

Inmates, who had varying degrees of access to radio and newspapers, were very much aware of contemporary styles, and seemed to hold onto free-world identities by imagining themselves dressed fashionably and attractively. Their

Sharply-dressed men recording for radio. Albert Lee, "Recording Radio Program Camp 11" cartoon, Inside Word, May 1952, 40.

contemporary lives were defined by uniforms, but their confinement could not completely obscure their stylish true selves. They often spoke humorously of the world of fashion: "Hey you guys, all these originals not from Parée, but straight from Parchée and like no other."[77] Ferita in 1960 reported,

> We are working very hard. The installation of the new sewing machines has put us behind the manufacturing of the clothes. Incidentally, are any of you fellows keeping up with the decision of the London tailors to change the 1961 pants to form-fitting trousers. Skin-tight. Those of you who suffer from "bow legs" will certainly be at a disadvantage. Anyway, be on the lookout for stovepipe stripes. We believe in keeping up with the latest fashions."[78]

In 2006 in a museum warehouse, historian Heather Ann Thompson pulled a bloodied uniform from a box of unprocessed material from the New York State Police. Elliot "L. D." Barkley was wearing the uniform when a state trooper shot him during the 1971 Attica prison uprising. The cause of Barkley's death was contested—did correctional officers target him as one of the revolt's organizers, or was he a victim of a ricocheting bullet? His uniform, saved as evidence, indicated that clothing held meaning about the life and death of its wearer in its bloodied folds.[79]

Scholars studying the experience of incarceration find limited archival resources and few points of entry into the day-to-day lives of incarcerated people, forcing them to "read between illegible lines only to still be confronted by . . . broken silence."[80] Many scholars have relied primarily on administrative records when studying incarceration.[81] For the Mississippi State Penitentiary, even official records are largely inaccessible.[82] Because of limited resources and because of systemic injustice in the United States prison system, histories of incarcerated people often focus on the brutal and coercive aspects of prison life, with an emphasis on institutional violence.

Centering violence illuminates the vulnerability of incarcerated people, and the institutions that abuse and neglect instead of rehabilitate. But to know of the cruelty they faced raises the question of how they survived. What emotions did they experience, beyond suffering? Mary Ellen Curtin notes that many historians have only seen prisoners as "casualties of a cruel system, not as historical actors in their own right."[83] In a recent book on the incarceration of black women in the South, Sarah Haley calls for scholars to "read along the archival grain of death and destruction, as well as against it, to uncover and imagine . . . social and interior lives and intellectual contributions."[84] A full accounting of institutional violence is central to understanding incarceration, and makes it even more important to see the "interior lives" of incarcerated people. They were human beings capable of thought and action, not just abused bodies.[85]

People incarcerated at Parchman faced violence, deprivation, and alienation from their families and communities. They were also profoundly creative in their everyday lives, giving meaning to the limited resources available to them. Fashion scholar Elizabeth Wilson notes that regardless of environment, "we consistently search for the crevices of culture that open us to freedom."[86] Men and women at Parchman in the 1950s and 1960s built lives around glimpses of freedom in the midst of the mundane and violent. Examining clothing captures their flashes of imagination and personality, and demonstrates that there is much more to know about incarcerated people than how they suffered.

Notes

1. Albert Lee, "Parchman Fall Fashions," *Inside World*, November 1954, 31.
2. Shobana Shankar, "Parchman Women Write the Blues? What Became of Black Women's

Prison Music in Mississippi in the 1930," *American Music* 31: 2 (Summer 2013), 183–202. http://www.jstor.org/stable/10.5406/americanmusic.31.2.0183.

3. Sources differ on when the state first imprisoned women at Parchman. In 1901, prison officials constructed stockades in which male and perhaps female inmates lived as they cleared land for the prison. 1905 was the first year the penitentiary was fully operational, and David Oshinsky states that the women's camp opened in 1915. William Banks Taylor contends that women were incarcerated at Parchman in 1906 after being moved from the satellite Oakley Farm. A recent unpublished history by Telisha Dionne Bailey contends that African American women lived there beginning in 1901. In 1986, the state transferred female inmates to the Central Mississippi Correctional Facility in Rankin County. Bailey's work explores the broad history of incarceration of African American women in the state, from the early twentieth century to the 1980s. Telisha Dionne Bailey, *"Please Don't Forget about Me": African American Women, Mississippi, and the History of Crime and Punishment in Parchman Prison, 1890–1980*, PhD dissertation, University of Mississippi, 2015; David Oshinsky, *Worse than Slavery: Parchman Farm and the Ordeal of Jim Crow Justice* (New York: Free Press, 1996); William Banks Taylor, *Down on Parchman Farm: The Great Prison in the Mississippi Delta* (Columbus: Ohio State University Press, 1999).

4. "Martha Alice Stewart: Time on Parchman Farm, 1930s" Collection, University of Mississippi Archives and Special Collections. Stewart was the head nurse at Parchman from 1930 to 1939 and had extensive access to many parts of the penitentiary, from the hospital to the fields, to the superintendent's home and band practices.

5. Fashion scholar Lou Taylor in *The Study of Dress History* notes that historically many museums and archives focused only on finely designed and made clothing of the wealthy, with garments worn by the poor and middle class given little value, to say nothing of clothing worn by incarcerated people. Lou Taylor, *The Study of Dress History* (Manchester: Manchester University Press, 2002), 51.

6. Artist unknown, "Cotton," *Inside World*, January 1972, 36.

7. Elaine Scarry, *The Body in Pain: The Making and Unmaking of the World* (New York: Oxford University Press, 1987), 40. The first issue of *Inside World* was published in 1949, but I was unable to locate this issue in the archives. The final issue was published in 1981, but through the 1970s–1980s, the publication schedule became much more erratic. This study will examine *Inside World* from 1950 through the 1960s, the years that the inmates published *Inside World* most consistently and wrote most extensively of sewing and clothing.

8. Pam, White Women's Camp Report, *Inside World*, April 1957, 12–13. Some inmates used their full names, some only their first, a nickname, or a pseudonym. When quoting inmates, I will not indicate when they diverge from accepted English grammar. I will also use their own descriptor for their unit (e.g. Forbidden City, the White Women's Camp, etc.).

9. Nita Kelly, "News from the Women's Camp—White Women's Unit," *Inside World*, April 1958, 13. A 1936 *Clarion Ledger* article described the Women's Camp as having a long shed-like space for black women and a small brick building for white women.

10. See Nita Kelly, "White Women's Unit," July 1958, in which she writes about the superintendent sending the women to the cotton fields after they complained about sewing. "I was under the impression that a hoe was something you cleaned your flowerbed with. Lordy

Mercy! It should be against the law to make tools like that. You have never seen a bunch of more grateful girls, to get back to their sewing machines," 11.

11. Ora Lee Adams, "Garden of Eden" Report, *Inside World*, April 1966, 18.

12. Juliet Ash, *Dress Behind Bars: Prison Clothing as Criminality* (London: I.B. Tauris, 2009), 3.

13. Ash notes that there are three forms of prison dress: "highly-articulated, distinctive embodied punishment; malign neglect; own clothes or prison issue dress resembling everyday wear outside" (140).

14. Ash, *Dress Behind Bars*, 73.

15. Ash, *Dress Behind Bars*, 98.

16. Ash, *Dress Behind Bars*, 104. Uniforms at the now all-male Mississippi State Penitentiary at Parchman were still made of striped cloth as of June 2018, when I visited as a chaplaincy volunteer. Trustee uniforms are indicated by green, rather than black, stripes. Women at the Central Mississippi Correctional Facility wear similarly striped uniforms, with green for trustee inmates and black for all others. In some units at both facilities, inmates wear white shirts with the striped pants. "MDOC Convict" is printed on the back of the shirt in large black letters.

17. Robert T. Chase describes prisoners in Tennessee burning striped uniforms in 1985 when the legislature replaced blue denim with stripes. Robert T. Chase, "We Are Not Slaves: Rethinking the Rise of Carceral States through the Lens of the Prisoners' Rights Movement," *Journal of American History* 2015; 102 (83): doi: 10.1093/jahist/jav317.

18. Talitha LeFlouria, *Chained in Silence: Black Women and Convict Labor in the New South* (Chapel Hill: University of North Carolina Press, 2015), 88.

19. Mary Ellen Curtin, *Black Prisoners and Their World, Alabama, 1865–1900* (Charlottesville: University of Virginia Press, 2000), 126.

20. A. E. Bolton, Camp 10 Report, *Inside World*, April 1960, 22.

21. Ash, *Dress Behind Bars*, 140.

22. Albert Lee, Camp 11 Report, *Inside World*, November 1955, 26.

23. Mary Marshall, Forbidden City, *Inside World*, Feb 1964, 7.

24. Song quoted in Oshinsky, *Worse Than Slavery*, 143. I could quote a number of blues songs referencing sewing or clothing, but many scholars have studied the significance of blues music at Parchman. Blues is indeed the only cultural expression that scholars have studied at the prison.

25. James Hendricks, editorial, *Inside World*, November 1961, 23. Ash in *Dress Behind Bars* notes that iconic prison uniforms like the stripes Hendricks wore "replaced the body of the prisoner as criminal in the public sphere," 4.

26. Jesse F. Durham, editorial, "At Last the Country Is Waking Up," *Inside World*, June 1955, 3.

27. See, for example, *Inside World* issues February 1958 (March of Dimes collection), January 1962 (506 inmates assisted with response to flooding in Flowood), February 1961 (Red Cross makes monthly blood collection, 806 pints), July 1953 (editorial on willingness to volunteer for trials on Hansen's disease), December 1954 (Camp 6 collected $34 to purchase flowers upon hearing of the death of Sergeant Van Landingham's baby son. Landingham was the sergeant for the women's camp for decades).

28. An intriguing question remains about how this system worked within the women's camps in the 1950s and 1960s. Did they sew under the gun? When they worked in the fields, were they under the gun? If so, were the armed trustees male or female? Administrators categorized women as trustees and as gunmen, but it is not clear whether female trustees were armed, or if they just used the hierarchical term to designate status. I found no camp reports that mention armed women. Because they wrote so minutely of daily matters, my supposition is that the female trustees were not armed. Perhaps labor "under the gun" was reserved for outdoor labor.

29. Pam and Gene, "White Women's Unit," *Inside World*, October 1959, 11.

30. Ferita, "Colored Women's Unit," *Inside World*, November 1960, 28.

31. For example, in July 1954 and May 1972.

32. David Rothman in *The Discovery of the Asylum* notes that distinctive uniforms (though at the time not striped) were used as a security measure in prisons beginning in the late eighteenth century in the US. David H. Rothman, *The Discovery of the Asylum: Social Order and Disorder in the New Republic* (Piscataway: Transaction Publishers, 1971), 90.

33. James Hendricks, Interview with Superintendent Fred Jones, *Inside World*, May 1960, 27.

34. Flip, "Meet Dr. MacCormack," *Inside World*, February 1961, 14.

35. R. Harris, "Across the Editor's Desk," *Inside World*, May 1966, 10.

36. Joe Bumgarner, editorial, *Inside World*, January 1967, 9.

37. Reporter not named, "Colored Women's Camp" Report, *Inside World*, June 1954.

38. Pam and Gene, White Women's Unit Camp Report, *Inside World*, October 1958, 11.

39. Laura Livingston, "Forbidden City," *Inside World*, June–July 1967. In this study, I focus on sewing done for other inmates as part of compulsory prison labor. Beginning in 1969, Parchman had a "Needle Trades Camp" in which women learned how to sew for commercial endeavors, including drapery and upholstering. Some women did write about plans to become upholsters or professional seamstresses after leaving Parchman. It is understandable why a person who had labored in a prison setting might avoid that type of labor in the free world, but some did choose to take skills learned in prison and use them on the outside, transforming prison labor into something of value to them. Mary Ellen Curtin writes of black male prisoners in Alabama leased to mines as convicts, who continued as free miners upon release (5). Leflouria in *Chained in Silence* also emphasizes that much carceral labor required great skill, such as brickmaking and blacksmithing, jobs of women convict laborers in Georgia (84).

40. Ferita, "Col'D Gal's Camp," *Inside World*, March 1960, 12.

41. See Camp 8 (Charles Chinn, 19) and Camp 10 (Jeff Robinson, 22), April 1958.

42. Mary McGraw, "Meet McGraw—White Women's Unit," *Inside World*, November 1960, 21.

43. Albert Turner, "Camp 10 Report," April 1957, *Inside World*, 18.

44. Joe Evelyn, White Women's Unit Report, June 1957, *Inside World*.

45. Letter from Superintendent C. E. Breazeale to Governor Ross Barnett, protesting state budget cuts, stating $84,500 monthly cost of caring for inmates, meaning $38.50 per inmate per month, or $1.27 per day. January 18, 1963. Correspondence of Ross Barnett, Mississippi Department of Archives and History.

46. James Williams, Camp 3 Report, *Inside World*, November 1958, 17.

47. James Hendricks, editorial, *Inside World*, February 1960, 4.
48. Sue Theriault, "Forbidden City News," *Inside World*, November 1966.
49. Thelma Huston, Women's Camp Report, *Inside World*, February 1951, 33.
50. Reba Morgan, "Women's Camp Report," August 1961, *Inside World*, 22. Their camp was nicknamed "Forbidden City."
51. Thelma Huston, "Women's Camp Report," *Inside World*, October 1951, 36.
52. Sarah Haley in *No Mercy Here: Gender, Punishment, and the Making of Jim Crow Modernity* writes about a skilled female blacksmith that "even if she found blacksmithing meaningful, the pursuit of satisfaction from meaningful work in the context of captivity cannot redress her pained condition." I think it is possible for a laborer to find meaning in their work if it benefits them in some way, like relationship formation for women at Parchman. This would likely not be the case for the blacksmith. Haley, *No Mercy Here: Gender, Punishment, and the Making of Jim Crow Modernity* (Chapel Hill: University of North Carolina Press, 2016), 99–100.
53. Louise Smith, "News from Women's Camp," *Inside World*, October 1955, 18.
54. Mary Marshall, "Forbidden City" Report, *Inside World*, October 1965, 9.
55. Joe Bumgarner, Camp 5 Report, *Inside World*, February 1967, 23.
56. Richard Lott, Camp 5 Report, *Inside World*, April 1963, 16.
57. Carolyn Crowder, "Garden of Eden" Report, *Inside World*, December 1967, 20.
58. James Lewis, Camp 8 Report, *Inside World*, November/December 1968, 15.
59. Laura L. Livingston, "Forbidden City," *Inside World*, June-July 1967, 20.
60. Mary Marshall, "Forbidden City," *Inside World*, November 1964, 8.
61. Robert L. Hayes, Camp B Report, *Inside World*, January 1966, 18.
62. Nathaniel Richardson, Camp 3 Report, *Inside World*, August 1968, 56. And El Toro (James Edwards), RCD (Reception Center) Report, *Inside World*, September 1968, 48.
63. Kali Nicole Gross, "African American Women, Mass Incarceration, and the Politics of Protection," *Journal of American History* 2015, 102 (1): 25–33. doi: 10.1093/jahist/jav226.
64. Wendy, Bitsie, Bonnie, "Forbidden City Camp Report," *Inside World*, April 1964, 12.
65. John Keith, "Ten Reports," *Inside World*, May 1964, 20.
66. Albert Lee, Camp 11 Report, *Inside World*, March 1956, 20.
67. Thelma Huston and Lulu Berry, "Women's Camp News," *Inside World*, May 1951, 33–34.
68. Curtin, *Black Prisoners and Their World, Alabama, 1865–1900*, 129.
69. George Golden, Camp B Report, *Inside World*, January 1959, 21.
70. Thelma Huston, "News from Forbidden City," *Inside World*, April 1952, 33.
71. Mary Marshall, "Forbidden City," *Inside World*, December 1964, 9.
72. Mary Marshall, "Forbidden City," *Inside World*, November 1965 11.
73. Francis Welliver, "Down and Out," *Inside World*, June 1961, 3.
74. Joe L. Bumgarner, editorial, *Inside World*, February 1967, 3.
75. Paula Berry, "Women's Camp Choir" cartoon, *Inside World*, April 1951, 30.
76. Albert Lee, "Recording Radio Program Camp 11" cartoon, *Inside Word*, May 1952, 40. The women did sew band uniforms in 1960, when Parchman bands began performing outside of the penitentiary, but this cartoon predates that.
77. Mary Marshall, Forbidden City, *Inside World*, February 1965, 11.
78. Ferita, "Colored Women's Unit," *Inside World*, November 1960, 28.

79. Heather Ann Thompson, *Blood in the Water: The Attica Prison Uprising of 1971 and its Legacy* (New York: Pantheon, 2016), xv.

80. LeFlouria, *Chained in Silence*, 189.

81. Looked at in a new way, administrative records can illuminate prisoners' lives. LeFlouria in *Chained in Silence*, 16, used "whipping reports" in her research, not to understand cruelty but to foreground the resistance that preceded the punishment.

82. The Mississippi Department of Corrections has not transferred records for most of the twentieth century to the Mississippi Department of Archives and History, and they are thus inaccessible.

83. Curtin, *Black Prisoners and Their World, Alabama, 1865–1900*, 4.

84. Haley, *No Mercy Here: Gender, Punishment, and the Making of Jim Crow Modernity*, 14–15.

85. Scholars of incarceration in the South often look to scholarship on slavery for ways of discussing institutional violence and the body, and the use of "humanity" when discussing the worth of enslaved people raises questions for some. Saidya Hartman in *Scenes of Subjection: Terror, Slavery, and Self-Making in Nineteenth-Century America* challenges the academy's emphasis on the "recognition of humanity" of enslaved people, warning that "the selective recognition of humanity undergirded the relations of chattel slavery [that] had not considered them deserving of rights or freedom." Hartman demonstrates the incalculable power of enslavement to make people subject, creating an environment brutal in every aspect. However, I resist the idea that people who are subject to institutional violence do not also have a sense of self that is generative and meaning-making. The enslaved or incarcerated, seen outside of the relationship to the enslaver or imprisoner, were autonomous human beings who had interior lives. Walter Johnson considers the language of "dehumanization" to be problematic because it centers the power of the slave owner: "The idea that enslavement 'dehumanized' enslaved people suggests that their humanity needs to be proven again and again." In this work I hope to illuminate the humanity of incarcerated people as evidenced through their creative will to make meaningful lives in a violent space, not as resisters to an institution, but as historical actors in their own right. Walter Johnson, "To Remake the World: Slavery, Racial Capitalism, and Justice," *Boston Review*, http://bostonreview.net/race/walter-johnson-slavery-human-rights-racial-capitalism, 26 October 2016.

86. Elizabeth Wilson, *Adorned in Dreams: Fashion and Modernity* (Rutgers, NJ: Rutgers University Press, 2003), 244.

THE MISSISSIPPI POOR PEOPLE'S CORPORATION

Clothing Manufacture and Consumer Capitalism in Defense of Black Voting Rights, 1965–1974

WILLIAM STURKEY

On May 9th, 1966, a forty-five-year-old white New York woman named Jacqueline Bernard performed a remarkable act when she sent a check for $2,325 to a woman she had never met. Ms. Bernard submitted her check to a black Mississippi woman named Oberia Holliday, the president of the Una Sewing Cooperative in Clay County, Mississippi, to support a fundraising campaign called "Blocks for Freedom." Thirty-seven days after sending the first check, Bernard sent Holliday another payment for $254. Two months later, she mailed a third check. And then in late October of 1966, Jacqueline Bernard went to her local bank, took out a personal loan for $300, and sent a fourth check to Mrs. Holliday.[1]

Jacqueline Bernard had been paying close attention to the Black Freedom Movement in Clay County. Her son Joel began working as a volunteer during the 1964 Mississippi Freedom Summer civil rights campaign. In letters home, Joel described the bleak conditions facing local African Americans, telling his mother he could not even "begin to describe the poverty" and that "the town is practically run by the KKK." Jacqueline wanted to help. She forwarded some of Joel's letters to family members and even a local newspaper in the hopes of drawing awareness to the challenges of black Mississippians living in Clay County. Through Joel, Jacqueline also began exchanging letters with other white activists and eventually local African Americans. Although it appears she never visited Clay County herself, Jacqueline's involvement continued after Freedom Summer, well after Joel left Mississippi. She recruited others to join her cause, soliciting neighbors, friends, and businesses for clothing donations to help struggling black families in Clay County. And then in the summer of 1965, she became involved with the "Blocks for Freedom" campaign that eventually led her to send large checks to Mississippi, even at her own expense.[2]

Jacqueline Bernard's level of involvement in the southern civil rights movement was exceptional, but she was just one of the movement's innumerable liberal white supporters. Although not usually involved in marches and sit-ins, white northern liberals identified with the moral authority of the movement. Beginning in the spring of 1963, the civil rights movement dominated the American news for two years, developing an unprecedented amount of moral capital. Over those two years, Americans saw, heard, and read about firehoses used on children in Birmingham, the murder of Mississippi NAACP Field Secretary Medgar Evers, the massive March on Washington and Martin Luther King Jr.'s "I Have a Dream Speech," the murder of four girls in Birmingham, the death of President Kennedy, the assassination of three civil rights workers in Mississippi, "Bloody Sunday" on the Edmund Pettis Bridge, and the murder of a Michigan woman trying to help southern black voters. Civil rights coverage was relentless. The news kept coming in waves, exposing every single American to the horrific realities of southern Jim Crow and white supremacist resistance to black activism. From a teenage folk singer in small town Minnesota to a middle-class white woman living on Manhattan's Upper West Side, millions of Americans were awakened to the struggle of southern African Americans for basic constitutional and human rights. Thousands, like Viola Liuzzo, the woman killed in Alabama, went to the South and joined the movement themselves. Even more, like Jacqueline Bernard, felt the cause pulling on their moral purse strings.

The eighteen women in the Una Sewing Cooperative were members of a larger organization named the Poor People's Corporation (PPC) that sought to convert liberal white moral support into direct financial and political empowerment. Founded in 1965, the Poor People's Corporation was created to meet the new challenges of the post-Jim Crow era.[3] In many Mississippi counties, the potential of the 1965 Voter Rights Act was undercut by a 1962 state law that required local newspapers to print the name of local citizens who attempted to register to vote. Potential African American voters became susceptible to a variety of retributions for their political activity. As in the case of the women of the Una Sewing Cooperative, many were fired from their jobs for registering to vote or for other forms of civil rights activism. Faced with this new type of challenge, a group of Mississippi activists developed the PPC to offer seed grants and marketing assistance for black

Mississippians to start their own companies that would allow them to both earn an income and register to vote. And because of the moral momentum generated by the movement over the preceding years, they also found thousands of allies who were willing to spend money and consume goods to help support the black freedom struggle. This essay tells an annotated version of their story.

In telling the story of the Poor People's Corporation, this essay offers three primary scholarly interjections. First, it helps illuminate the ways that African Americans, especially women, used clothing manufacture as a mode of activism and resistance. Second, this essay will situate the women of the PPC within the context of the Black Power movement, which tragically often excluded working-class southern black women whose grassroots economic and political programs demonstrated major tenants of the very movement that overlooked their activities and goals. As Christina Greene has written, "The tendency of both scholars and the public alike to focus on the more sensational aspects of Black Power and on black violence has diverted attention from some of Black Power's more lasting and significant aspects and from projects initiated by women."[4]

Finally, this essay uses the story of the PPC to complicate the historiographical understanding of the connection between civil rights and economic equality. I suggest that the support garnered for pro-civil rights organizations in the mid-1960s created unique economic opportunities for southern black activists that do not fit neatly into the current historiographical declension narrative of the "lost promise of civil rights." Whereas many historians of the "long civil rights movement" have argued that the movement of the 1950s and 1960s was reduced from radical labor organizing into "a very different type of Civil Rights Movement," with a stripped-down agenda largely devoid of a strong labor component capable of producing real economic change, I argue here for the conceptualization of a different type of opportunity—one that did not threaten to fundamentally alter America's liberal capitalist state, but rather offered a unique opportunity to advance black political *and* economic goals through unprecedented access to what Lizabeth Cohen has dubbed the "Consumer's Republic." Because of the "transcendent moral power" generated by the movement's desegregation activities of the 1960s, black southern producers gained direct access to middle and upper-class consumers. In other words, another opportunity was actually found. Unfortunately for black activists, however, that window of opportunity was also ultimately lost.[5]

The PPC

In the fall of 1964, three African American women in Canton, Mississippi (where the average annual income for African American families was only $1,100 per year)[6] had an idea to help local black women combat poverty. Canton residents Mrs. Levy, Mrs. Harris, and Maggie Douglas recruited local black women to a series of small gatherings, asking each to brainstorm ideas for products they could manufacture and sell to northern consumers. At first, they received only a small response. But after securing a major order for over six thousand children's smocks from the Child Development Group of Mississippi, a federally funded Office of Economic Opportunity Program, their membership rapidly increased. The following spring, dozens of women were fired from their jobs at a Madison County sewing factory for registering to vote. These dismissals came on the heels of the proposal of the 1965 Voting Rights Act, demonstrating to black Mississippians the ways local white supremacists would use grassroots efforts to thwart federal legislation. With families to provide for and nowhere else to work, many of these women turned to the Madison County Sewing Firm for help.[7]

A Madison County-based activist named George Raymond contacted allies in Jackson and explained the problem facing Canton's black women voters. Raymond asked his friend Jessie Morris for advice about how to market and distribute the goods being produced by the growing Madison County Sewing Firm. Morris liked the idea. He and several other Jackson activists realized that if they "could get other people to make dresses too," then "we could probably ship em' off and sell em.'" "So it was decided," Morris remembered, "that we form a group that could lend money to get small groups like this started, making things." And so the PPC was born.[8]

To raise seed money, PPC organizers used mailing lists borrowed from the Mississippi Council of Federated Organizations (COFO). By 1965, COFO had become incredibly proficient at soliciting donations from liberal groups across the nation. During the 1964 Freedom Summer, COFO experienced massive levels of support from across America, especially through the growing number of "Friends of SNCC" groups that organized to provide support in virtually every major American city and liberal college town. Other support came in the form of church groups such as the Delta Ministry, campus organizations, liberal political organizations, and even individuals such as Chicago millionaire Lucille Montgomery. All of these organizations played a major role in the execution of the 1964 Freedom Summer, and many maintained contacts in Mississippi for years afterward. The full contributions of these vastly underappreciated groups were never realized by many activists, and have yet to be illuminated by civil rights historians. Nonetheless, they played important fundraising roles well into 1965, despite the departures of hundreds of white volunteers and dozens of burnt out SNCC veterans. For example, in the eight months after Freedom Summer, one Hattiesburg organizer alone received $3,659.12 from northern benefactors.[9]

The PPC quickly tapped into these established pro-civil rights support networks and soon enjoyed similar benefits from northern supporters. Within ninety days, they received support from Friends of SNCC groups in Los Angeles, Boston, Detroit, Oakland, Seattle, and Quaker organizations in Washington, DC, and Philadelphia. This resulted in significant financial contributions and the arrival of several volunteers who travelled to Mississippi to work with and train prospective workers. With donations from mostly white benefactors, the PPC began in the summer of 1965 an incredible experiment in black self-help and community empowerment.[10]

The PPC held its first membership meeting at Tougaloo College on Sunday, August 29, 1965, just twenty-three days after President Lyndon B. Johnson signed the Voting Rights Act. Three hundred people attended. The primary goal of the gathering was to introduce prospective members to the organization and distribute the first wave of start-up grants. The Board of Directors was composed of Movement veterans Jessie Morris, Hunter Morey, R. L. Bolden, Jessie Harris, and Donald White. Treasurer Morey announced that the organization had raised $5,021, all from individual donations. After a brief introduction, the meeting quickly turned toward distribution.[11]

Various groups of black Mississippi workers had learned of the newly formed PPC through their involvement with local civil rights activities. The opportunity to merge political activism and manufacturing must have seemed serendipitous to some of the groups of black workers. African American communities in Mississippi had produced their own goods for decades. In many places, the production of items such as quilts played key roles in responding to the social and financial constraints of Jim Crow. Production techniques had been passed down through generations. Many prospective members of the PPC arrived at the first membership meeting with proposals, budgets, and samples. Some of these workers had learned to produce these goods from their mothers and grandmothers. For generations, black Mississippi women had produced their own materials—ranging from clothing to quilts—to provide for their families and supplement household incomes. Many prospective PPC members were domestic workers who had been conducting sewing for white families for years, and were extremely experienced and talented.

The women of the Madison County Sewing Firm were first on the docket. They asked for a loan of $1,000 to buy fabric, pay wages, and make a down payment on industrial sewing machines. To supplement their application, five co-op members displayed samples of their products. These included cotton dresses, women's suits, handbags, babies' dresses, smocks, boys' shirts and shorts, and men's shirts, ranging in price between $1.50 and $12.00. Co-op President Maggie Douglas offered an encouraging testimony of the co-ops ability to help its workers pursue economic and political freedom, testifying that most of the sixteen employees had previously worked as domestics in white Canton homes before being fired for "voter registration drives and other civil-rights activities." While working as domestics, these women had earned only about $12 per week. After joining the Madison County Sewing Firm, most doubled their take-home pay while working half the hours. And, of course, they were also able to register to vote without the fear of losing their jobs.[12]

Several other organizations applied for startup grants. The Adams County Bag Firm of Natchez applied for $400 to make leather coin bags. These made-for-men satchels were eight-to-ten inches long and could be looped through belts. The bags proved to be popular among young adults. The group even donated a special white leather bag to singer James Brown, who promised to wear it on tour over the next several months to help solicit donations. In honor of the Rock n' Roll star's latest album, the Natchez group nicknamed their products, "Papa's Brand New Bag." In their application, the Adams County bag firm noted that the bags only cost $1 to produce, but could be sold for as much as $10.00. A new sewing machine and payroll money would enable them to produce hundreds of bags per day.[13]

Numerous Pike County organizations applied for funds. One group of young women wanted $400 to make twelve-by-eighteen-inch ladies' handbags they estimated could sell for $20. Twenty-five Pike County women wanted to make the same products as the Madison County group and applied for $500 to cover the costs of sewing machines, wages, materials, and access to a building rented at $10 per month. Twenty-five unemployed middle-aged men applied for $1,445.00 to open a toy factory. Seeking to "use their wood-working skills and knowledge to support their families," these men had produced a factory blueprint and were actively seeking a contract with a northern toy company. They also planned to supplement toy production with furniture manufacturing and pay themselves a modest $1.25 per hour wage.[14]

The initial PPC meeting resulted in the distribution of nearly $4,500 to six co-ops. Additionally, Jessie Morris suggested that the organization spend

$400 to establish a sales depot in Jackson, which would store and distribute the products made by each cooperative. The store would have a small staff, display space, and administer sales through a mail-order catalogue. The Liberty Outlet House, as the distribution center came to be called, was the most important organizational aspect of the PPC. It institutionalized distribution by connecting PPC producers with a wide range of nationwide consumers. Ellen Maslow, a Brandeis dropout turned SNCC voter-registration worker, volunteered to open a New York office to expand the organization's national breadth.[15]

Three months later, approximately two hundred people attended the second PPC meeting in Mileston. Liberty Outlet House Manager Bill Hutchinson announced that the outlet was receiving goods from several cooperatives and planned to open within two weeks. Friends of SNCC groups in St. Louis and Boston had ordered a combined $792 worth of products, and additional purchases were expected from similar groups in Chapel Hill, North Carolina, San Francisco, and Berkeley, California. Doris Derby, director of the newly established PPC training facility in Jackson, announced that a woman named Mrs. Felson from the American Jewish Congress had arrived in Mississippi and was planning to help publicize the PPC in New York City.[16]

Other groups of women submitted requests for funds. Sarah Hart and Ruth Lee represented the newly formed Mount Olive Quilting Co-op. Rebecca Donald and Ruby Davis of Ruleville had organized seventeen experienced quilters who were ready to start work immediately. They had already received numerous orders from California and Ohio. The Una Sewing Cooperative in Clay County had already generated over $100 by selling suppers at local black churches and used the money to restore an old storehouse with new paint, wiring, and general repairs. They just needed additional funds for sewing machines. A Hopedale woman named Mrs. Morganfield had also organized a group and already had more than seventy orders for quilts.[17]

The PPC attempted to ensure political activism alongside economic self-sufficiency. Each PPC member was required to be a registered voter. The organization also educated members, especially through the distribution of a pamphlet titled "County Government in Mississippi" that explained the political process. Produced by the Tougaloo College-based Freedom Information Service, this late 1960s mailing was distributed among local black civil rights workers across the state. The twenty-page mailer included tutorials explaining primary elections, voting procedures, and information on the elections and duties of different offices, including sheriffs, boards of supervisors, circuit clerks, tax assessors, coroners, and superintendents of education. The PPC made sure that each co-op received copies of the political primer.[18]

By the end of 1965, the Poor People's Corporation had developed a promising network of distributors. The organization relied on various Friends of SNCC groups throughout the country to publicize PPC products to individual customers, small boutiques, and neighborhood stores. Boston and Detroit Friends of SNCC vowed to open their own store to distribute the Mississippi co-op products.[19] So did a group of students at the University of Washington. Quakers in Philadelphia and Washington vowed to pass out brochures at an upcoming Race Relations Conference. The Women's International League for Peace and Freedom sent brochures to its three hundred national branches. A woman in Yellow Springs, Ohio, solicited PPC goods and planned a branch of the Liberty Outlet House. Berkeley, California's Arts and Crafts Cooperative and Cost Plus import store wanted to include PPC goods, especially Ruleville quilts. So did the San Francisco Eye Soar.[20] By the end of 1966, the PPC roster of wholesale buyers included stores across America such as the Lantern in Grinnell, Iowa, Cokotoo Boutique in Hyattsville, Maryland, the Gallery Ltd., in Champaign, Illinois, Wilpe Bazaar in Indianapolis, Indiana, Her Closet in Pompano Beach, Florida, Caravan Traders Ltd. in Chicago, Illinois, and Terra Cotta in New York City. Just sixteen months after its creation, the PPC was selling goods to more than seventy retailers across the United States.[21]

A year after attending the PPC's first membership meeting, Ellen Maslow successfully opened a New York City storefront to distribute goods. Located on Bleecker Street in the heart of Greenwich Village, this New York City branch of the Liberty House was one of dozens of Village-area co-ops. Abbie Hoffman, Maslow's former Brandeis classmate who would later become famous as one of the Chicago Eight, was hired as its sales manager. The opening of the New York City Liberty House attracted unprecedented media attention. Maslow remembered, "At the opening, there were more reporters than customers; the TV cameras couldn't all fit in." The store opening was covered in local New York City newspapers such as *Cue Magazine*, the *New York Times*, the *Village Voice*, and *The Daily News*.[22]

The PPC drew national-level interest among a wide variety of media outlets. The Nation of Islam's *Muhammad Speaks* encouraged members to patronize the PPC, noting, "Without the support of Black people—who spend upwards of $35 billion per year in white markets—the PPC, and any other Black efforts to establish economic independence, stand little chance of success."[23] The *Michigan Chronicle* reported the opening of a Detroit branch of the Liberty House and growing support among Motor City residents.[24] Throughout the following year, additional news stories appeared across America. Later articles appeared in *The Wall Street Journal, New York Post, New York Amsterdam News, Washington Post,* and *Chicago Defender,* which called the PPC "the most ambitious of the self-help programs."[25] The *Chicago's American* previewed the Windy City's forthcoming Liberty Outlet House branch in a feature on the PPC. It extolled the virtues of the PPC, noting, "They are operating in the finest American tradition." The PPC was also featured in black magazines *Negro Digest* and *Jet,* which noted that "request for items have also come as far as East Africa, England, France and Hawaii."[26]

The New York City Liberty House sold children's dresses for $3.95, suede handbags from the McComb Leather Co-op for $19.95, and full-size, hand-sewn patchwork quilts priced at $35. Hoffman, who by that time was firmly entrenched in the late 1960s hippie counterculture, also began peddling PPC products at summer music festivals, including Woodstock and the 1966 Newport Folk Music Festival, where Hoffman sold PPC goods next to a table where Stokely Carmichael was distributing Black Power literature. Through activists like Ellen Maslow and Hoffman, both inspired and galvanized by mid-1960s movement activities, the Liberty House market was able to reach the streets of New York City.[27]

By 1969, Derby was also operating an impressive grassroots public relations campaign. Derby spent much of January in New York City and Boston appearing on local television shows including WOR-TV's Joe Franklin Show, WABC-TV's "Like It Is," and the hotel cable station Channel 6-TV. She also made numerous appearances on African American radio programs including WCOP's "Gus Sanders Show" and WGBH's "Say Brother."[28] After her New York City trip, Derby launched a forty-two-day West Coast publicity tour to promote the PPC. This sophisticated effort involved radio and television appearances, newspaper interviews, product shows, mailing list sign-ups, and numerous consultations with supporters. Articles appeared in mainstream newspapers including the *Los Angeles Times* and *Oakland Tribune,* and in black California papers such as the *Los Angeles Sentinel* and San Francisco's *Sun Reporter.*[29]

The publicity helped mobilize additional support. African American celebrities and civil rights movement veterans also helped rally support for the PPC. A 1967 mailing from celebrated black Hollywood couple Ossie Davis and Ruby Dee told the story of the PPC and urged recipients to order from the included catalogue. The organization's list of sponsors included well-known people such as Ella Baker, A. Philip Randolph, Dorothy Day, James

Farmer, Michael Harrington, John Lewis, Rev. A. J. Muste, Norman Thomas, and Nathan Schwerner, the father of slain activist Mickey Schwerner.[30]

Assistance came in numerous forms. Although the PPC had started by soliciting an established COFO mailing list, by the end of 1966 different groups were contacting the PPC and offering unsolicited assistance. A Reed College group read about the PPC in the *National Guardian* and asked for more information about purchasing goods and making donations. The Unitarian Church of Princeton asked for brochures for its congregation and sent a small donation. A representative of the twelve-thousand-member Pocketbook Workers Union caught wind of the PPC in *The Nation*, and offered to lend help "in some tangible way." New York Foundation president and Wall Street investment banker David John Heyman simply bought the organization a car.[31]

Back in Mississippi, the PPC kept growing. Although some of the businesses failed, others took their place. A White Station co-op, led by fifty-nine-year-old Alma Young, made candles. An Athens sewing firm made clothing for dolls and suede jewelry. Twenty Mt. Nebo women produced neckties. Rosehill women produced aprons, smocks, and clutchballs, while a group of Baertown women sewed ladies' dresses. Just as "Black Power" activists were organizing conferences, lectures, and publications, hundreds of black Mississippians, mostly women, were churning out a different form of black economic self-sufficiency. For members of the PPC, Black Power looked vastly different. As opposed to the traditional Black Power imagery consisting of clenched fists, afros, dashikis, and dark glasses, PPC Black Power was manifested in the form of rag dolls, tote bags, aprons, and wax candles. Clothing produced by women was the most tangible form of "Black Power" in many Mississippi communities.[32]

Although Liberty House was initially conceived as a distribution center, its duties were soon expanded to include a new role as co-op supplier in order to control prices and negotiate for better terms. When explaining the expansion of its role, PPC administrators explained, "Because the supply requirements of the member groups are pooled, Liberty House's raw material procurer is able to place much larger orders than any one group would place. It thus obtains discounts not available to any one group."[33] Liberty House's role as supplier certainly offered valuable potential benefits by connecting the rural Mississippi co-ops to northeastern suppliers and offering discounts. But it also explicitly linked the fate of each co-op to each other and the Liberty House itself. If one co-op struggled or failed, then it could negatively affect the other PPC businesses. Some of the co-ops, of course, were bound to fail. Ideally, the organization would have been able to cut ties with the least successful cooperatives. The Liberty House recognized this, noting, "If self-sufficiency is the goal, cooperatives must maximize the profitability of their investments even if they have to forego their effect upon the community."[34] But PPC officials defended their nontraditional business model, arguing that it defeated their fundamental purpose. "In a strictly commercial operation," Derby explained to the *Washington Post*, "we'd simply lay off the workers during slow periods and fire the slow ones altogether. But our objective isn't to make money for Liberty House but to train people and make them independent." Because it was a humanitarian effort involving personal relationships, Liberty House simply refused to cut people loose.[35]

Additional Jackson Liberty House financial problems stemmed from poor managerial practices and inexperience. At their peak, sales figures topped $110,000. Its sheer scale required additional expertise and help. And although sales numbers were sometimes impressive, they were also unstable. The civil rights activists who ran the Liberty House would have greatly benefitted from the expertise of accountants, marketing experts, and business managers. Another problem was that the initial capital investment was too small. The initial Liberty House grants totaled $5,000. From this relatively small fund, the PPC sought to employ over one hundred and fifty people, providing each with a living wage while also paying for supplies. The Liberty House had simply taken on too much responsibility. It marketed goods, conducted public relations campaigns, paid administrators, bought supplies, and absorbed losses when co-ops failed to turn a profit. The initial lack of investment meant that the organization did not have a large enough capital base to absorb losses. Tragically, at a time when the federal government doled out millions for anti-poverty campaigns, Black Power activists raised thousands of dollars for purposes less directly related to their stated mission, and even rich cotton planters such as Mississippi senator James Eastland received six-figure subsidies to control cotton prices, the PPC was unable to build a large enough start-up capital base to survive poor sales periods.[36]

Despite some initial successes, by 1974, the PPC was forced to close its doors. The organization did enjoy encouraging sales numbers, but was unable to overcome the realities of business management and waning support in the mid-1970s. Between July 1, 1967, and June 30, 1968, organizational sales reached $81,844. Two years later, gross sales increased to $119,492.43 (the historical equivalent of approximately $740,000). By 1970, it was America's largest independent distributor of handicrafts made by low-income people.[37] But the Liberty House absorbed constant losses in the early 1970s. Additionally, inflation hit it hard, making the loans repaid by co-ops worth less than their original value, especially because the company did not charge interest.[38] From 1970 on, Liberty House lost money as it overextended itself and PPC co-ops relied too heavily on it. In 1971, it lost $24,985.77. By 1973, many of the co-ops had folded and the Liberty House lost $3,827.42 as PPC sales plummeted to a mere $31,564.41. In 1974, the organization liquefied its holdings.[39]

Like many grassroots economic and political initiatives of the Black Power era, the story of the PPC and similar organizations has gone overlooked in favor of the more visible aspects of the Black Power movement. Across the South, numerous co-ops strove for similar goals as the PPC, including quilters in Gee's Bend, Alabama Quilters, handbag makers in Elton, Louisiana, a Brownsville, Tennessee, organization titled Haywood County Handicraft, and a group of Pecan Praline peanut-butter-brittle makers—all of which contacted the PPC at various points to inquire about inclusion.[40] The women in these groups built on decades-long community sartorial traditions to manufacture clothing items and other household staples that facilitated their political freedom and allowed for other forms of activism, while also providing a steady household income. Although most of these programs were overlooked by contemporary Black Power activists, they probably held the greatest potential for empowering blacks at the local level through a well-defined connection between generating economic and political power. As a Wall Street Journal writer observed in 1966, the PPC offered a "concrete manifestation of 'black power,'" in an era when the concept was "rather vaguely defined." Had the Black Power movement more fully incorporated the needs of organic producers and activists like the women who worked in southern cooperatives, organizations like the PPC would have had much better chances of success.[41]

Additionally, the story of the PPC demonstrates that the moral momentum created by the civil rights movement in the 1960s resulted in brief but significant economic potential for networks of activists. These networks did not transform the nation's economic structure in the ways suggested by Korstad and Lichtenstein, but they did offer impressive potential for economic empowerment on the local level.[42] Much of this potential was created by interracial northern support. It is difficult to measure precisely how much financial opportunity existed, but the civil rights movement of the mid-1960s did allow for hundreds of black Mississippians to parlay clothing production into political activism and increased economic opportunity. At a moment when the movement was in vogue like never before or since, everyday

Americans could employ their traditional politics of mass consumption in a way that assisted persecuted southern African Americans and allowed even suburban housewives to participate in a sort of consumptive activism. Unfortunately for most cooperatives, the opportunity closed during the late 1960s during the rise of urban unrests, the Vietnam War, and the backlash of the New Right.[43]

Notes

1. Jacqueline Bernard to Mrs. Holliday, New York, NY, June 15, 1966; Jacqueline Bernard to Mrs. Holliday, New York, NY, August 13, 1966; Oberia Holliday to Mrs. Bernard, Prairie, MS, August 17, 1966; Jacqueline Bernard to Mrs. Holliday, New York, NY, October 27, 1966; and Oberia Holliday to Mrs. Bernard, Prairie, MS, December 20, 1966, all found in Box 1, Folder 2, Jacqueline Bernard Papers, 1964–1967, (hereafter Bernard Papers), State Historical Society of Wisconsin, Madison, WI (hereafter WHS).

2. Joel Bernard to Folks, August 1, 1964, Box 1, Folder 1, Bernard Papers. Examples of the correspondence between Jacqueline Bernard and Mississippi activists can found in Box 1, Folders 1–3, Bernard Papers.

3. I refer to the post-Jim Crow era as the period after the passage of the 1964 Civil Rights Act and 1965 Voting Rights Act, both of which struck down major components of legal segregation. Segregation did, of course, persist in many places.

4. Christina Greene, *Our Separate Ways: Women and the Black Freedom Movement in Durham, North Carolina* (Chapel Hill, NC: University of North Carolina Press, 2005), 189.

5. Risa L. Goluboff, *The Lost Promise of Civil Rights* (Cambridge, MA: Harvard University Press, 2007); Robert Korstad and Nelson Lichtenstein, "Opportunities Found and Lost: Labor, Radicals, and the Early Civil Rights Movement," *Journal of American History* 75: 3 (December 1988) 786–811, quoted on 811; Lizabeth Cohen, *A Consumers' Republic: The Politics of Mass Consumption in Postwar America* (New York: Knopf, 2003).

6. Dittmer, *Local People*, 221.

7. "Coop Formed in Madison County, Miss.," *The Student Voice* 6: 5, August 30, 1965, 1; "The Madison County Sewing Firm," Box 2, Folder 14, PPC Records, 1960–1967 (PPC Records), State Historical Society of Wisconsin (SHSW), Madison, WI.

8. Jessie Morris, Interview by Author, March 22, 2010, Jackson, MS (Morris Interview).

9. Letter from Robert L. Beech to Rev. William Carhart, April 22, 1965, Box 1, Folder 2, Robert Beech Papers, 1963–1972, WHS (Beech Papers); For more on SNCC's changing status during the fall of 1964 and into the spring of 1965, see Clayborne Carson, *In Struggle*, especially 133–214.

10. Morris Interview; various correspondence in Box 1, Folder 3, PPC Records.

11. Morris Interview; and "Minutes of the First Membership Meeting of the PPC, 1, Box 1, Folder 7, PPC Records.

12. Minutes of the First Membership Meeting of the PPC, 2.

13. Minutes of the First Membership Meeting of the PPC, 2–3.

14. Minutes of the First Membership Meeting of the PPC, 3–4.

15. Minutes of the First Membership Meeting of the PPC, 2–6.

16. Minutes of the First Membership Meeting of the PPC, 2–5.

17. Minutes of the First Membership Meeting of the PPC, 2–9.

18. Although the organizational bylaws required each member to register, there is no supporting evidence documenting individual or group voting patterns. Mabley, "They Get Just 25c an Hour and Prosper," *Chicago's American*, June 9, 1967, copy in Box 3, Folder 12, Derby Papers; "County Government in Mississippi," October 1966, Box 3, Folder 1, Derby Papers; and Morris Interview.

19. Don Shaw and Martha Kocel to Jessie Morris, Boston, MA, November 15, 1965, Box 1, Folder 3, PPC Records; Dorothy Dewberry to Jessie Morris, October 15, 1965, Detroit, MI, Box 1, Folder 3, PPC Records.

20. Andrew Silver to PPC, Seattle, WA, Undated, Box 1, Folder 5, PPC Records; Letter to Jessie Morris, Washington, DC, October 21, 1965, Box 1, Folder 3, PPC Records; Ann Reery to Friend, Yellow Springs, OH, February 7, 1966, Box 1, Folder 4, PPC Records; Jesse Morris to Ann Reery, Jackson, MS, February 25, 1966, Box 1, Folder 4, PPC Records; Sandra Rudwick to Jessie Morris, Berkeley, CA, September 9, Year Unknown, Box 1, Folder 5, PPC Records.

21. "The Liberty House Co-Operative," 6–7, Organizational Overview and History, Box 2, Folder 12, PPC Records.

22. Ellen Maslow, "Liberty House: A Community Institution," January 10, 1967, Box 2, Folder 5, Derby Papers.

23. "Self-Help Program Grows in Mississippi," *Muhammad Speaks*, date unknown, newspaper clipping in Box 2, Folder 11, Derby Papers.

24. Carol Schmidt, "Seek Outlets for PPC," *Michigan Chronicle*, April 22, 1967, newspaper clipping in Box 3, Folder 11, Derby Papers.

25. Ellen Maslow, "Liberty House: A Community Institution," January 10, 1967, Box 2, Folder 5, Derby Papers; and "Negro-Operated Co-Ops Increase in South," *Chicago Defender*, December 11, 1966, 40.

26. Jack Mabley, "They Get Just 25c an Hour and Prosper," *Chicago's American*, June 9, 1967, copy in Box 3, Folder 12, Derby Papers; and David Llorens, "On the Civil Rights Front," *Negro Digest*, November, 1965, 37; and "Liberty House Markets the 'Crafts of Freedom,'" *Jet*, March 16, 1967, 53.

27. Joan Cook, "Handicrafts of the South Are Offered," *New York Times*, December 22, 1966, 52. For more on Hoffman and his involvement with the PPC, see Jonah Raskin, *For the Hell of It: The Life and Times of Abbie Hoffman* (Berkeley: University of California Press, 1996); and Marty Jezer, *Abbie Hoffman: American Rebel* (New Brunswick, NJ: Rutgers University Press, 1993), especially 42–70.

28. Memo from Doris Derby to PPC Staff, "New York Public Relations-TV Appearances," January 27, 1969, Box 3, Folder 11, Derby Papers.

29. West Coast Publicity Trip Report, Box 3, Folder 11, Derby Papers.

30. Ossie Davis and Ruby Dee, "A Message from Ossie Davis and Ruby Dee," Box 1, Folder 6, PPC Records.

31. Tim Janke to Jessie Morris, Portland, OR, September 27, 1965, Box 1, Folder 3, PPC Records; Jackson P. English, Co-Chairman, Social Concerns Committee, the Unitarian Church of Princeton, NJ, to Liberty House, Princeton, NJ, March 12, 1966, Box 1, Folder 4,

PPC Records; Philip Lubliner, Manager, Secretary-Treasurer, Pocketbook Workers Union, New York, to Liberty House, New York, NY, July 25, 1966, Box 1, Folder 4, PPC Records; Linda M. Henry, PPC New York Coordinator, to Mr. D. John Heyman, December 5, 1966, Box 1, Folder 4, PPC Records.

32. "The Liberty House Co-Operative," 18–19, Organizational Overview and History, Box 2, Folder 12, PPC Records.

33. "The Liberty House Co-Operative," Organizational Overview and History, 12, Box 2, Folder 12, PPC Records.

34. "Liberty House: A Proposal for Cooperative Assistance," 3, Box 3, Folder 19, Derby Papers.

35. Derby quoted in William Raspberry, "Travail of a Cooperative," *Washington Post*, October 1, 1971, A27.

36. "Parting Shots," *LIFE Magazine*, November 6, 1970, 73–76; and "The PPC: Purpose and Structure," Box 3, Folder 14, Derby Papers.

37. "Liberty House: A Proposal for Cooperative Assistance," 5–6, Box 3, Folder 19, Derby Papers.

38. Milne, "Can a Black Co-op Beat Inflation?"

39. "1971 U.S. Corporation Income Tax Return," Box 2, Folder 12, Derby Papers; "1972 U.S. Corporation Income Tax Return," Box 2, Folder 12, Derby Papers; and "1973 U.S. Corporation Income Tax Return," Box 2, Folder 12, Derby Papers.

40. "Education & Training for Co-operatives—A Report," April 25, 1970, Box 2, Folder 7, Derby Papers. The location of the Pecan Praline cooperative is unspecified in this document.

41. Neil A. Maxwell, "Self-Help Struggle: Dixie Negroes Start Co-Ops to Break Their Dependence on Whites," *Wall Street Journal*, August 19, 1966.

42. Robert Korstad and Nelson Lichtenstein, "Opportunities Found and Lost: Labor, Radicals, and the Early Civil Rights Movement," *Journal of American History* 75: 3 (Dec. 1988), 786–811.

43. For more on related cooperatives and small businesses of the 1960s and 1970s, see Joshua Clark Davis, *From Head Shops to Whole Foods: The Rise and Fall of Activist Entrepreneurs* (New York: Columbia University Press, 2017) .

THE DRESS MAKES THE BAND

Used Clothes, Drag Acts, and Bohemians in the Athens, Georgia Music Scene

GRACE ELIZABETH HALE

In the late 1970s and early 1980s, the only way to find the Athens scene in the daytime, before the parties started and the few clubs that booked the new music opened, was to look for the weird clothes. At the hippie café the Eldorado, Fred Schneider of the B-52's waited on tables wearing a hard hat with a flashing light on his head and offered up ironic little sayings along with the food. On Broad Street at Russo's Gyro Wrap, the first place in town with a sidewalk café, Jerry Ayers, a member of the band Limbo District, wore a ragged jacket and a battered fedora as he sat outside sipping espresso and writing in a journal. After 1981, when the city lined a block of College Street with shade trees, raised beds, and benches, young people wearing old suit jackets, men's work and dress shirts, suspenders, baggy pants, fifties dresses, and work boots stapled band flyers to the kiosks or talked and ate lunch among the alternately preppy and hippie University of Georgia students. Scene-makers used their thrift-store style to write their difference on the public spaces of their tiny college town in northeast Georgia like graffiti artists marking the hip hop scene on New York's boroughs by tagging the trains.[1]

Athens was an unlikely location for a new bohemia, and yet a group of small-town and suburban, mostly white and middle-class kids nurtured a music and art scene there that grew into an important site of alternative culture in Reagan's America. In 1981, Michael Lachowski, bassist in the band Pylon captured the reaction of people outside Athens to the new music being made there for a reporter for the *Atlanta Constitution*: "They're freaked out, especially in the States, that bands with any measure of sophistication should come from a small Southern town." A few of the groups they formed—the B-52's, R.E.M., and Widespread Panic—became famous. Other bands including Pylon, the Method Actors, Oh OK, Mercyland, and the singer-songwriter

Vic Chesnutt achieved success as critics' darlings or musicians' musicians without ever breaking through to a mass audience. Most bands played parties and local clubs, recorded, toured, and put out their music themselves or on independent labels in relative obscurity. Together, all these Athens musicians and other locals who wrote about and photographed them, made band flyers and album covers, ran clubs, and turned out for shows helped create the shifting and related genres of college, alternative, and indie rock.[2]

More broadly, in opting out of the politics, popular culture, and ways of dressing, eating, and living that dominated middle-class, suburban America, Athens musicians and their fans built a rich alternative culture. Unlike past American bohemians who gathered in neighborhoods in cities like New York and San Francisco, they rooted their scene in a small college town in a region still understood in that historical moment as a haven for white supremacists and the opposite of underground or avant-garde. Acting out with the materials readily available, they wore secondhand clothes, played pawn shop instruments, collected used records, read old books, lived in historic houses, and watched television reruns and classic movies. This creativity produced a local culture that prized amateur, do-it-yourself production over professionalism, formal originality or emotional intensity over craft, and reworking the old rather than celebrating the new. Athens bohemians drank too much, tried most drugs, and had sex not just with the people they were dating but with their friends and people they met at clubs or parties and both same and opposite sex partners. They made play in opposition to work their measure of the good life. In the process, they reimagined bohemia as small town, local culture and helped preserve the very concept of "alternative."[3]

In Athens, used and visibly out-of-style clothing functioned as a badge of bohemianism, a way for people to communicate their alternative identity to others. Less visibly, wearing old dresses, shirts, jackets, pants, and shoes actually helped these middle-class suburban and small town kids remake themselves as bohemians. Like childhood dress-up games, Halloween, and school theatricals, trying on odd garments and putting them together to create different styles enabled people to play with alternate identities. Clothing framed the edge of the self, for the wearer as much as for the people she encountered in town, at work, or in class. Qualities like the texture, feel, color, and shape of a garment and the way it enabled or constricted movement, exaggerated or veiled gender and sexuality, and conveyed casualness or formality could make the wearer feel bold, brave, and different, ready to try something new. Used clothing was easy to acquire and cheap, less expensive than using the laundromat. At the Potter's House Thrift Store on Washington

Street, patrons could dig through the pile in the back room and buy anything they could stuff in a brown paper grocery sack for a quarter and then later a dollar. Scene participants became bohemians by dressing up.[4]

Boys in Dresses

Long before Athens was anything but a sleepy southern college town, Jerry Ayers did what young people whose creative ambitions were too big for their hometowns did before the 1980s—he moved to New York. When Andy Warhol photographed him there, around 1970, he was hanging out at Warhol's studio the Factory and had remade himself as a drag queen, the Warhol superstar Silva Thin. In Warhol's Polaroid, Thin's pose was jaunty, a brash kind of feminine, the Audrey Hepburn–end of 1940s stardom. His two-toned, feminine jacket parted to reveal high-waisted pants and half a "Y" of the leather fastener of a set of suspenders. A brown scarf knotted at his neck topped a dark blouse that tied close to reveal a dagger of bare skin. Longish natural hair swept loosely back and deep red lipstick traced his heart-shaped mouth. Dark eye shadow covered his lids and natural browline under faked brows that arched high, while white eyeliner beneath his eyes added a theatrical touch. Thin's left hand in his pocket cocked his right hip forward, as he bent his right arm at the elbow and again at the wrist, holding a cigarette sexily in his long, thin fingers. The crotch of the pants, pulled upward by the suspenders, revealed the barest curve of a bulge. Together, the clothing, the makeup, and the pose produced an androgynous look, an image simultaneously masculine and feminine, unassignable to either category, queer.[5]

In the late 1960s and 1970s, drag queens and other gender nonconforming artists and entertainers helped create new movements like pop art and performance art. Because it was difficult, sometimes illegal, and expensive for men to buy women's clothes for themselves, drag queens helped invent and popularize thrift store style, picking through used clothing to discover something so out-of-style and fabulous that it could be presented as original, as new in terms of fashion if not ownership. At the Factory, Silva Thin hung out with more famous drag queens and Warhol superstars Jackie Curtis, Candy Darling, and Holly Woodlawn. He played a small role in Curtis' musical *Vain Victory*, which starred Darling. And he interviewed the San Francisco drag troupe the Cockettes—a group of gay and straight men and women who invented a kind of psychedelic Victorian gender-bending—about their visit to New York for the February 1972 issue of Warhol's *Interview* magazine. Thin also traveled to Europe during this period and appeared in an advertisement in the French version of *Vogue*, photographed by Chris von Wagenheim, who had also worked for *Interview*. In the early seventies, Thin embraced what people at the time were beginning to call "genderfuck," a form of drag in which people played with gender and sexual codes to call attention to the fact that men and women could be women and men, that identity was fluid and about performance rather than anatomy. Genderfuck positioned androgyny as a radical act.[6]

In New York, Thin kept in touch with his younger gay friends back home, Keith Strickland and Ricky Wilson. Still in high school, Strickland and Wilson took the Greyhound to the city to visit him. In the bus station bathroom, they changed into drag and then went straight to the Factory. With Thin, they hung out with Darling, Curtis, and Woodlawn and soaked up the downtown scene. In the mid-seventies, when Warhol turned away from drag queens and embraced the uptown Studio 54 crowd, Thin moved back to Athens where his father still worked as a University of Georgia professor. By then, Strickland and Wilson had returned home from Europe, where Wilson had studied in Germany while Strickland worked. Reunited in Athens, the three men and other friends including Fred Schneider, Robert Waldrop, a University of Georgia art student, Kate Pierson, a former folksinger who had lived in England, and Wilson's younger sister Cindy Wilson began dressing up and acting out around town. Schneider was so openly gay that he shocked everyone, running around town in only a speedo. Strickland went to campus events and parties wearing a purple "yak" wig or a Mack truck mirror around his neck like a giant pendant. Pierson and her then husband Brian Cocaine set up living room furniture—a sofa, a chair, and a rug—at the intersection of College and Broad and sat and watched the traffic. Together, the band of friends invaded a neighborhood Mardi Gras parade in mime makeup and mismatched Victorian-looking clothing and ended up in a photo spread in the local paper. Another time, Ricky Wilson hauled his reel-to-reel tape player out to a country field and played a tape of African tribal music that one of them had borrowed from the UGA library. As the friends danced in the grass, a circle of cows drew close and bobbed their heads to the music. As Pierson recalled years later, repeating what became a mantra of Athens bohemianism, "We had to make our own fun."[7]

In the mid-seventies, before heading to the Potter's House, Strickland and Wilson listened to records and looked at photographs of Bowie, Alice Cooper, and the New York Dolls for inspiration. At Wilson and Strickland's ramshackle old house on Pulaski, they pieced together costumes out of secondhand clothes, jewelry, and wigs and practiced their album art poses. Together with Ayers and Waldrop, they transformed used party dresses into fabulous costumes and wore them to a disco called the Circus. Woodlawn even came down from New York City to visit. Like Ayers at the Factory, these Athens friends were not dressing up to create a seamless illusion. They were not trying to be women. Instead, embracing androgyny, a space where male and female visually met, the guys put on used women's clothing, wigs, and makeup without shaving their faces or their legs. A few women sometimes joined in, dressing like men in long-sleeved shirts, suit coats, and ties, like punk musician Patti Smith on the cover of her 1975 album *Horses*.[8]

Historically, drag or dressing up in ways that self-consciously play with gender and sexuality has enabled practitioners to comment on these categories as well as culture and politics more broadly. Highlighting contradictions, performing the fact that the act is an act, drag questions the relationship between reality and illusion, original and copy, and authenticity and artifice. As part of camp, a set of cultural practices and sensibilities that extend beyond cross-dressing, drag produces new meanings, new identities, and new ways of feeling out of images, stories, and artifacts understood as out of date or fake or even trashy. In New York, Ayers as Thin had participated in a scene that blurred the lines between the avant-garde art world, burlesque shows, and underground networks of alternative sexualities. In this context, a great variety of people questioning gender and sexual conventions—men and women who would later identify as gay, bisexual, transgender, or gender nonconforming—played with drag. Dressing up, they created an aesthetic logic that suggested that there might not be any difference between reality and performance.[9]

In Athens, drag worked as a solvent, a playful way of dissolving conventions and categories, a "fun" form of rebellion, as people cross-dressed for drag-themed house parties, Halloween, and art school parties and openings. Drag pushed the experimentation that happened in apartments, classrooms, and studios into the streets. It linked out gay locals and students to other Athens residents and students questioning sexualities and other cultural norms, creating a very queer, sexually open and experimental scene. And it sent people rummaging through the racks and shelves at thrift stores and yard sales, the castoffs of popular cultures now past, for ideas and materials, making it cool to reject "the new" in a search for original music, art, or style.[10]

When Strickland, Ricky and Cindy Wilson, Pierson, and Schneider debuted as the B-52's at a 1977 Valentine's Day house party, the group was more like a punk version of the Cockettes—a drag-infused, pop-art influenced, theatrical review—than a band in any traditional sense. When it was time for the show to start, band members came out of a back room where they had dressed in secret. Strickland wore his infamous purple yak wig, Ricky Wilson parodied a collegiate look, then out of style but soon to be resurrected as "preppy," and Schneider sported a wife-beater tee and a huge moustache. What people in the small audience crowded into that living room most remembered, however, was the naked Barbie doll tied by a string to a light socket and the transformed appearance of Cindy Wilson and Pierson. Frizzed platinum blond wigs surrounded their heads like giant, fake-fur halos, made all the more visible by the contrast offered by their black blouses. The music, except that both performers and audience members danced, seemed secondary to the look. Though Ricky Wilson played guitar and Strickland played drums live, much of the music was prerecorded. Cindy Wilson, Schneider, and Pierson used toy instruments to add sound effects to a tape played on the same machine that had captivated the cows. Like the Ramones, a band they admired that took the lessons of drag reviews and impersonated sixties leather boys and their crude garage-rock sound instead of Hollywood starlets, the members of the B-52's blew up the boundary between homage and parody. They reenacted what they loved, their own collage of fifties and sixties pop culture themes, moves, and sounds. Their friend John Taylor named the style they invented "thrift store rock."[11]

Boys in dresses remained common in Athens over the years. Scene participants remember drag parties and produce the snapshots to prove it: Mike Green of Atlanta punk band the Fans and later Athens band Boat Of wearing a turquoise chiffon blouse and satin skirt, pink sunglasses, makeup and a wig; David Gamble of the Method Actors bare from the waist up except for a bra and cat-eye sunglasses; and Nicky Gianaris of the Tone Tones posing in a leopard-print minidress, opening his painted, pouting lips to display his tongue. Members of the band Love Tractor, including Mark Cline, Armistead Welford, and Mike Richmond, sometimes performed in drag, and by the mid-eighties, young men wearing dresses waited tables and worked the bar and the door at Athens coffee shops, cafes, and clubs. *New York Rocker* photographer Laura Levine visited Athens in fall of 1983 and shot a Super 8 film, *Just Like a Movie*, featuring Matthew Sweet of Oh OK, Michael Stipe and Bill Berry of R.E.M., and their friend Chris Slay in dresses.[12] R.E.M. guitarist Pete Buck practiced a subtler drag. When he was a student at Emory, he bought Patti Smith's album *Horses* because he liked the "arty" way Smith looked on the cover. "I wore Patti Smith jackets, and I even had a barber give me a Patti-Smith haircut." Smith had created the look that Buck copied through her own drag act, by copying male rock stars like Keith Richards. Buck did not need a dress to act like a woman who was acting like man.[13]

Ayers introduced drag practices to successive waves of Athens bands. Along with Robert Waldrop, he helped shape the B-52's visual image and wrote the lyrics for some of their early songs. Ayers' "52 Girls," for example, appeared as the B side of the B-52's first single. On the surface, the song presented a list of women's names, old starlets and tv characters, the slain president's wife "Jacki-O," a Warhol favorite, and "Kate" and "Cindy," the women in the band. Yet the words, like a drag show, played a game of hide and seek, and whether these girls were women because they were born with female anatomy or because they wore dresses and skirts was unclear. As Mark Cline remembered, Ayers "was a huge influence on us, how we dressed, how we looked, how we formed our bands, how we made music. We all wanted to be like him."[14]

By the late 1970s, Ayers was working a different form of drag, as much in opposition to the traditional codes of heterosexual manhood as his old superstar act. In opposition to hippie excess and yuppie success, he modeled ragged and flapping failure, a style the *Village Voice* called more than a decade later when it was still an alternative culture staple, "Boho as hobo." In worn fedoras and work caps, ragged suit jackets and pants, and cracked brogans or work boots, he looked like a copy of a copy, a contemporary version of a sixties folk music fan's fantasy of a Depression era working-class man. He even played a magical version of this hobo figure in Laura Levine's 1983 movie. Drag as playing with gender was still there, though, most powerfully in Ayers' affect. Cool and constrained, Ayers hung back at the edges. He whispered, and people had to lean in to hear. He made self-effacement sexy. Emotionally, he played "the girl." Michael Stipe would take up this act in the 1980s and use it to become a star.[15]

Girls in Drag

In the early 1970s, when members of the B-52's were inventing a radical kind of pop-art punk, they came up with a brilliant innovation. For people who knew anything about underground drag theatricals, the quotations were clear: wigs or their own elaborate, teased, and styled hair; dramatic make-up; and used clothing repurposed as glamourous costumes. The B-52's put the drag act on the women. In this way, a band with a very queer sensibility made up of three gay men, one heterosexual woman, and one bisexual woman managed to bypass the widespread homophobia of the late 1970s and early 1980s, release albums on major label Warner Brothers, and achieve a level of popularity outside the world of underground music.[16]

Long before the B-52's became famous, Georgia State students used their campus television station's video equipment to tape an early 1978 show in Atlanta. As the concert started, Schneider introduced the band members like an emcee announcing the stage names of drag queens, with Cindy Wilson as "Cinderella," Strickland as "formerly Pebbles," and Pierson as "Swoop Bag Nell." Then the band broke into a ragged and dissonant "Rock Lobster," more a piece of musical theater with an extended demonstration of strange dances and animal noises than the later version that became a hit song. As Ricky Wilson's guitar and Pierson's organ with their sci-fi soundtrack parts and Schneider, Pierson, and Cindy Wilson's vocals made clear, aliens—queers and drag queens—had taken over the teen beach party. Crossing racial boundaries as well as gendered and sexual ones, Wilson and Pierson performed like queens performing a drag version of a sixties girl group, white women playing white men playing African American or Latina women. While Pierson shimmied in a printed and buttoned-up sleeveless shirt with a Peter Pan collar and Cindy Wilson shook it down in her prim and belted Sunday dress, the drag came out as much in the vocals and the moves as the clothes. Sharing a mic, they danced just a little too stiffly and sang, sometimes, just a little off key. Wilson's loud and dissonant cackles about midway through the song hit just short of hysteria. Pierson's hi-pitched "ah's" at the end mimicked a man's falsetto version of a high female voice. In this Downtown Café performance, Cindy Wilson and Kate Pierson played the drag queens.

Early scene participants' embrace of drag shaped the context in which women in Athens began wearing what people were just beginning to call vintage dresses. In the late nineteenth century, African American men began blacking up, putting black face paint on their dark faces, in order to compete with white blackface acts whose coon songs, blackface theatricals, cakewalks, and comic skits and speeches dominated the popular stage. By doubling their race, by pretending to be white men pretending to be black men and women, they found a way to critique whites while also gaining access to the lucrative business of entertaining white audiences. Within the queer sensibility of the early Athens scene, women wearing old and outdated female clothing were dressing up like men dressing up like women, performing masculinity like blacked-up black men performed whiteness. In the late 1970s and early 1980s in the South, white women rarely performed rock music on local stages. At the same time, female college students—in that moment before the preppy fad brought back sundresses—mostly wore tee-shirts and jeans. Despite the brave presence of a small number of outspoken feminists, Athens college-town culture then appeared little changed by second-wave feminism. The federal government, for example, had to force the University of Georgia to hire women as tenure-track and tenured professors in the 1970s. Punk rock, too, despite pioneers like Patti Smith, was not much more open to women than mainstream rock. Within these constraints, wearing vintage dresses and other old items of women's clothing enabled women to play with masculinity and power.[17]

From the earliest days of the scene, women sometimes wore men's clothes to the same kinds of parties and events that men wore dresses. Art students Margaret Katz and Debbie McMahon, for example, copied Patti Smith's *Horses* era style and dressed like men in identical white shirts and dark ties in the photograph art student John Martin Taylor shot for the poster for their September 1977 exhibition of paintings, drawings, and prints at the local Lyndon House Galleries. Many female scene participants wore men's suit jackets and shirts over long-john pants or leggings. Michael Stipe's close friend Lynda Hopper, who founded the band Oh OK with Michael's sister Lynda Stipe, cross-dressed as a man for Laura Levine's film. More often, Hopper—like her bandmate Lynda Stipe—wore vintage dresses. Doubling down on gender—wearing women's clothing on visibly female bodies—enabled two young women just learning to perform to play with the contradiction between their girlish look, sound, lyrics, and amateurism and the power inherent in the position of fronting a band. Hopper and Lynda Stipe, however, did not have to figure out how to perform this act on their own. No one in Athens worked the woman-in-drag persona—a woman pretending to be a man pretending to be a woman—better than Vanessa Ellison, later Vanessa Briscoe Hay, frontwoman and singer for the next Athens band after the B-52's to win acclaim with critics and fans of underground music, Pylon.

In person, Briscoe Hay was shy and spoke with a soft southern accent. On stage, she thrust her curvy body and alternately moaning, screaming, and chanting voice so far into the mic that, like the young Elvis Presley, she seemed to be making love to the device. In August 1981, when Pylon played Danceteria, a New York dance club that also showcased live bands, video artists Emily Armstrong and Pat Ivers who programmed the video lounge there used their equipment to record some of Pylon's show. As the band launched into their song "Danger," Briscoe Hay stared at the audience, her eyes barely visible under a thatch of brown bangs, hissing "ssssss," like a snake or a machine valve, and chanting phrases like "the sound of danger."

She wore a church dress gone wrong, its color a bit faded and its shape a little soft, and a whistle instead of a necklace. As she shook and twirled her head to the slowly building beat, a limp lace sleeve slipped down her shoulder. Her facial expressions alternated between lack and excess, an underplaying that suggested choked amateurism and an overplaying that evoked the entwined histories of drag and blackface. As the song built, Briscoe Hay began spinning like a windup whirling dervish, slowing down and speeding up according the tension in her spring. Her dress and her moves accentuated her breasts and hips. Her accent was somehow flat and yet also lushly southern. Her vocal style and her moves quoted Patti Smith's androgyny and the arty shock and awe of Yoko Ono as filtered through Cindy Wilson and Kate Pierson. Her performance conjured a world in which drag queens and southern beauty queens were one.[18]

Fronting Pylon and acting like a man acting like a woman, Briscoe Hay came off as both feminine and powerful. In a photograph taken by *New York Rocker* staff photographer Laura Levine, Briscoe Hay stood tall with her arms outstretched, holding out the swirling skirt of her vintage dress like wings. Beneath her on the floor sat her three male bandmates Michael Lachowski, Curtis Crowe, and Randy Bewley, looking like her puppets or her young. The critic Van Gosse described her performance style for the *Village Voice*: "She was certainly not yet a spandex tinkertoy. Shoeless with whistle, in parochial-school blue smock and white blouse, large, nonalluring, but quite hypnotic, she shook it down most gravely, (a real modern dance) and bestrode the stage like a tigress summoning her prey, growling and biting the air." Briscoe Hay taught women in Athens that women could work drag's exaggerated femininity as well or better than the boys to generate their own authority and control over an audience. In the right context, vintage dresses could work like superhero costumes, simultaneously granting and advertising their wearers' power.[19]

Androgynous

Playing with gender and sexuality and questioning conventions did not have to mean wearing a dress. Drag could make use of other kinds of clothing and other mediums of public presentation. Jerry Ayers had given up drag as the act of wearing women's clothes as the Athens music scene emerged in the wake of the B-52's' success, but he kept drag's hide-and-seek, cover-and-reveal logic and its emphasis on layering. In the bohemian hobo persona he would practice through the 1980s, Ayers continued his pop-art influenced performance practice, erasing the distinction between exterior and interior, surface and depth, image and inner self. He changed his name to Jeremy and stopped talking about the Factory and Warhol. And he worked an affect conventionally defined as feminine, asserting himself through denial, through being quiet, hanging back and moving at the margins. People who wanted to know him had to work for the privilege. They had to seek him out. They had to watch him and listen carefully. They had to be quiet too.

Sometime in the late fall of 1979 or winter of 1980, Michael Stipe met Ayers. That same winter, Stipe began playing music with two UGA students, Bill Berry and Mike Mills, and a record store clerk and sometime UGA night-school student Pete Buck. R.E.M. debuted at an Athens party in April, playing a ragged mix of original songs and covers like the Sex Pistols' "God Save the Queen." Particularly memorable given the drag roots of the scene was the new band's sloppy, extended version of Patti Smith's version of Van Morrison's "Gloria." From the start, R.E.M. mined Buck's record collection, picking quirky and often obscure songs to fill out their gigs. They also wrote a batch of original songs that sounded so much like the music of sixties garage bands that listeners who knew their rock history, not as easy to come by in those days before iTunes and Spotify, could not tell if the new band was playing their own or other musicians' songs. Their covers and their originals that sounded like covers got the new band in trouble with many of the art-student founders of the Athens scene. As Curtis Crowe, the drummer for Pylon, remembered, "At the time, the whole art school party crowd had this thing about cover songs. We were on the 'leading edge of a musical revolution[,]' and we thought playing cover songs was taking two steps back[,] and everyone kind of put their nose in the air about it." Yet Crowe, like many locals who saw R.E.M. play during their first few months as a band, also remembered being impressed—the music "had a lot of energy about it."[20]

At the time, the guys in R.E.M. did not publicly admit being bothered by this local reception, yet their statements to the press in 1982 and afterward as they became more successful made clear in retrospect that their reputation as "unoriginal" hurt. It also cut the band off from the model for making it as a band established by the B-52's—work Ayers's and other locals' connections, play New York, put out a single with University of Georgia graduate and then Atlanta record-store owner Danny Beard's label DB Records, and win enough support from New York underground critics, promoters, and fans to tour and make more records. And unlike Buck, Berry, and Mills, Stipe was an art student at UGA. He took classes with the people who formed what

Crowe called "the art school party crowd" and ran into them at exhibitions and shows. He wanted to be an artist, and his friendship with Ayers provided him with a model.[21]

Through the summer and fall of 1980 and the winter of 1981, Stipe gradually adopted many aspects of Ayers' persona—his layered, ragged old clothing, his quiet way of cultivating mystery, and his androgyny. He picked up Ayers' habit of writing down overheard snatches of conversations in a journal. Halfway through 1980, Stipe began working these phrases and other ambiguous, poetic language into song lyrics. That summer, sitting on a couch or mattress in the yard in front of an old church where some of them then lived, band members wrote "Gardening at Night," a song they later called their first "real" song and that they admired enough to name their publishing business Night Garden Music. Unlike the words he wrote for earlier songs like "A Different Girl," Stipe here crafted the kind of mysterious narrative that would characterize the songs the band recorded for their EP and first few albums. Over the years, band members offered multiple explanations for the meaning of the lyrics for "Gardening at Night." As Peter Buck explained to Q magazine in 1992, "There was an old guy in my neighbourhood [sic] who would be out gardening at 2 a.m. in his suit and tie. I'd see him when I was out trying to get a beer at the Magic Mart or somewhere. It's basically a metaphor for the uselessness of everything." Band members also described the song as a reference to urinating outside at night, a frequent practice as they drove their dirty Dodge van across first the Southeast and then much of the rest of the eastern half of the nation, playing any club, bar, pizza parlor, or disco's new wave night that would have them. Around the same time, Stipe collaborated with Ayers in the writing of "Windout," one of two R.E.M. songs on which Ayers received a cowriting credit.[22]

Though Stipe rarely appeared on stage in a dress, from around 1981 forward, he often wore layers of androgynous clothing. He started with one or more t-shirts and then buttoned long-sleeved shirts over those and over each other, creating doubled and tripled collars and multiple sets of flapping sleeves. He also pulled old pajama pants and baggy suit pants over slimmer old work pants. As he performed, he methodically stripped off his clothing piece by piece, in a kind of striptease that left him dripping sweat from his blond ringlets and last soaked tee. The undecipherability of Stipe's words—he increasingly wrote ambiguous lyrics and blurred his pronunciation as he sang—created an aural style that matched his androgynous clothes.[23]

A video of the band playing the song "Wolves, Lower" on October 10, 1982, at the Pier in Raleigh, North Carolina, demonstrated the subtle ways Stipe incorporated used clothing and the hide and seek layering and ambiguity of drag into his early performances. The song started with Stipe speaking the words "mirror" and "flower" as Bill Berry pounded a four-four beat, an opening that owed a great deal to Pylon, despite R.E.M. members' insistence that they were not influenced by other Athens bands. As Buck on guitar and Mike Mills on bass joined in and the music built in volume, Stipe made two indecipherable sounds before gasping out "ehhhhhhh." Stepping away from the mic, the singer bounced as he continued dancing, his body spinning in a circle horizontally as it also flowed vertically, as if some spark started at his head and worked its way rhythmically down to his feet. Low in his range, Stipe sang, "Suspicion yourself / suspicion yourself / don't get caught." Then he almost repeated himself: "Suspicion yourself / suspicion yourself / let us out." He stayed low, almost growling, as he continued, "While the lower wolves / here's a house to put / wolves at the door." As the song progressed, Berry increased the tempo. At the chorus, Stipe pushed his voice higher as Mills and Berry joined in. Together, they sang, "House in order," and Stipe answered in a falling then rising series of syllables, "Ah / Ah / Ah / Ah / Ah." Through most of the song, Stipe left Mills and Berry to sing the chorus as a call while he waited and answered alone with the response.[24]

At the end of the first chorus, Buck played his guitar close to Stipe as the singer popped his eyes wide and smirked in what could only be described as a leer. Buck looked down, smiled, and moved away. Stipe and Buck flirted like Mick Jagger and Keith Richards in the sixties, a once radical and then tired gesture somehow revived by R.E.M.'s homage, Stipe's androgyny, and Buck's drag—his Patti Smith influenced version of Richards. Onstage and off, Stipe crafted a sexual identity as consciously indecipherable as his lyrics. Unlike the male members of the B-52's—Fred Schneider, Ricky Wilson, Keith Strickland—and Michael Lachowski of Pylon, Stipe did not claim a gay identity either publicly or privately, though his friends knew he had sex with both men and women. He did not speak publicly about his sexuality until 1994.[25]

Throughout the set at the Pier, Stipe was charismatic. His supple body speeded up and slowed down, in and out of sync with the rhythm, a flowing version of Briscoe Hay's snapping twirls. He wore eye makeup and a layered sorority jersey (another kind of women's clothing) under a baggy suit jacket with a scarf hanging out of the pocket. Channeling Briscoe's take on male rock moves, Stipe mouthed the microphone and made love to the stand, moaning what could be words in an unknown tongue or sounds of pleasure. Buck wore mascara and a cut off black t-shirt, and by a few songs in his dark curly hair hung in his eyes in wet tendrils. Mills, on the other hand, expressed little emotion. He wore a white long-sleeved, button-up shirt with French flapping sleeves and short, straight bangs that revealed a lot of forehead as he played bass like a guitar. He came across as a mash-up of nerdy new waver and earnest folk revivalist, the eighties version of the sixties' Pete Seeger. The vocal harmonies of Stipe, Mills, and Berry sounded simultaneously sweet, transgressive, and sexy, male voices merging like the singing of a Motown girl group (a form also worked by the B-52's), men playing women and also perhaps playing too close, playing around. Channeled through the women of the B-52's and Pylon, R.E.M.'s drag made rock masculinity seem real again.[26]

The January 17, 1983, issue of *People* included a brief description of the Athens music scene and a full-page photograph the magazine, labeled a "family portrait." A sloppy pyramid of people squinted into the sun as they sat on the sidewalk and the base of a Revolutionary War monument in a narrow median flanked on both sides by Broad Street. A dull, Deep South winter sky took up more than a third of the photo, pierced only by the shaft of an obelisk, glowing white against the gray. The point of the monument and parts of some people's feet were missing. Inches away from the crowd, cars drove into and out of the frame. The awkwardness of the photograph's composition and framing highlighted the awkwardness of the self-conscious crowd in which seasoned bohemians, ex-hippies, and crashers mixed with band members who snuck out of square jobs, hoping to make the shoot.[27]

Invited to represent the Athens scene for *People*, some people brought musical instruments—a banjo, a tambourine, an accordion, a clarinet, basses, and guitars. Michael Lachowski of the band Pylon lifted up a toy ray gun. Tim Lacy of the band Art in the Dark grasped a stick topped with what looked like the head of spider man. Others dressed up in their thrift-store best. In the center of the foreground, Velena Vego wore a conical straw hat, a tourist or stage production's version of the kind of headgear a person might wear to tend rice in a Vietnam paddy, over a fifties-era plaid church dress, fishnet stockings, and old, low-heeled leather pumps. To her left, Armistead Wellford of Love Tractor wore a plaid work shirt over worn jeans held up by suspenders and scuffed brogans. Al Walsh of the Squalls clenched a pipe in his teeth. Behind him, Davey Stephenson, then Limbo District bandmate and boyfriend of Jerry Ayers, wore his own version of the boho hobo look, a white shirt, a bow tie, and a battered fedora. And in the center, barely visible through the hand he used to shade his face, still simultaneously hiding and revealing himself in a battered old man's hat and an ancient, oversized coat, stood the person who started it all, Jerry Ayers.

The late 1970s and early 1980s were not an easy time to be a bohemian in the deep South. The rise of the religious right, the election of Reagan, the AIDS epidemic, and stubbornly persistent white supremacy, sexism, and homophobia pushed white young people to conform across the region. Questioning all the givens—the middle-class values, cultural taste, and gender and sexual norms that people had grown up, was difficult. It meant making new, conscious choices and risking loss. It took courage. White frat boys and rednecks and young African American men yelled "faggot" at anyone who looked different and sometimes followed up their threats with their fists. Employers refused to hire and fired people for wearing secondhand clothes. Middle-class parents stopped paying college tuition and cut off contact. Thrift store style—life as a kind of bohemian, anti-middle-class drag act—did not just announce to the world that the wearer had succeeded in casting off their old life. Dressing up also helped them to get there.

Notes

Material from this essay appeared in a different format in *Cool Town: Athens, Georgia, and the Promise of Alternative Culture in Reagan's America* (Chapel Hill: University of North Carolina Press, 2020). We use it here with the kind permission of the author and the University of North Carolina Press.

1. Bob Hay, "Memories of Eldorado: The Athens Eatery Where the Squalls, B-52s Once Worked," *Eldridge ATL* (July 14, 2016), http://www.eldredgeatl.com/2016/07/14/memories-of-eldorado-the-athens-eatery-where-the-squalls-b-52s-once-worked/, accessed September 23, 2016. Denise Sullivan, *R.E.M.: Talk about the Passion, an Oral History* (New York: Da Capo Press, 1998), 6. The best book published on the Athens scene is Rodger Lyle Brown's *Party Out of Bounds: The B-52's, R.E.M., and the Kids Who Rocked Athens, Georgia, 25th Anniversary Edition* (Athens: University of Georgia Press, 2016). A narrative history of the early eighties, Lyle calls his work "a book-length folktale that I have spun out of the slush and muck of many gathered half-remembered and misbegotten memories" and does an excellent job of capturing the spirit of the era, even if the participants in the parties he describes disagree now about the details. Like Brown, though in a later period, I was a minor participant in this scene in the second half of the 1980s. See also Blake Gumprecht, *The American College Town* (Amherst: University of Massachusetts Press, 2008), 189–226.

Writing the book from which this article is drawn has required constructing an archive. I have used the newspaper clipping files on music and musicians, art and artists, and politics in Athens in the University of Georgia's Hargrett Rare Book and Manuscript Library. I have also used the records related to UGA's college radio station WUOG and other scattered materials. The UGA libraries also house the *Red and Black Collection*, the archives of the student newspaper, and copies of local papers like the *Athens Banner-Herald* and the *Athens Observer*. I have located all surviving issues of local fanzines and newspapers, including most importantly *Tasty World Magazine* (early 1980s) and the earliest issues of *Flagpole* (began publishing in 1987) on World Cat and through private holdings. I have worked in the Lyndon House Art Center's unprocessed collection of catalogs, photographs, and slides, documenting its annual juried art show, an event central to the local visual arts scene. I have drawn on the online materials collected for and at the Athens Rewind reunion event held in 2005. I have also interviewed about one hundred participants in the scene and also used interviews, remembrances, photographs videos, audio recordings, and flyers posted on blogs and comment sections of social media sites and published in online journals and magazines.

2. Bill King, "Athens: A City Attuned to a New Wave-length," *Atlanta Journal Constitution* (August 30, 1981), 1F, 6F; and Art Harris, "O' Little Town of Rock 'n' Roll," *Washington Post* (August 29, 1984), B1. On the history of punk, post-punk, new wave, and college, alternative, or indie rock, see Legs McNeil and Gillian McCain, *Please Kill Me: The Uncensored Oral History of Punk* (New York: Grove Press, 1996); Clinton Heylin, *From the Velvets to the Voidoids: A Pre-Punk History for a Post-Punk World* (New York: Penguin, 1993); and Heylin, *Babylon's Burning: From Punk to Grunge* (New York: Cononogate, 2007): Dick Hebdige, *Subculture: The Meaning of Style* (New York: Routledge, 1979); Simon Firth, *Sound Effects: Youth, Leisure, and the Politics of Rock 'n' Roll* (New York: Pantheon, 1981); Simon Reynolds, *Rip It Up and Start Again: Postpunk 1978–1984* (New York: Penguin, 2006); Barry Shank, *Dissonant Identities: The Rock'n'Roll Scene in Austin, Texas* (Hanover: Wesleyan University Press, 1994); and Theo Cateforis, *Are We Not New Wave? Modern Pop at the Turn of the 1980s* (Ann Arbor: University of Michigan, 2011).

3. Participants in the Athens music scene were mostly but not entirely white and mostly but not entirely middle-class in family background. In the wake of the civil rights movement and the global success of southern rock as a genre, self-consciously bohemian or underground music fans were thrilled to find something that was forward looking, unconventional, antiracist, and gay that was also southern. Elsewhere in the larger project, I address the role of race in eighties underground music. On understanding bohemia as the anti-middle-class, see the classic Jerrold Seigel, *Bohemian Paris: Culture, Politics, and the Boundaries of Bourgeoisie Life, 1830–1930* (New York: Viking, 1986).

4. On the history of wearing used clothing in the US, see the pioneering Jennifer LeZotte, *From Goodwill to Grunge: A History of Secondhand Styles and Alternative Economies* (Chapel Hill: University of North Carolina Press, 2017).

5. Andy Warhol, *Silva Thin*, circa 1970, a unique polaroid print mounted on board, for sale at Christies June 16–25, 2015, as part of a lot called "Andy's Randy Summer," https://onlineonly.christies.com/s/andy-warhol-christies-andys-randy-summer/silva-thin-40/17910#, accessed October 15, 2015.

6. Silva Thin, "Interview with the Cockettes," *Interview* (February 1972), 47–49; and Silva Thin in Jackie Curtis, *Vain Victory*, clip of 1972 performance online at https://www.youtube.com/watch?v=a-9SilkF4ZI, accessed October 15, 2015 (Ayers appears at around 1:40); and Silva Thin, "Theater: Interview with the Cockettes," February 1972, 48–49. The fashion photographer Chris von Wagenheim shot Silva Thin for Vogue. See Mauricio and Roger Padilha, *Gloss: The Work of Chris von Wagenheim* (New York: Rizzoli, 2015). On genderfuck, see Laud Humphreys, *Out of the Closets: Sociology of Homosexual Liberation* (Englewood Cliffs: Prentice-Hall, 1972), 164; and Tom Burke, "Gays in Arms: The Violet Millennium,"

Rolling Stone (August 30, 1973), on the new "macho" transvestitism and drag as satire of female impersonation, men in dresses, makeup, heels, and beards. On drag queens shopping for secondhand and "genderfuck," see LeZotte, *From Goodwill to Grunge*, 183–238; and the documentary film Jennie Livingston, *Paris Is Burning* (1990), shot in the 1980s in New York City. I thank LeZotte, formerly my graduate student at UVA, for introducing me, via her own important research, to the Cockettes.

7. Bennet interview, Cline interview, Welford interview, Seawright interview, McLaughlin interview; John Martin Taylor, "The B-52's and Me," on *Hoppin' John's: John Martin Taylor's Personal Blog*, http://hoppinjohns.net/?p=263, accessed May 27, 2015; Brown, *Party Out of Bounds*, 1–58; Sullivan, *R.E.M: Talk About the Passion*, 1–23; and Shane Harrison, "When Art Made Athens Rock," *Atlanta Journal-Constitution* (April 12, 2014), http://www.myajc.com/news/entertainment/music/when-art-made-athens-rock/nfYYW/, accessed June 1, 2014. This article quotes Pierson as saying Wilson used a boom box, which none of them would have had circa 1975, and the UGA library would not have had African tribal music on cassette tape then either. Ricky Wilson did own a reel-to-reel tape player, however.

8. J. Eddy Ellison, "B-52s Still Feel Like an Athens Band," *Athens Banner Herald* (July 23, 1983); John Martin Taylor, "The B-52s and Me;" Mats Sexton, *The B-52's Universe: The Essential Guide to the World's Best Party Band* (New York: Plan B Books, 2002), 32; Brown, *Party Out of Bounds*, 17–35.

9. Walter Benjamin, "The Work of Art in the Age of Mechanical Reproduction," 1936, reprinted in Benjamin, *Illuminations* (New York: Schocken, 1968); Miles Orvell, *The Real Thing: Imitation and Authenticity in American Culture, 1880–1940* (Chapel Hill: University of North Carolina Press, 1989); Stuart Hall, "Notes on Deconstructing the Popular," *People's History and Socialist Theory*, Raphael Samuel, editor (London: Routledge and Kegan Paul, 1981), 227–40; Dick Hebdige, *Subculture: The Meaning of Style* (London: Routledge, 1979); and Simon Firth, *Sound Effects: Youth, Leisure, and the Politics of Rock 'n' Roll* (New York: Pantheon, 1981); Marjorie Garber, *Vested Interests: Cross-Dressing and Cultural Anxiety* (New York: Routledge, 1997); Susan Sontag, "Notes on 'Camp,'" *Partisan Review* 31:4 (Fall 1964), 515–30; Andrew Ross, "Uses of Camp," in *No Respect: Intellectuals and Popular Culture* (New York: Routledge, 1989), 135–70; Fabio Cleto, ed., *Camp: Queer Aesthetics and the Performing Subject* (Ann Arbor: University of Michigan Press, 1999).

10. Kennedy Fraser, "On and Off the Avenue: Feminine Fashions," *New Yorker* (April 14 1975), 80–89; and LeZotte, *Goodwill to Grunge*.

11. John Taylor, "New Wave Rock Comes to Town," *Athens Observer* (January 26, 1978), 17.

12. Athens Rewind memories and photographs; Cline and Welford interviews; "Post-Punk's Visual Chronicler: Interview with Laura Levine (part 2)," *Rockcritics.com* (January 22, 2009), https://rockcritics.com/2009/01/22/post-punks-visual-chronicler-interview-with-laura-levine-part-2/, accessed January 31, 2016.

13. Athens Rewind memories and photographs; Cline and Welford interviews; "Post-Punk's Visual Chronicler: Interview with Laura Levine (part 2)," *Rockcritics.com* (January 22, 2009), https://rockcritics.com/2009/01/22/post-punks-visual-chronicler-interview-with-laura-levine-part-2/, accessed January 31, 2016; Amy Gross, "Introducing Rock 'N' Roll's Lady Raunch: Patti Smith" *Mademoiselle* (September 1975).

14. B-52's first single, Cline interview.

15. "Bohemian Diaspora," *Village Voice* (February 4, 1992): 26–31.

16. By 1979, onstage Strickland was working the role of the dandy, Schneider appeared as an odd fusion of Tennessee Williams' characters and the film *Saturday Night Fever*, and Ricky Wilson appeared as his own kind of pop-art icon, dressing frequently like an officer from Star Trek or some other sci-fi character.

17. Interviews with people who were professors at the University of Georgia in the 1970s: Judith McWillie interview; Robert Croker interview; Art Rosenbaum interview.

18. "Pylon-1980," online at https://vimeo.com/50389577, accessed May 27, 2015. See also http://eastvillage.thelocal.nytimes.com/2012/10/15/nightclubbing-pylon/, accessed May 27, 2015, which described the video as part of "*Pat Ivers and Emily Armstrong's archive of punk-era concert footage being digitized for the Downtown Collection at N.Y.U.'s Fales Library*."

19. Van Gosse, "Pylon Draws the Line," *Village Voice* (February 25–March 3, 1981), 61–62, describes Briscoe in a performance at the Rock Lounge in New York on Valentine's Day 1981.

20. Sullivan, *Talk about the Passion*, 9–11; William Haines, "Underdog R.E.M. Upstages the Brains," *Red and Black* (May 8, 1980, 9); Fletcher, *Remarks*, 26–27; Cline interview; Seawright interview. Smith's lyrics describe either a woman's desire for another woman or Smith performing a male narrator's desire for a woman.

21. Andrew Slater, "REM: Not Just Another Athens, Georgia, Band," *Rolling Stone* (October 1982): Stipe: "We're not a party band from Athens, we don't play New Wave music, and musically, we don't have shit to do with the B-52s or any other band from this town. We just happen to live here. . . . It's ridiculous. You'd think anyone with an ear for music, anyone who was really listening, would be able to distinguish between REM and the B-52s, or REM and Pylon." See also Andy Schwartz, "R.E.M.: It's Happened Again," *New York Rocker* (January 1982).

22. Mat Snow, "R.E.M.: Interview," *Q* (October 1992). http://www.rocksbackpages.com.proxy.its.virginia.edu/Library/Article/rem-4, accessed October 8, 2016. Ayers also received a cowriting credit for "Old Man Kensey," written in the spring of 1984. In the entire R.E.M. catalog, the band gave cowriting credit on only four songs. "Windout" was released in 1984 on the soundtrack for the movie *Bachelor Party* and in 1987 on the I.R.S. Records R.E.M. compilation *Dead Letter Office*.

23. Laura Levine, a photographer who shot post-punk bands for *New York Rocker* and other publications, online at http://lauralevine.com/photography/gallery.php, accessed October 8, 2016; Seawright interview, Cline interview; video and other images by Levine.

24. The show at the Pier is available online at https://www.youtube.com/watch?v=iPE-l-tfNoI, accessed May 27, 2015.

25. Simon, "A Session with Michael Stipe;" Giles, "Everybody Hurts Sometime;" DeCurtis, "Monster Madness": "In terms of the whole queer-straight-bi thing, my feeling is that labels are for canned food. . . . I think sexuality is a much more slippery thing than that. . . . I've always been of questionable sexuality or dubious sexuality"; Goldberg, "Cybersex, Sex, and the Mysterious Stipe-Man;" Chris Heath, "Michael in the Middle;" Aron, "R.E.M. Comes Alive;" Pemberton, "Michael Stipe: Cash for Questions;" and Fred Maus, "Intimacy and Distance: On Stipe's Queerness."

26. In the 1982 Pier video, you cannot really see Bill Berry.

27. "These days Athens (Ga.) is a creative center," *People* (January 17, 1983).

AFTERWORD

JONATHAN PRUDE

Where should we end? Or more precisely, *how* should we end a collection of essays on "clothing and fashion in southern history"?

Perhaps, to begin with, by noting what this volume is not about. And the starting point here might be one of the terms flagged in its title and mission statement. For the book is in fact not to any large degree about "fashion" as that word is commonly used: the shifts and pirouettes of high style. Notions of elegance—and the ways such notions circulated through the social order—are broached here and there. But generally speaking "fashion" is treated in these pages as the aggregate of dress associated in various ways with various individuals and constituencies. Taken as a whole the collection handles fashion less as Fashion—the *dernier cri*—than as the medley of costumes in history as history was widely lived: not as something exclusive but as all that clothing could and did signal at any given moment and across time.

And so with "southern." For despite its leading mention in the volume's self-labelling, this term, too, is handled in what may seem a counterintuitive manner. All the essays have southern settings. But we find no sustained claim of an identifiable southern style of clothing (much less an identifiable Southern High Fashion.). What's more, to underscore what Ted Ownby and Becca Walton stress in their introduction, the relatively understudied field of clothes in the South means that exploring the subject does not (and one senses they believe should not) launch from all too familiar evocations of all too stereotyped markers of an all too hyperdistinctive regionalism known as the South. And since this point of departure is not readily available, "southern" in this book is not an a priori abstraction meant to be corroborated by clothing. Instead, the collection conceives the South as a geographic arena—itself divided among specific locales and moments (from antebellum years to more recent times)—that is open to be investigated, and illuminated by pursuing apparel. The South in these essays is explained by, rather than explains, clothing. It's a place where clothing happens.

Afterword 143

But how, then, does clothing happen for our authors? Or again more precisely, what does looking back across this collection suggest might be usefully highlighted about its examination of apparel in southern history? What are some of the significant after-echoes of this volume?

* * *

One after-echo is surely the prominent presence of women. Now the tale of clothing in America is by no means an exclusively female saga. Men wore clothes. They participated in the artisanal production of garments. In one way or another (whether as employees, employers, or merchant-entrepreneurs) they loomed large in the industrial manufacture and selling of both the material of apparel and apparel itself. And until recently they were responsible for many—if not most—of the discourses bearing on dress. On the other hand, historians have for some while recognized the key place of women in the domestic fabrication of yarn, cloth, and clothing along with their participation in the small-shop craft assemblage and retailing of certain garments, not to mention their role in the industrial manufacture of textiles and clothing. By the same token, scholars have documented the importance of clothing in the self-presentations and overall maneuverings used by women as they responded to their situations. Indeed, it's also true (and perhaps reflected at a meta-level by the gender balance among contributors to this collection) that "clothing" as a field of study has often been associated with "women's history."

So the salience of women in this collection is not surprising. Yet it remains striking. While men are not absent from these essays, and have substantial roles in several, a good number of the pieces foreground particular instances of women's dealings with the material and finished items of apparel. The foregroundings seem altogether reasonable, even inevitable. And they suggest that it is a reasonable, even inevitable expectation that investigations of clothing will point toward strengthened understandings of how women fit into southern history. Such enhanced understandings might well depart from received historical narratives. Which in turn suggests that considering clothing—not least because of its alignment with women's history—fosters important new versions of the southern past.

Clearly, though, the women in these essays are not all the same. In fact, taken together the protagonists of these pieces, the men as well as the women, are a thoroughly mixed group. They are white and black; they are slave, incarcerated, and free; they are lesser- and not-so-lesser-ranked. It follows, not surprisingly, that the interactions with clothing that the essays ascribe to this arresting range of figures are themselves arrestingly mixed. That said, the collection is also threaded with connections and parallels. So that another and, in truth, an especially resonant kind of after-echo emanating from *Clothing and Fashion in Southern History* is a set of common denominators that surface amidst and weave across the diversity: a bundle of shared themes and topics that themselves often intersect and are in some measure anticipated in the introduction but can nonetheless be usefully pointed out in this afterword.

There is, for example, the shared characteristic of clothing existing as elements in assorted dense networks. Several of the essays disclose how, even if the South is not construed as existentially distinct, the story of clothing (and related goods) can still define the South as a region by identifying it as the southern component of geographically extensive economic exchanges. Thus, Katie Knowles notes how the slave-rooted antebellum South engaged in transregional trade by providing cotton for the production of textile materials and garments, much of it carried out outside the South, and by then serving as markets for those same materials and garments, including the ready-made apparel and rough cloth relegated to slaves. So also, William Sturkey's discussion of the Mississippi Poor People's Corporation in the 1960s and 1970s considers a cluster of operations that were based in the Southeast but imported contributions from far and wide and dispatched finished items back to distant customers.

But the networks could also be more confined and encompass interactions that might or might not be formally commercial. Hence Knowles reveals transactions involving slaves purchasing and bartering for items from local stores, incorporating cast-off garments from their masters, and distributing clothes to one another. By the same token, Sarah Jones Weicksel takes up the manufacture of Civil War uniforms, focusing on the intraregional sewing projects of southern women dedicated to providing costumes for Confederate troops. And Becca Walton lays bare the cloth and clothing provisioning carried out within the tightly closed circuitry of Mississippi's Parchman Prison in the 1950s and 1960s. Or the networks could be at once confined and extensive and both economic and administrative. Weicksel's essay shows her uniform-fashioning women engaging with various extra-local Confederate governmental structures. So too, Susannah Walker's investigation of WPA southern clothing manufacturing reveals undertakings slated to supply clothing for local or regional markets while simultaneously tied to overarching state and federal officials and policies.

Another common denominator running through these essays turns on the fact, fundamental and unavoidable, that clothing is made—that it is shaped by human labor. While *Clothing and Fashion in Southern History* does not directly probe the large textile plants and apparel factories that emerged in the United States in the years covered by the book, it attends frequently to the work-full creation of garments (as well as some fabrics and other products): to the (largely female) value-adding labor—whether slave, incarcerated, or free, whether paid or unpaid—embedded in the probings the book does host. And the work thus examined sheds its own informative light on clothing in the South.

Though the point is laced quietly into her discussion, it seems plain enough, for instance, that the clothes-making role of the slaves Knowles treats, together with the networks in which they participated, allowed antebellum southern chattel laborers to act as though they possessed the garments passing through their hands. Which is to say their clothes-making work was part of how slaves accomplished the remarkable feat of presenting themselves as property actually able to own property—and hence as intrinsically human. For Weicksel, the ramifications of clothes making unfold on a different register. For she shows that the elite women claiming the patriotic mantle of crafting uniforms for the Confederacy were in practice frequently crafting a myth. These individuals' limited experience of, and knowledge about, clothes making left the real job of making garb for soldiers to fall heavily to slave and free white, lesser-ranked women: the former because they were assigned this task, the latter because they needed the pay they received. Significantly, the labor of these last two groups was largely effaced in the narrative the South came to tell about well-placed southern ladies gallantly and selflessly contributing their toil to clothe Dixie's troops. As a result, uncovering what really happened on this score adds helpfully to our understanding of how the South managed its war effort—even as it also discloses the sad irony of southern white laboring women denied recompense after 1865 precisely *because* they had sewed for the Rebellion.

Moving into the twentieth century, Walker's discussion offers the intriguing revelation that women involved in WPA clothes making in the Depression-era South could be caught between visions of their labor as basically about serving their households versus being workers with jobs. In a significant sense, then, Walker spotlights a 1930s southern instance of a basic tension winding through American historiography of treating working women as either women who labored or laborers who were women. From another angle, Sturkey's analysis of the Mississippi Poor People's Corporation thirty to forty years later advances the valuable argument that the clothes making work managed by that organization, and the cooperatives it fostered, invested a crucial dimension of economic self-sufficiency into the projected goals of the civil rights movement.

But the clothes of this volume do not just travel through networks and are not just made.

The essays assembled here are also linked by their shared demonstrations that clothing transmitted meaning and projected identities. And gave pleasure. This last attribute might go unnoticed, for it is often more implicit than explicit in these contributions. In practice, though, virtually all the pieces touch on apparel likely to have been enjoyed to some degree; and the commonality of this feature certifies its importance and renders it worth remarking in this afterword. Certainly it's probable that the items turned out by Mississippi cooperatives gave deep satisfaction to those who bought them, just as we can assume the apparel generated by the WPA sewing shops (of store-bought quality but inflected with local accents) and the uniforms supplied to rank-and-file Confederate soldiers pleased their recipients. Nor is it any less likely that the personalized costumes slaves produced for themselves and the stylish variations of prison garb assembled by Parchman inmates carried considerable charges of pleasure.

In this context, though, Grace Elizabeth Hale's homage to the self-costuming musicians of Athens, Georgia, in the 1970s and 1980s deserves special mention as a piece that pivots centrally around pleasure. Her account turns on the way members of local bands in this time and place created their dress—their clothes making entailing rummaging through thrift stores for old outfits—in ways that facilitated their crossing, recrossing, and generally trespassing across all manner of boundaries: fashion, gender, real versus artifice, and overall propriety. Their "looks" were as important as their sound, Hale explains, with the resulting mash up of songs and appearance cascading into fluidly shifting styles of music and regalia (as well as frequent changes in the names and persona of band members). But her narrative also suggests that through it all there coursed a sense of powerfully provocative mischievousness. And a sense the mischievousness was powerfully enjoyable not only for the groups' audiences but equally for the band members themselves. Some of the groups broke through to fame and fortune; others soon faded away. But all of them, according to Hale, were "playing" at what they did—with that term evidently used to signal both an intent to experiment and the pleasure taken doing so. It was, she tells us, "a 'fun' form or rebellion."

A further thread braiding together many of these essays is that they deal with subordinate or marginal figures whose clothes tilt with—indeed challenge—power. The resulting contestations with received authority were typically not directly confrontational. But they mattered. And they form a significant part of what clothes are and how they function in this collection. Unquestionably, for example, the clothing and other products generated by the Poor People's Cooperatives in Mississippi weaponized both consumption and manufacturing to contest the coercive subjugation of Jim Crow. And Walker, for her part, shows that the laboring women in southern WPA sewing projects pushed back against debilitating administrative policies (and closures of their shops), their efforts occasionally including protests by African Americans against the racist practices infiltrating these operations.

But there is also the consequential pushing back documented by Knowles and Walton. Both these writers explore responses by subaltern populations to demeaning impositions of uniform or uniform-like cloth and clothing. For Knowles the responses entailed antebellum slave women using what time and ability they possessed to edit, dye, and patch the materials given them and thereby transform their workaday garb into personalized outfits (thus paralleling their customization of leisure wear and going some distance to legitimize cloth that whites dubbed unfashionably "negro" simply because of the black skins it covered). These women, in sum, used their time and ability to counter the flattened dehumanization of assigned everyday garb with clothing that allowed slaves to announce themselves as particularized individuals (and individuals, it might be added, wearing clothes expressive now and again of African and West Indian motifs). For Walton, the responses seemingly encompassed the humanizing dividend that imprisoned women harvested just from the act of producing linens and standard garments. They drew strength, we might say, by harvesting a special ramification of clothesmaking work: a ramification that allowed a thoroughly disenfranchised constituency to counter alienation just by securing acknowledgement of clothes that were "the visual representation of [its] labor" and the caregiving import of that labor. But the responses by Parchman inmates also encompassed heartfelt resentment of the striped version of prison uniforms. And the responses encompassed, too, the carefully modified presentations—extending from hair and cosmetics to jauntily tweaked costumes (and here high fashion does make an entry)—used to mark "visiting days" or a prisoner's final release. For Walton as for Knowles, clothing was an arena to navigate regulated "looks" with modest but significant counterstipulations of who they were.

Now it should be apparent that the clothing comprising such pushing back was by all indications frequently the same clothing that pleased. In truth, pleasure and contestation might well have often reinforced each other. Clothing could please in some measure because it contested; contestation could run along channels of pleasure. And this was nowhere more true than in Athens, Georgia, in the 1970s and 1980s. It was risky to bring bohemianism to rural Georgia at this historical moment. It took bravery to cross dress and wear stridently thrift store costumes. There was scorn and there were beatings. But this was ultimately because the "fun" *did* enclose a "rebellion." There was an edgy earnestness to what was going on. Within the jolts of merriment serious lines were being seriously crossed. In the world of clothing fun could have teeth.

* * *

So: the prominent place of women; the importance of labor; the potential for using clothing to challenge power; the possibilities of fun; the overlapping common denominators criss-crossing the essays in this collection—these are among the significant after-echoes of *Clothing and Fashion in Southern History*. But there's another kind of echo we might consider at least briefly. It's the echo of certain elements of historical heritage that, while arising outside these essays, serve as particularly compelling frameworks for a few of them.

We might note, for example, that the cooperative enterprises Sturkey shows operating in Mississippi in the 1960s and 1970s had ample precursors—though most of them equally short-lived—in the cooperatives arising amidst the labor movements of the 1800s as various working people sought to counter the various inequities they encountered. We might note as well the backstory surrounding standardized apparel. From early in the Republic, many Americans viewed the obligation to wear regularized costumes as signs of intolerable servility. Self-assigned apparel by certain occupations and voluntary militias and the outfits designated for the small professional military were acceptable. But by and large uniforms meant being uniformed, a condition associated with "lacky" retainers of European aristocrats and in the United States with incarcerated deviants and—crucially—with slaves. As a result, broad contingents of free citizens—including policemen, members of public militias, non-professional fire "laddies," railroad conductors, and non-chattel domestic servants—initially resisted the indignity of uniforms. Only slowly, and in some measure because of the patriotic connotations suffusing Civil War uniforms, did prescribed costumes gain wide approval—and even then not among those for whom this kind of apparel remained connected to involuntary and punitive subservience. Understanding this framework helps us appreciate the level of defiance on the table when chattel laborers recalibrated their garb. It also helps us appreciate both the hefty cultural implications flowing from the Civil War costuming that Weicksel details and, going the way other way, the abiding aura of denigration attaching to imposed costumes, the lingering equation of subjugation and uniforms that led Parchman prisoners to react as they did to their imposed 'looks.'

Or consider the context surrounding the "scene" Grace Hale finds bubbling up in Athens in the later decades of the last century. It does not change what she describes. But it enhances our grasp of all that she discloses to realize that the "bohemianism" her subjects carried out by rummaging through second-hand stores was foreshadowed by generations of lower-ranked Americans who mixed cast-off and second-hand garments with top hats and fashionable-looking frocks. Nor should we overlook the traditions of cross dressing lodged in a variety of folk customs, some encompassing vigorous popular protest. And then there's the fraught record of minstrelsy. Hale mentions that among the antecedents of the borrowings and gender swappings occurring in Athens (specifically the practice of women dressing as men dressing as women) were the performances of late-nineteenth-century blacks who participated in blackface theatrics, "doubling their race" by imitating whites imitating blacks. The fact is, however, that especially in its early phases during the 1830s and 1840s, blackface minstrelsy joined racist appropriations with elaborate ricochets of imitation (with white mockeries of blacks often based on derisive black versions of whites) and with complex white plebeian jabbings at those above and equally complex (and at times ambivalent) interracial and transgender masquerading.

It follows that what happened in a sleepy Georgia college town during the 1970s and 1980s can be read as drawing on—and on some underlying channel of cultural memory quite possibly as knowingly drawing on—historical transcripts of bricolage costume practices, of customary protest, and of stage conventions heavy with the contradictory freight of toxic racism and biting subversion. It follows, too, that what happened in Athens can be read as pulling off its blend of playfulness and barbed trespasses in part *because* it drew on what went before.

* * *

How should we end this afterword? Perhaps by calling attention to several aspects of clothing that are mentioned in passing in this volume but that we would do well to bear in mind going forward. Thus, we should be careful to attend to the materiality of clothes. A number of the essays delve into the concrete processes of putting together garments and the physical feel of apparel. We should build on this and keep track of exactly what was involved in sewing by hand and by machine. And we should likewise keep track as best we can of exactly how items of dress pressed, slid, rubbed against the skin; how they smelled when new, old, or soiled; how much they weighed; how they offered protection from the cold and accommodated heat; how they facilitated or constrained movement. We should keep track of clothes as *things*.

In much the same way we should be prepared to move on from the importance that several of our authors place on the appearance of clothing and on the way, implicitly or explicitly, dress was often performed. Hence we should be ready to explore how to communicate the "look" of clothes in future studies. To cite one tactic, we should be ready to make widened use of images—and to use pictures not merely to illustrate descriptions recounted in words but (as a few of these essays do) as evidence of how graphic representations of clothing themselves functioned historically and thus themselves served in the historical narratives of dress. And we should likewise be prepared to realize that the performative quality of clothing meant garments often involved intricate interplay between messages projected and received, between intentions signaled overtly or only implied (or delivered with deniable ambiguity) by those wearing clothes and interpreted confidently or only inferred (and sometimes misunderstood) by those observing dress from the outside. In the end, the messages ramifying out from the clothes of people in the past could be bitingly clear, or elusive, or blends of the two.

Such, to reiterate, are considerations for explorations going forward. But it's precisely by registering confidence that this field *will* go forward that we can best end this afterword. *Clothing and Fashion in Southern History* is not definitive. For all its common denominators and elements of framing historical heritage, it does not advance a comprehensive argument or promote an enveloping perspective. But this is hardly a flaw. On the contrary, we should read this book, as we read any genuinely valuable collection, as a clearing of the throat, as an array of gestures pointing in many directions, as an invitation to do more.

CONTRIBUTORS

Grace Elizabeth Hale is Commonwealth Professor of American Studies and History at the University of Virginia, where she teaches courses in US cultural history, the US South, and documentary studies. She is the author of *Making Whiteness: The Culture of Segregation in the South, 1890–1940* (New York: Pantheon, 1998); *A Nation of Outsiders: How the White Middle-Class Fell in Love with Rebellion in Postwar America* (New York: Oxford University Press, 2011); *Cool Town: Music, Art, and Alternative Culture in Athens, Georgia* (Chapel Hill: University of North Carolina Press, 2019).

Katie Knowles holds a PhD in History from Rice University, where her dissertation focused on clothing worn and made by enslaved people in the antebellum US South. She is curator and assistant professor at the Avenir Museum of Design and Manufacturing at Colorado State University.

Ted Ownby is William Winter Professor of History and Southern Studies and former director of the Center for the Study of Southern Culture at the University of Mississippi. He is coeditor of *The Mississippi Encyclopedia* (2017) and editor or coeditor of eight other works and the author of *Subduing Satan: Religion, Recreation, and Manhood in the Rural South, 1865–1920* (1990), *American Dreams in Mississippi: Consumers, Poverty, and Culture, 1830–1998* (1999), and *"Hurtin' Words": Defining Family Problems in the Twentieth-Century South* (2018).

Jonathan Prude is associate professor of history at Emory University, where he teaches courses about class and culture in American history. He is the author of *The Coming of Industrial Order: Town and Factory Life in Rural Massachusetts, 1810–1860* (1983; new edition 1999), and coeditor, with Steven Hahn, of *The Countryside in the Age of Capitalist Transformation: Essays in the Social History of Rural America* (1985).

William Sturkey is assistant professor of history at the University of North Carolina, where he teaches classes in modern American, African American, and southern history. He is the author of *Hattiesburg: An American City in Black and White* (2019) and coeditor with Jon H. Hale of *To Write in the Light of Freedom: The Newspapers of the 1964 Mississippi Freedom Schools* (2015).

Susannah Walker received her PhD in History from Carnegie Mellon University. She is the author of *Style and Status: Selling Beauty to African American Women, 1920–1975* (2007), and has taught at Virginia Wesleyan College and Buckingham Browne & Nichols School and now works in the University of Toronto Libraries.

Becca Walton holds degrees in history and cultural studies from the University of Virginia and the University of Mississippi, where she was also an associate director at the Center for the Study of Southern Culture. After time as a member of the Community of St. Anselm in London, she is training to be an Episcopal priest.

Sarah Jones Weicksel holds an MA from the Winterthur Program in American Material Culture and a PhD in History from the University of Chicago, where she wrote a dissertation entitled *The Fabric of War: Clothing, Culture, and Violence in the American Civil War Era*. She is a project historian at the Smithsonian Institution's National Museum of American History.

INDEX

Page numbers in *italics* refer to illustrations.

Adams County Bag Firm of Natchez, 114
Adorned in Dreams: Fashion and Modernity (Wilson), xi
American Jewish Congress, 115
androgyny, 127, 128, 133, 135–36
antebellum period, viii, xii, 3–22, 27, 37, 142, 144–45, 147
Appalachian South, viii
Art in the Dark (band), 137
Ash, Juliet, 87
Atlanta Constitution, 61, 124
Aunt Jemima, x

badges, 3–4, 8, 20, 22
Baker, Ella, 117
balmoral petticoat, 20–21
Barefootin' (Blackwell), viii
Barnard, Malcolm, 5
Belk, viii
Berry, Bill, 129, 134, 136–37
Berry, Daina Ramey, 17–18
Berry, Lulu, 98
Berry, Paula, *101*, 101
Bewley, Randy, 133
B-52's (band), xiii, 124, 128–34, 136–37
bias grain, 5–6
Birmingham World, 70
Black Freedom Movement, 109, 111
Black Power, 111, 117–20
black voting rights, 109, 112–13
Blackwell, Unita, viii
Blocks for Freedom, 109–10
Boat Of (band), 129
Bolden, R. L., 113
Bowie, David, 127

Briscoe Hay, Vanessa (Ellison, Vanessa), xiii, 132–33, 136
Brooks Brothers, 10, 17
Brown, James, 114
Brown, Joseph E., 37–40
Buck, Pete, 129–30, 134–36
Bumgarner, Joe L., 99

Cahn, Susan K., xi
camp reports, xiii, 86–92, 98, *100*
Camp, Stephanie M. H., 19
Carmichael, Stokely, 117
Charleston Museum, 16–17
Chestnut, Vic, 125
Chicago Defender, 70, 117
Chicago Eight, 116
Chicago's American, 117
Child Development Group, 112
Circus, The, 128
Civil Rights Movement, viii, xiii, 69, 109–15, 117, 119–20, 146
Civil War, 6, 11, 32, 35, 38, 47, 144, 148
Clark, Henry T., 40
Cline, Mark, xiii, 129–30
clothing: antebellum, xii, 3–22, 37; gender and, ix, xi, xiii, 49–50, 125–28, 130, 132–33, 138, 143, 146, 149; homespun, x, 6, 16, 37; military, x, 32–50; prison, 84–103; production of, 32–50, 120; ready-made, 3, 10, 35, 44, 144; secondhand, xi, xiii, 111, 125, 128; store-bought, x, 57–59, 146; work, x, 3–22
"Coal Miner's Daughter" (Lynn), viii
"Coat of Many Colors" (Parton), ix
Cocaine, Brian, 157

153

Cockettes, 126, 128
Coke, H. D., 70
Confederate soldiers, xii, 32–33, 36, 44, 46–49, 145–46
consumer capitalism, 3, 7, 9, 14, 20, 22, 109–21
consumer-science class, xi
Cooper, Alice, 127
Cost Plus, 116
cotton, ix–x, 3–22, 32, 37, 43–44, 46, 71, 84, 87, 92–94, 114, 119, 144
cotton mills, ix, 10–11, 34
Council of Federated Organizations (COFO), 112, 118
cross-dressing, xi, 128
Crowe, Curtis, 133–35
Cue Magazine, 116
Curtin, Mary Ellen, 88, 98, 103
Curtis, Jackie, 126–27

Daily News, 116
Darling, Candy, 126–27
Davis, Jefferson, xi
Davis, Ossie, 117
Davis, Ruby, 115
Day, Dorothy, 117
Dee, Ruby, 117
Delta Ministry, 112
Department of Agriculture, 56
Derby, Dorris, 115
Designing Women, viii
Dior, Christian, 101
Donald, Rebecca, 115
Douglas, Maggie, 112, 114
drag queens, 126–27, 131, 133
Durham, Jessie F., 89
dyeing, xii, 12–15, 21–22, 58, 147

Eastland, James, 119
Economic Opportunity Program, Office of, 112
Ellison, Vanessa. *See* Briscoe Hay, Vanessa (Ellison, Vanessa)
enslaved labor, ix–x, xii, 3–22, 33–34, 36, 41, 44–47, 144–46, 148
Evers, Medgar, 110

Factory (studio), 126–28, 134
Fairchild's Dictionary of Textiles, 6
Fans (band), 129
Farmer, James, 117–18
Farm Security Administration (FSA), 56–57
Fashion as Communication (Barnard), 5
fast fashion, 4
Fayetteville Observer (circular), 40
Federal Emergency Relief Administration (FERA), 54, 59–60, 63–64, 69
flax, 12
Forbidden City, 84, 94–95, 98
Ford, Tanisha C., x
Freedom Information Service, 115
Freedom Summer, 109, 111–13
Friends of SNCC. *See under* SNCC: Friends of
FSA. *See* Farm Security Administration
Fuentes, Marisa J., 5
fugitives, 5, 9

Gamble, David, 129
garment industry, ix, 63, 65–66, 74
Gianaris, Nicky, 129
global economy, ix, 3, 6, 14, 22
"Gloria" (Morrison), 134
"God Save the Queen" (Sex Pistols), 134
Green, Elna C., 55, 62
Green, Mike, 129
Gunn, Tim, viii

Haberland, Michelle, ix
Hale, Grace Elizabeth, xi, xiii, 146, 149
Haley, Sarah, 103
Harrington, Michael, 117
Harris, Ron, 90, 99, *100*
Hart, Sarah, 115
Haywood County Handicraft, 120
heckles, 12
Hendricks, James, 88–90, 92
Heyman, David John, 118
Hill, Sarah Laws, 26
home economics, xi
home production, x

homespun, x, 6, 16
Homewood Colored Civic League, 70
hoop skirts, viii, ix
Hopkins, Harry, 54, 60, 62, 64, 68, 70, 74
Hopper, Lynda, xiii, 132
Horses (Smith), 128–29, 132
Hutchinson, Bill, 115

Incidents in the Life of a Slave Girl (Jacobs), 3, 22
indigo, 13
industrial manufacturing, ix, 3, 50, 59, 63, 65–66, 74, 114, 143
Industrial Revolution, 7
inmates, xii, 84–103, 146–47, 149
Inside World, xii, 84, 85, 86–87, 89–92, 94, 96, 97, 98–99, 99, 100, 101
Interview, 126–27

Jacksonville Times-Union, 60
Jacobs, Harriet, 3–4, 8, 22
Jagger, Mick, 136
Jet, 117
Jim Crow, x, 23n7, 95, 110, 113, 147
Johnson, Lyndon B., 113
Jones, Fred, 90
Just Like a Movie (1983), 129
"Justification of Sewing Projects" (Hopkins), 64

Kennedy, John F., 110
kersey, 7–8
King, Martin Luther, Jr., 110
Knowles, Katie, xii, 144
Korstad, Robert, 120

Lachowski, Michael, 124, 133, 136–37
Lacy, Tim, 137
Ladies' Soldier's Friend Sewing Society, 32, 46
Lee, Albert, 84, 85, 88, 96, 97, 99, 99, 102
Lee, Ruth, 115
Levine, Laura, 129–30, 132–33
Lewis, John, 118

Liberated Threads: Black Women, Style, and the Global Politics of Soul (Ford), x
Liberty Outlet House, 115–20
Lichtenstein, Nelson, 120
Limbo District (band), 124, 137
linsey (linsey-woolsey), 3, 7–8
Los Angeles Sentinel, 117
Los Angeles Times, 117
Love Tractor (band), xiii, 129, 137
Lynn, Loretta, viii

Macon Weekly Telegraph, 8, 40
Madison County Sewing Firm, 112, 114
Mardi Gras Indians, x
Maslow, Ellen, 115–17
McComb Leather Co-op, 117
Mercyland (band), 124
Method Actors (band), 124, 129
Michigan Chronicle, 116
Mills, Mike, 134, 136–37
Mississippi State Fair, 88
Mississippi State Legislature, 92
Mississippi State Penitentiary. *See* Parchman
Mobile Press, 62
Montgomery, Florence M., 6
Montgomery, Lucille, 112
Morey, Hunter, 113
Morris, Jessie, 113–14
Morrison, Van, 134
Mount Olive Quilting Co-op, 115
Muhammad Speaks (Nation of Islam), 116
Murray, Pauli, viii
Muste, Rev. A. J., 118
"My Day" (E. Roosevelt), 65

NAACP, 70–71, 110
Nation, 118
National Guardian, 118
Nation of Islam, 116
Native American trade, ix, 8
Negro Chamber of Commerce, 74
negro cloth, x–xii, 3–22
Negro Digest, 117

156 Index

New Deal, viii, xii, 54–75; programs, xii, 57, 59–60, 74–75
New Orleans Times-Picayune, 8, 57
Newport Folk Music Festival, 117
New York Amsterdam News, 117
New York Dolls, 127
New York Post, 117
New York Rocker, 129, 133
New York Times, 116
Norfolk Journal and Guide, 71

Oakland Tribune, 117
O'Hara, Scarlett, ix
Oh OK (band), xiii, 124, 129, 132
Ono, Yoko, 133
Osnaburg, 8, 15
Ownby, Ted, 142
Oxford English Dictionary, 6–7

"Papa's Got a Brand New Bag" (Brown), 114
Parchman, xii–xiii, 84–102; Women's Camp, 87, 89, 91, 93, 95, *101*, 101
Parton, Dolly, ix
patches. *See* badges
People, 137
Perkins, Carl, viii
Pierson, Kate, 127–29, 131, 133
plains, 7–8
plantations, viii, ix–x, xii, 3–22, 44–46, 85, 92; ledgers, xii, 5, 10, 15
Pocketbook Workers Union, 118
pop-art punk, 130
popular culture, viii, 50, 125, 128
Presley, Elvis, viii, 132
prison dress. *See under* clothing: prison
Project Runway, viii
Proud Shoes (Murray), viii
Pylon (band), xiii, 124, 132–34, 136–37

Q, 135

Race Relations Conference, 116
Ralston, Blanche, 67
Randolph, A. Phillip, 117
Raymond, George, 112

R.E.M., xiii, 124, 129, 134
Richards, Keith, 130, 136
Richmond, Mike, 129
"Rock Lobster" (B-52's), 131
Roosevelt, Eleanor, 64–65
Roosevelt, Franklin D., 56, 67–68, 70
runaways, 5, 8–9, 21

Schneider, Fred, 124, 127–29, 131, 136
School Relief Fund, 58
Schuykill Arsenal, 35
Schwerner, Mickey, 118
Schwerner, Nathan, 118
seamstresses, 20, 32–37, 41, 44–45, 47–48, 63–64, 67–68, 74, 91
Sears and Roebuck, 59
secondhand clothes, xi, xiii, 111, 124–26, 128, 138; in stores, 125; and style, 124, 126
Seeger, Pete, 137
sewing, ix, xi–xiii, 4, 12–14, 16, 20, 32–50, 54–75, 84–103, 109–10, 112–15, 118, 144, 146–47, 149; patriotism and, 32–50; projects/co-ops, xiii, 54–75, 144, 146–47; societies, 32–50, *33*
sewing rooms, 54–75; penitentiary, 84–103; segregation of, 69–74, 87
Sex Pistols (band), 134
Sexual Reckonings: Southern Girls in a Troubling Age (Cahn), xi
shoes, viii, 10, 16, 37, 97, 99, 125
Slay, Chris, 129
Smith, Patti, 128–29, 132–34, 136
SNCC, 115; Friends of, 112–13, 115–16
Southern Claims Commission, 47
southern musicians, x, xiii, 124–38, 146
spinning, 9, 12–14, 16, 41–43
Squalls (band), 137
Steel Magnolias (1989), viii
Stewart, Martha Alice, 85
Stipe, Lynda, xiii, 132
Stipe, Michael, xiii, 129–30, 132, 134–37
Strickland, Keith, 127–29, 131, 136
Student Nonviolent Coordinating Committee. *See* SNCC
Studio 54, 127

Sturkey, William, xiii, 144–45, 148
Sun Reporter, 117
Sweet, Matthew, 129

Taylor, John, 129, 132
textile mills, ix, 7, 10–11, 34
Textiles in America, 1650–1870 (Montgomery), 6
Thin, Silva, 126–28
Thomas, Norman, 118
Thompson, Heather Ann, 102
thrift store rock, 129
Tone Tones (band), 129
Tougaloo College, 113, 115

Una Sewing Cooperative, xiii, 109–10, 115
uniforms, x, 35–50, 84–103, 85, 147–49; military, x, 35–50; prison, x, 84–103, 85, 147, 149; stripes/striped, 84, 85, 88–90, 92, 95, 97, 99, 101–2, 147; work, x, 148
Unitarian Church, 118
United Nations Standard Minimum Rules for the Treatment of Prisoners, 88
used clothing. *See under* clothing: secondhand
US Office of Army Clothing and Equipage, 35

Vain Victory (1972), 126
Vego, Velena, 137
Village Voice, 116, 130, 133
Vogue, 98, 127
von Wagenheim, Chris, 127
Voter Rights Act 1965, 110

Waldrop, Robert, 127–28, 130
Walker, Susannah, xii, 144–45, 147
Wall Street Journal, 117, 120
Walsh, Al, 137
Walton, Becca, xii, 144, 147
Warhol, Andy, 126–27, 130, 134
Washington Post, 117, 119
weaving, 7, 9, 13–14, 16, 20, 36, 41–43, 45
Weekly News and Courier, 38
Weicksel, Sarah Jones, xii, 114–15, 148
Welford, Armistead, 129
"When Can I Change My Clothes?" (White), 88
White, Bukka, 88
White, Donald, 113
Whitney, Benjamin, 8
Widespread Panic (band), 124
Wilson, Cindy, 127, 131, 133
Wilson, Elizabeth, xi, 103
Wilson, Ricky, 127–29, 131, 136
Women's and Professional Projects (WPP), 54, 57, 61, 65, 67, 68, 73
Women's International League for Peace and Freedom, 116
Woodlawn, Holly, 126–28
Woodward, Ellen, 54, 58, 60, 63–65, 67–68, 71–74
work-relief programs (WPA), 55, 63–64, 69, 74
Works Progress Administration (WPA), viii, 44, 54–75, 144–47
WPP. *See* Women's and Professional Projects

www.ingramcontent.com/pod-product-compliance
Lightning Source LLC
Chambersburg PA
CBHW030625230426
43661CB00053B/2149